MAKING SENSE OUT OF MEANING

Making Sense out of Meaning

An Essay in Lexical Semantics

WALTER HIRTLE

McGill-Queen's University Press
Montreal & Kingston • London • Ithaca

© McGill-Queen's University Press 2013

ISBN 978-0-7735-4205-1 (cloth)
ISBN 978-0-7735-8917-9 (ePDF)
ISBN 978-0-7735-8918-6 (ePUB)

Legal deposit fourth quarter 2013
Bibliothèque nationale du Québec

Printed in Canada on acid-free paper that is 100% ancient forest free (100% post-consumer recycled), processed chlorine free

McGill-Queen's University Press acknowledges the support of the Canada Council for the Arts for our publishing program. We also acknowledge the financial support of the Government of Canada through the Canada Book Fund for our publishing activities.

Library and Archives Canada Cataloguing in Publication

Hirtle, W. H. (Walter Heal), 1927–, author
    Making sense out of meaning: an essay in lexical semantics / Walter Hirtle.

Includes bibliographical references and index.
Issued in print and electronic formats.
    ISBN 978-0-7735-4205-1 (bound). – ISBN 978-0-7735-8917-9 (ePDF). – ISBN 978-0-7735-8918-6 (ePUB)

1. Polysemy. 2. Semantics. 3. Discourse analysis. 4. Cognitive grammar. 5. Metaphor. 6. Psycholinguistics. I. Title.

P325.5.P65H57 2013   401'.43   C2013-904658-5
                                                                         C2013-904659-3

This book was typeset by Interscript in 10.5 / 13 Baskerville.

To the memory of Roch Valin

Contents

Acknowledgments ix

Introduction 3

I SITUATING THE QUESTION

1 Language as a Human Phenomenon 11
2 Linguists and the Tradition 24
3 Meaning: An Object of Scientific Enquiry? 33

II MAKING WORDS

4 Coming to Grips with Meaning 43
5 How *Access* "Got Verbed" 57
6 Wording 73

III LEXEMES OF VERBS

7 Monosemy and Polysemy 87
8 Discerning Different Senses of *See* 111
9 Grammatical (In)compatibility with Other Verbs 128
10 *Do, Be, Have* 139
11 Working Out the Right Sense 146

IV LEXEMES OF SUBSTANTIVES

12 Common and Proper   159
13 'Unbounded' and 'Bounded'   172
14 Metaphor   182

V THE GRAMMATICAL CONNECTION

15 Making Lexemes into Nouns   199
16 Space Words, Time Words, and Adverbs   214

VI CONCLUDING REMARKS

Conclusion   223

Glossary   227

Notes   231

References   241

Index   251

Acknowledgments

If I have risked venturing into an area of language that has not been explored in any detail from the viewpoint adopted here, that of Gustave Guillaume's theory of the word, it is because of Roch Valin. Some years before his illness, I was hesitant about applying Guillaume's method to some problem in English we had never envisaged. Roch's reaction was something like "Go ahead! Dive in!" Coming from him, this gave me the confidence I needed to set to work on it, and on subsequent problems. His recent death reminded me of this turning point in my career and of how highly he was esteemed by those who worked with him for his view of language. For him, language was man's most important creation, the word its central component, and meaning the heart of the word. Any value this essay may have is a tribute to his inspiration and of course to Guillaume's teaching, which inspired all he did in linguistics.

I owe much to discussions with my colleagues in the Fonds Gustave Guillaume at l'Université Laval and am particularly grateful to Claude Guimier for comments on an earlier version of this study. Finally, the very fact that this essay has resulted in a publication is due in large part to the encouragement and support of my wife.

MAKING SENSE OUT OF MEANING

Introduction

This essay will be one more attempt to situate meaning, that protean component of words, within an overall view of language, to bring it within the scope of a linguistic theory permitting us to understand how we manage to communicate by means of such a changeable element. The traditional view of meaning as the mental counterpart of linguistic signs has been called into question by work in the field of neuroscience[1] and even in the field of linguistics. If it is a mental entity, then meaning is strictly subjective and so, in the eyes of many scholars, cannot be treated scientifically. It remains that the traditional view of meaning is based on language as a phenomenon, on what we, as ordinary speakers, experience of language. Since it is our experience of any reality that provides the basis, the initial data, for reflecting on it in a scientific way, this view of meaning as a mental reality will be adopted here as the starting point to explore what it can tell us of the nature of language itself.

As a number of linguists have pointed out, meaning occupies a central place in language because it is what every speaker intends to express and what every listener tries to understand. As a consequence, there is no shortage of books that deal with various aspects of semantics and provide reference material for courses on the subject, and so one may well question the need for yet another study in semantics, particularly one limited to lexical meaning. Being a mental reality, meaning is the most difficult part of language to analyze, and no study can claim to have elucidated it completely. This includes the present study, which, however, will propose answers to two important difficulties encountered by a mentalist approach.

First, having no existence outside the mind, meaning requires a physical, perceivable sign to make it accessible to someone else. Those of a positivist bent have pointed out that meaning, being purely subjective, cannot be observed objectively and so, unlike its sign or any other physical object, does not lend itself to being measured by other observers. They therefore conclude that meaning does not give rise to data that can be treated scientifically, a conclusion that has led to linguists focusing on syntax or some other aspect of language and marginalizing meaning or even excluding it as an object of scientific (rational) enquiry. This question will be re-examined here and an argument put forward to show that meaning can give rise to observations calling for a rational explanation.

Second, even granted that meaning is the central reality of language, linguists are confronted with a difficulty when describing the observed meaning of any word: the apparently insurmountable problem of polysemy. How can the same sign express different senses and yet be the same word in the eyes of the speaker? In his important study of this problem, *On Monosemy*, Ruhl argues that a word has a single meaning and attributes its apparent diversity of meaning to the context, a view adopted here in part. However, while making use of his valuable data base, the present study will explore a dimension of meaning Ruhl did not envisage – certain widespread variations found with verbs, others with nouns – and will examine the relation between a word's basic lexical meaning and the different senses it can bring to the sentence. This will lead to the proposal that it is a word's underlying lexical monosemy which enables it to express the polysemy observed in discourse.

Examining a word in this way, before it takes its place in a context, entails adopting a speaker-centred approach, as opposed to the listener-centred approach adopted by so many studies. Focusing on the speaker involves examining how an idea is construed, along with the necessary grammatical components, to provide the meaning of a word ready for use. Taking into account the speaker's role in the act of language does call into question the validity of certain widely accepted notions concerning conversion and a mental lexicon. On the other hand, through this speaker-oriented approach, we can discern the relationship between a word's monosemy and its polysemy and explain, without appealing to hypothetical rules or to situation and context, how a speaker can use a word to express different senses and how a listener, making use of context and situation, can understand it rightly. Thus there is no opposition between the two types of approach; to the contrary, the speaker-oriented approach developed here provides a complement to listener-oriented approaches developed in other studies, a necessary complement if one wants to take into account the whole of the phenomenon, the act of language from beginning to end. References to other approaches have been brought in only incidentally, as an aid to clarify my approach, which must be understood before a full-fledged comparison with others can be undertaken.

This is an exploratory study, a first attempt to situate meaning within an overall view of the act of language, permitting us to understand how we manage to communicate by means of such a changeable element. Various scholars and poets have written on meaning, often with valuable insights suggesting its crucial role for mankind, and many linguists have approached meaning in an attempt to account for the vagaries of this mental IMPORT[2] of the word (what it brings into the sentence), some abandoning the attempt as "futile." So far, however, no comprehensive view has emerged providing an understanding of meaning as an essential component of the general phenomenon of speaking, itself an essential of the human phenomenon. Any contribution the present essay may make to this ongoing attempt to understand the nature of language will be due to an effort at the outset to approach the question of meaning from that more general point of view in order to discern its place in the language act and its role in the formation and expression of human thought.

This essay will therefore begin by evoking the big picture, the way a number of writers have envisaged the relationship between man and language, or more precisely between thought and language, and will then discuss how linguists have accepted this tradition. This will bring us to the crucial question of how meaning, which exists only in the mind, can be approached as an object of scientific observation. Besides the usual presuppositions of any scientific venture[3] – that the object of analysis is somehow orderly, that the human mind is capable of discerning this order, that the attempt to do so is worthwhile – the approach adopted here presupposes that language is primarily a mental construct, a human artefact resulting from the way speakers over the generations have fashioned words in order to express what they have in mind.

Observing for scientific purposes, however, involves more than just looking at something. It has often been pointed out that "a scientific approach does not consist in simply observing, accumulating experimental data to deduct a theory from it. One can easily spend years examining an object without obtaining even the smallest observation of scientific interest. To make observations of any value, one must at the outset have a certain idea of what there is to observe."[4] Part II of this essay goes on to outline the point of view adopted here at the outset for observing usage, because "unless we already have some hypothesis in mind, we are unable to know which portions of our 'observation' are relevant and which are not."[5] Our hypothesis, which is provided by Guillaume's theory of the word and its place in the act of language as applied to English, entails a different conception of what linguists and others call a mental lexicon, thus making superfluous the process of conversion evoked by many grammarians. This discussion will bring out the distinction between the two types of meaning, lexical and grammatical, and provide a first idea of how we form words while speaking.

With the focus on the word, the minimal sayable unit of meaning, the delicate problem of distinguishing between its lexical and grammatical imports is examined in Part III in order to explain what permits a word to be so adaptable, so pertinent to each specific context, and yet, in spite of this variability, so effective as a means of communication for all speakers of a language. Examining in detail actual uses of a number of verbs, as found in Ruhl and other studies, brings out variations of sense which are common to all of them. Such variations, it is suggested, are manifestations of lexical polysemy. Turning to the substantive in Part IV, the consideration of different types of substantive as well as types of usage throws further light on how the lexical meaning of a word is formed and brings out other common variations of sense, including metaphor, which are proposed as manifestations of lexical polysemy. Finally, in Part V, these observations are interpreted in the light of a word's grammatical components, thus permitting certain reflections on how its lexical meaning is formed as a part of speech.

This attempt to make sense out of meaning involves situating meaning observed in a sentence in the wider context of the word-forming process during the act of language. Being largely exploratory, this study sometimes involves looking at frequently observed facts from a new, more general viewpoint. Nothing guarantees the success of such a venture, since it appeals to new analytical methods and often results in findings calling for wider observation of usage to verify their validity. This seems, however, to be the way of progress in any scientific approach, if one can judge by the way a very different discipline developed:

> Ptolemy's systems gave results that are surprisingly good, but he went about his work in what is for us a curious way. He tackled each construction piecemeal; that is, he took up each problem one by one, and dealt with it as though other aspects of the planet's motion were irrelevant to what he was doing. This raises the question of what Ptolemy was trying to achieve. He was certainly not attempting to devise a unified cosmology. Rather he seems to have assumed that his job as an astronomer was "to save the appearances," as the phrase went, namely, "to account for the way heavenly bodies appeared," not to offer a *physical explanation* of their motion. If a planet showed an irregularity in speed, and another in size, the astronomer was at liberty to explain the first by an epicycle and the second by two epicycles or vice versa! The question of the reality of these constructions was never raised by Ptolemy.
> Copernicus was dissatisfied with this arbitrary way of doing astronomy and he proposed a radically different system. (Shea and Artigas, 17–18; italics in the original)

The present essay is thus an attempt to get beyond piecemeal, ad hoc accounts of what particular words contribute to the sentences they are used in, and to discern what is built into, theoretically, any word permitting it to express different senses. That is, the aim here is to distinguish clear cases of polysemy from all the variations observable in discourse, and to discern what in the mental system of a word makes this polysemy possible.

I SITUATING THE QUESTION

1

Language as a Human Phenomenon

> Thought makes language while being made by language.
> Delacroix

LANGUAGE-DEPENDENT THOUGHT

To situate the topic of this essay at the outset, it will be useful to evoke general attitudes toward language reflecting the cultural tradition of the last two centuries. This chapter will compare remarks by writers from various fields – literature, philosophy, history, etc. – to give an idea of the cultural setting in which linguistic thought has developed. One may well wonder what such comments can bring to a discussion of linguistics. Their value lies in the fact that each of these persons, besides having the daily experience of language as a phenomenon like any other speaker, also has a particular sensitivity to language or has reflected on it. We will turn to linguists in the next chapter.

It has often been pointed out that scientific enquiry begins with an attitude of wonder with regard to something in our experience, so it may help to consider what we think is the most wonderful thing mankind has ever produced. Our thoughts may go immediately to the most advanced computer or other technological device, to our favourite Beethoven symphony, to the philosophical work or scientific theory that leads us furthest into an understanding of the universe, to the great proclamations recognizing the dignity of every human being. These are indeed great human accomplishments, but a moment's reflection will suffice to show that what lies behind each one of them is the possession of language, of a mother tongue giving each of us access to our forebears' achievements and putting us in a position to contribute something. Indeed, without language each generation would have to begin again that long mental trek from primitivity which our most distant ancestors undertook at the dawn of human prehistory. As one historian puts it: "Culture is the human way of life communicated by language, so that the word of man is both the creator and the transmitter of culture."[1] From the point of view of the prior conditioning factor, then, it can be argued that language is mankind's most admirable achievement since it permits us to develop everything else that characterizes us as human beings.

This may well be what Bertrand Russell had in mind when he remarked that "language comes first and thought follows in its footsteps."[2] He is not, of course, the only one to put forward the idea that language has permitted human mental development. Before him, Condillac, the eighteenth-century thinker, maintained that the language we speak is a measure of how we think: "The entire progress of the human mind depends on the skill with which we make use of language."[3] This can be understood both for mankind as a whole, as we have just seen, and for any individual in the sense that by extending our vocabulary, we gain access to new concepts, opening up new fields for reflection. Even more, the precision with which we use words affords a measure of how well we think. This view of language has a direct implication for any program of education: of primary importance is extending and refining the use of the mother tongue, since this is in good part the foundation of further intellectual development.

Remarks of this sort may strike some people as merely an appeal to use big words, to "speak fancy," whereas we seldom feel any need to be on our best linguistic behaviour because in most situations ordinary language suffices for the needs of everyday communication. It remains, however, that simply meeting the requirements of our usual social intercourse by means of the words that emerge into consciousness involves much more than is generally realized. The following remark by Hegel gives us a clue as to why language is considered to play such an important role in human affairs: "In our day it cannot be sufficiently stressed that what distinguishes man from beast is thought. Language permeates all inner experience or thought which man makes peculiarly his own, and whatever he expresses in linguistic form – be it obscure and confused or clear and explicit – has categorial content. So natural is logical thought to man; or rather, we may say, it constitutes his distinctive nature."[4] Whatever we say, then, be it an ordinary "Good morning" or the most abstruse philosophical or scientific treatise, has "categorial content." That is, no matter how ephemeral, particular, or vague the experience we happen to be talking about, the very fact of expressing it by means of language categorizes it, and shows it has something in common with other experiences. Indeed, this situating of any experience in a more general framework constitutes the distinctively "logical" nature of human thought. As Waldron (197) puts it: "In the most natural way, so natural that most people remain unaware of it their entire lives, language and language-dependent thought develop *pari passu*." Such remarks are concerned with what permits our thinking and our conversation, what enables us to grasp and express different areas of experience, to make distinctions and perceive similarities in various fields of human endeavour from the most commonplace to the most abstruse. This is an ability that depends to a large extent on our having acquired the ideas proper to each area of experience.

George Orwell brings this out forcefully when he describes the opposite effect of Newspeak, the language of the totalitarian state depicted in his well-known novel *Nineteen Eighty-Four.* "Newspeak, indeed, differed from most all other languages in that its vocabulary grew smaller instead of larger every year. Each reduction was a gain, since the smaller the area of choice, the smaller the temptation to take thought. Ultimately it was hoped to make articulate speech issue from the larynx without involving the higher brain centres at all."[5] Any totalitarian state aims at enslaving the minds of people in order to make alternative ideas impossible: "Don't you see that the whole aim of Newspeak is to narrow the range of thought? In the end we shall make thoughtcrime literally impossible, because there will be no words in which to express it."[6] It is language which permits us to call to mind alternatives to the scenario presented by our experience of the moment. Thanks to language, our intellect can readily evoke possibilities, compare, establish relationships, and thus provide the necessary condition for making a choice. Waldron (81) goes so far as to say: "It is language which confers on us that consciousness of alternative options which we call freedom. It is language, in short, which makes us in the truest sense human."

These are major claims for language – it permits categorial or logical thought and, through this type of thinking, the possibility of choice. The idea that language is the means for bringing to mind and expressing thought in this way has been taken by some to imply that there is no thinking without language; they even interpret the Sapir-Whorf hypothesis as a sort of linguistic determinism. This, however, is not the whole story, since there is another way of looking at the relation between language and thought, as we shall now see.

THE STRUGGLE FOR WORDS

Not all those who have reflected on the relation between thought and language would agree with the view that language is a necessary precondition for human thought. Zeno Vendler (31), for example, claims "that whereas speech essentially involves the use of a language, thought is essentially independent of it." He makes this more explicit as follows: "Very often we hear 'I do not find the exact word for what I want to say.' The most natural assumption is that the speaker does know what he wants to say. For after a while he might exclaim 'I have it! It is ...' The word fits. Fits what? Fits into the sentence(s) the thinker entertains? Hardly, since many words could do that. But that word alone expresses his thought" (43). More vividly, a medical doctor describes his experience "in a slum hospital and the prison next door" as follows: "My patients often had no words to describe what they were feeling, except in the crudest possible way, with expostulations, exclamations, and physical displays of emotion. Often, by guesswork and my experience of other patients, I could put things into words for them, words that they grasped at eagerly. Everything was on the tip of their tongue, rarely or never reaching the stage of expression out loud."[7]

At the other extreme, Einstein (327) brings out the same relationship when he asks: "What is it that brings about such an intimate connection between language and thinking? Is there no thinking without the use of language, namely in concepts and concept-combinations for which words need not necessarily come to mind? Has not every one of us struggled for words although the connection between 'things' was already clear?" Although many people may not have experienced concepts as clearly as Einstein did prior to expressing them through language, most of us can probably recall situations (such as writing an essay) where, despite being aware of something to say, we have had trouble finding the right words to express the different notions and impressions we had in mind.

In the following passage Emily Carr, the painter, particularly sensitive to the fluidity of what she wants to express, describes the inadequacy of both paint and language to capture her thought:

> There's words enough, paint and brushes enough and thoughts enough. The whole difficulty seems to be getting the thoughts clear enough, making them stand still long enough to be fitted with words and paint. They are so elusive – like wild birds singing above your head, twittering close beside you, chortling in front of you, but gone the moment you put out your hand. If ever you do catch hold of a piece of a thought it breaks away leaving the piece in your hand just to aggravate you. If one only could encompass the whole, corral it, enclose it safe – but then maybe it would die, dwindle away because it could not go on growing. I don't think thoughts could stand still – the fringes of them would always be tangling into something just a little further on and that would draw it out and out. I guess that is just why it is so difficult to catch a complete idea – it's because everything is always on the move always expanding.[8]

It is not uncommon for writers, especially poets, to feel this inability of language to provide the means to express exactly what they want to express. T.S. Eliot alludes to this when he speaks of every attempt to use words as a "venture":

> ... And so each venture
> Is a new beginning, a raid on the inarticulate.
> With shabby equipment always deteriorating
> In the general mess of imprecision of feeling,
> Undisciplined squads of emotion.[9]

Each such venture ends in "a different kind of failure" because words are not capable of depicting fully what the poet has in mind, deteriorated to the point of being unable to express the precise feeling in context. It remains, however, that language does make it possible to articulate what would otherwise remain incommunicable. Northrop Frye expresses this as follows: "it is clear that all verbal structures with meaning are verbal imitations of that elusive psychological and physiological process known as thought, a process stumbling through emotional entanglements, sudden irrational convictions, involuntary gleams of insight, rationalized prejudices, and blocks of panic and inertia, finally to reach a completely incommunicable intuition."[10]

Similarly, for Robert Frost, it is the thought that calls for the word: "A poem ... begins as a lump in the throat, a sense of wrong, a homesickness, a lovesickness ... It finds the thought and the thought finds the words."[11] Here Frost's view focuses not on what a poem expresses but on the poet's mental activity of making the poem. The following lines from Tennyson summarize the difficulty in making words express one's thoughts:

> And I would that my tongue could utter
> The thoughts that arise in me.[12]

The point of these citations is to highlight the fact that thought – in a slightly different sense from that evoked in the preceding section, as we shall see – exists before we call on words to express it, and not just as a result of using words. Moreover, this alternative way of looking at the relation between thought and language makes sense since, obviously, one undertakes an act of language by calling on words only if one already has something in mind to say. Gethin (32) makes this point as follows: "Something that is not words must first trigger the particular words I actually use ... The thought must come first, quite independently, on its own." Furthermore, this mental content varies not only from one speaker to another and from one moment to another, but also in the vividness with which a given speaker at a given moment becomes aware of it. While an Einstein who grasps clearly an abstract concept, or an Eliot who feels with enhanced sensitivity a cultural context, may experience difficulty in finding the appropriate words, ordinary speakers generally find the words that come to mind adequate for their needs. Indeed, the very efficiency of language in finding the fitting words for ordinary discourse leaves the required search process in the dark, so much so that we are normally quite unaware of it. And yet calling to mind the words appropriate to the particular experiential message we want to express is a necessary component of every act of language – a point to be developed in a later chapter.

In our attempt to probe the relation between language and thought, the matrix in which we want to situate these chapters on meaning, we have seen so far that we need language to have thought and that we need thought to have language. Reflecting on this paradox, which is only apparent, will bring out the important point to be made in this first chapter: between thought and language there is a two-way relationship.

THE MEASURE OF THE UNIVERSE

In his *Prometheus Unbound*, Shelley evokes both facets of the thought-language relationship. In the following remarkable lines (II, iv, 72–3), he brings out how language gives rise to our rational or logical or categorial thought through concepts permitting us to grasp the world we live in:

> He gave man speech, and speech created thought,
> Which is the measure of the universe.

The terms *space* and *time* are good examples of how common words provide both ordinary speakers and scientists with concepts commensurate with the universe around us. Elsewhere in the poem (IV, 415–17) Shelley evokes the relationship between language and thought again, but from the other point of view:

> Language is a perpetual Orphic song,
> Which rules with Daedal harmony a throng
> Of thoughts and forms, which else senseless and shapeless were.

Here, for Shelley, the "throng of thoughts and forms" making up our stream of consciousness would remain "senseless and shapeless" without the intervention of language, whose unceasing role is to impose an intricate harmony and order on their turbulence. Language thus enables us to make sense of our experience by giving it a categorial or conceptual form and permitting rational thought.

The following excerpt from a poem by Mandelstam (cited in Vygotsky, 119) evokes this role of language from another point of view: "I have forgotten the word I intended to say, and my thought, unembodied, returns to the realm of shadows." Unless captured by a word, the thought slips back to the fringe of conscious awareness.

Shakespeare brings out much the same thing but with a different emphasis in *The Tempest* (I, ii, 353–8) when Prospero depicts how he taught the half-human Caliban language:

> I pitied thee,
> Took pains to make thee speak, taught thee each hour
> One thing or other: when thou didst not, savage,
> Know thine own meaning, but wouldst gabble like
> A thing most brutish, I endowed thy purposes
> With words that made them known.

Without words, Caliban was unaware of his own thoughts, and so all he could do was "gabble" like other animals. However, provided with words, with human language, he became aware of what was going on in his own mental life, becoming able to express it to himself and to others. Here the emphasis is on the humanizing effect of language, on the way words make us conscious of what is in our own minds, an obvious prerequisite for rational thinking.

In his *Linguistique et philosophie*, Gilson discusses this double relationship between thought and language from the point of view of the philosopher. He points out that "although all inner language is speech as thought [by the speaker], it is itself born of another thought, or mental activity, prior to language." To discuss this pre-language thought, however, there is a difficulty:

> We cannot talk about it. To grasp this thought in itself, one
> would have to be able to trace it back up, against the current
> so to speak, right to its source, that is to say, back to the point
> where the thought is beginning to descend into language, but
> where thinking and speaking are not yet quite the same thing.
> But the two elements of the experience are not equally
> matched, because if there exists a form of thought prior to
> language, we cannot say anything about it, even to ourselves
> ... Whatever we try to think about the not-yet-said is condi-
> tioned by the impossibility of doing it without calling on lan-
> guage ... All one can do is work back up from the spoken
> thought to the thought which is being spoken, try to discern
> the future, after-language thought in the thought which is
> being incarnated. (122–7; my translation)

The philosopher's quandary of how to reflect on one aspect of reality, pre-language thought, without putting it into words does not, fortunately, pose any problem for the ordinary speaker since the role of words is precisely to give the inarticulate a shape and form, permitting the mind to grasp it and, if one so wishes, to express it and reflect on it. This brings us to the last point to be raised in this chapter on how language has been traditionally viewed as a human phenomenon: how words carry out their role.

FROM PRE-LANGUAGE THOUGHT TO LANGUAGED THOUGHT

The tradition that language reduces the turbulence of our stream of consciousness often attributes this role to words not simply because we can speak only in words, but also because of the apparent stability of words as witnessed by the dictionary. On the other hand, we have seen that words often give the impression of being imprecise, unstable, difficult to use. Einstein speaks of a "struggle" and Eliot of an "intolerable wrestle with words and meanings" – comments perhaps suggesting that words are ill-adapted to their role. A brief discussion of this question will help bring out how tradition has confronted it.

In his *Philosophy of Rhetoric*, I.A. Richards brings out that words provide not a facsimile of the particular experience a speaker has in mind but, going beyond this, a generalized view of it:

> So far from verbal language being a 'compromise for a language of intuition' – a thin, but better-than-nothing substitute for real experience – language, well used, is a completion and does what the intuitions of sensation by themselves cannot do. Words are the meeting points at which regions of experience which can never combine in sensation or intuition, come together. They are the occasion and the means of that growth which is the mind's endless endeavour to order itself. That is why we have language. It is no mere signalling system. It is the instrument of all our distinctively human development, of everything in which we go beyond the other animals. (130–1)

According to Richards, then, an ordinary word such as *home* or *fun* or *nice* can depict a surprising diversity of experiences, each unique in itself, by abstracting impressions common to them. Thus these words evoke the "meeting point" for otherwise unconnected experiences. In this way, the mind "endeavours to order" the endlessly varied and, as some say, turbulent input into consciousness by organizing it, categorizing each singular experience whether it arises from sensation, imagination, or any other source.

Elsewhere, Richards evokes this ordering by the mind from the point of view of its effect:

> I can make the same point by denying that we have any sensations. That sounds drastic but is almost certainly true if rightly understood. A sensation would be something that just was *so*, on its own, a datum; as such we have none. Instead we have perceptions, responses whose character comes to them from the past as well as the present occasion. A perception is never just of an *it*; perception takes whatever it perceives as a thing of a certain sort. All thinking from the lowest to the highest – whatever else it may be – is sorting. (30)

This sorting or categorizing of experience would appear to be what Gilson (126) alludes to when he compares the "pre-language thought of the adult" with that of the infant: "What the *in-fans*, the non-speaking one, thinks is probably linked to what the same infant continues to think after having learned to submit it to the disciplines of a language." By learning its mother tongue, an infant learns to sort its perceptions, to submit its experience to a categorization, and so to accede to an adult mode of thinking. We will return to this important relation between thought and language in later chapters.

For the moment, the point to be made is that a word is not something to be used just once (a sort of kleenex-word) for evoking a particular experiential content with all its specificity; this is the role of a sentence.[13] Rather a word is capable of depicting a diversity of experiences or thoughts. Each word (e.g. *flower*) has been fashioned to leave out what is particular (a specific colour, shape, etc.) and evoke only what is common to a given "sort" or series of experiences. What a word calls to mind, then – its meaning – is not the specific experience one wants to express but a categorial representation of it, a generalization from particular experiences of a given sort. That is, a word's meaning is not something in one's momentary experiential awareness but a general idea applicable to that experience, and Einstein's struggle for words or Eliot's "intolerable wrestle with words and meanings" is the often demanding effort to find what word – or words whose general ideas when combined – will best depict the particular content of experience one has in mind.

This calls to mind the example provided by Pascal's well-known dictum where two regions of experience, containing and understanding, meet in the single French word *comprendre*, 'comprehend': "*Par l'espace, l'univers me comprend et m'engloutit comme un point; par la pensée, je le comprends.*" ("Through space the universe comprehends me and engulfs me like a point; through thought, I comprehend it.") Parallel examples in English are provided by the words *grasp* and *see*, which are used in ordinary discourse to designate both a physical activity (to grasp the oar, to see a bird) and an activity of the mind (to grasp the importance of something, to see what is meant) thanks to some impression common to both. Examples such as these often depend on the role of metaphor in language, a question to be discussed later once we have a sufficiently clear view of the elements involved in a word.

In our attempt to discern the relationship between thought and language[14] it has become clear that the word *thought* is commonly used to depict different sorts of experience and so provides another example of what we have just been discussing. Those who maintain that language is required for thought take it in the sense of rational, conceptual, languaged thought, whereas those who maintain that thought is required for language take it in the sense of intuitional, experiential, pre-language thought. In both cases *thought* is used to depict something of which we are aware, but is sometimes used to depict anything mental, even realities of which we cannot be aware. Since it is a key term for our purposes here, to avoid confusion it is important to bring out this sense as well.

In addition, *thought* is used to evoke an activity, as in the above citation from Frye, "that elusive psychological and physiological process known as thought." In this third sense, it can designate mental operations[15] that do not themselves emerge into consciousness, though their results do (Frye's "incommunicable intuition"), operations such as the thinking involved in producing the words required for a sentence, as we shall see. Finally, a fourth sense that will be pertinent in these chapters is to name the faculty or potentiality enabling us to undertake mental activities. This of course does not exhaust the possible senses of *thought* in usage, but it does help clear the ground not only by distinguishing between the experiential content of thought that necessarily precedes any act of language and the categorial content of thought that results from an act of language, but also by permitting us to include, when useful, pre-conscious thinking, and to name the faculty making all these possible.

LANGUAGE AS AN INTERFACE

In the light of the views discussed so far, views characterizing a traditional mentalist approach, we can now attempt to situate language as part of the human phenomenon. We have just seen that words enable us to categorize and depict, if only in a general way, whatever particular experience we may want to talk about. This indicates that the meaning of any word is something abstract, and explains why, although limited, our vocabulary is capable of confronting the infinite variety of our experience and sorting it into categories. Being abstract, the meaning of a word must have been drawn from particular experiences by a process of generalization, an historical process, speakers of each generation acquiring a word from the preceding generation's manner of using it and applying it to their own experience to provide "a generalized reflection of reality" (Vygotsky, 153) or an "informal theory of common experience" (Waldron, 3). This helps us understand why the categories inherent in word meanings vary from one language to another: even when confronted with substantially the same set of experiences, different language communities have sorted them according to different impressions. Such considerations lead to the conclusion that words are man-made entities, formed by the mental activity of speakers confronting their own personal experiences with the resources of their mother tongue and their innate capacity to generalize.

This conclusion is in seeming contradiction with the view expressed in a preceding section: where certain writers maintained that language has made man what he is, here we have concluded that man has made language what it is. Thanks to the distinction made between categorial, languaged thought and experiential, pre-language thought, we can now see that these views are not contradictory but complementary. On the one hand, each language community has been able to develop and transmit its traditional wisdom, philosophy, science, technology, etc. by means of the abstract categories provided by word meanings.[16] That is, thanks to its words, a given language permits its speakers to develop what is specifically human: a set of more or less general ideas that serve to categorize and depict any particular experience they may wish to talk about.

In this sense, language is the instrument that has permitted us to exploit our given mental potential, the characteristic usually taken as distinguishing us from the other animals. On the other hand, language is not a ready-made instrument provided for mankind at the outset. Rather it has had to be fashioned over the millennia thanks to our mental potential, providing the means for sorting out, grasping, what is going on in our own minds and expressing it. That is, language is a human artefact, a man-made instrument – "something that has to be built up out of the perception, behaviour and experience of each individual, with whatever aid he or she receives from other members of the same speech community" (Waldron, 18) – enabling the mind to organize whatever comes into our conscious awareness and, when appropriate, to communicate it. Or as Delacroix[17] puts it in the citation at the beginning of this chapter: "Thought makes language while being made by language."

Language is thus a sort of interface between experiential or pre-language thought and rational or languaged thought, an interface that is more than a boundary or limit since, as we shall see, it requires of the speaker/writer certain mental operations to transmute one type of thought into another. This languaging of experience can be depicted by the following diagram:

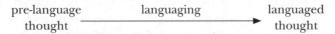

pre-language   languaging   languaged
thought   thought

As Waldron (xv) points out, this is "the central function of human language: the manner in which it *mediates* between sense experience and conceptual thought." Languaging thought is of course only part of a speaker's role. To complete an act of language, speakers/writers must express their languaged thought by means of perceptible signs that can then be understood and interpreted by addressees to complete an act of communication.

This, then, is the overall perspective within which our attempt to make sense out of meaning will be situated. It is a traditional approach that entails considering meaning not just as the reflex of a given set of sounds, or as just one other element of our mental experience, but as a construct of the mind, an "indispensable component" (Vygotsky, 120) of every word. The implications of this approach are many, but we shall mention only a few directly concerning language as an object of study.

2

Linguists and the Tradition

> Man is man through language alone.
> Wilhelm von Humboldt[1]

INTRODUCTION

This excerpt helps recall the first point of view brought out by the rather haphazard collection of citations in the last chapter, which was not intended to constitute a survey or history of the way language has been regarded, but merely to call to mind a traditional way of viewing the relation between language and man, or more precisely between language and thought. This traditional mentalist approach offered two perspectives, depending on how the word *thought* is understood, perspectives which were seen to be complementary. Language enables us to fix on and grasp more or less adequately what we have in mind, to order or categorize it, and then to express it. Without language, our stream of consciousness ('thought' understood as what we have in mind) would remain an ongoing series of personal experiences ordered only by the contingencies of the universe around us, and within us, our own impulses. By means of language, an incommunicable mental experience can be reduced through abstraction to the conceptual content of words and in this form brought into focus as sayable units of meaning (languaged 'thought') and so made communicable to others.

The reason for first calling to mind the traditional view is that it is comprehensive enough to include this double relation, thought$_1$ → languaging → thought$_2$, and so provide the broad perspective required to situate the question to be explored in these chapters, namely meaning. On the other hand, the traditional approach remains piecemeal, a series of insights from different points of view, and so does not provide a sufficiently coherent basis for examining meaning from the point of view of linguistics. In the present chapter, therefore, we will turn to several linguists to see how they have exploited this tradition as a foundation for analysis.

RECOGNIZING THE TRADITION

Although most nineteenth-century linguists were concerned with etymology and the historical development of meaning, Nerlich (39) mentions two who were concerned with the relation between meaning and thought. Reisig adopts a view of usage that "is very traditional, that is representational ... [L]anguage represents thought, a thought that itself represents the external world. For Reisig thoughts and feelings exist independently of the language that represents them, a view that his contemporary Humboldt tried to destroy in his conception of language as constitutive of thought." Here each linguist would appear to have taken into consideration one aspect of the double thought / language / thought relationship to the exclusion of the other: Reisig the languaging of experience, Humboldt the expressing of languaged thought.

In the following passage, Schaff (298) appears to echo Humboldt's view of language permitting thought: "The interpretation of the verbal signs as sounds with which certain independently existing thoughts are associated is due to a complete disregard of the nature of language processes and thought processes. Not only are there no thoughts existing independently of speech sounds ... but there is no thought independent of a system of such signs." Again we understand "thought" in the sense of what has been categorized thanks to language.

The other point of view is more common in an English-speaking context. Whitney (cited in Nerlich, 226) expresses his awareness of the way language depicts our experience by the abstract meanings of words: "[W]e do not and cannot always precisely communicate what we are conscious of having in our minds, and ... of what we call our expression, a part consists merely in so disposing a framework of words that those who hear us are enabled to infer much more than we really express, and much more definitely than we express it." Like others already cited, Whitney is particularly sensitive to the fact that words cannot render a particular experience in all its specificity but that the message inferred goes beyond the meaning understood.

Better known as a linguist with a traditional mentalist approach to meaning, Sapir also dwells on the process of abstraction involved in languaging experience in order to make it communicable:

> The world of our experiences must be enormously simplified and generalized before it is possible to make a symbolic inventory of all our experiences of things and relations and this inventory is imperative before we can convey ideas. The elements of language, the symbols that ticket off experience, must therefore be associated with whole groups, delimited classes, of experience rather than with single experiences themselves. Only so is communication possible, for the single experience lodges in an individual consciousness and is, strictly speaking, incommunicable. To be communicated it needs to be referred to a class which is tacitly accepted by the community as an identity. (12–13)

He goes on to speak of word meaning as "a convenient capsule of thought that embraces thousands of distinct experiences and that is ready to take in thousands more." Similarly for Whorf, who points out that "[w]e are inclined to think of language simply as a technique of expression, and not to realize that language first of all is a classification and arrangement of the stream of sensory experience" (55).

Gardiner also insists on the distinction between what we have in mind to say and the meaning of words:

> Everyone is familiar with the sensation of having something to say, but not knowing exactly what it is. And then the words come, and with them the feeling, not merely of expression, but even of creation. Words have thus become part of our mechanism of thinking, and remain, both for ourselves and for others, the guardians of our thought.
>
>   Let there be no mistake about it, however; even in abstract statements, the word-meaning can never be identical with the thing-meant, no matter how closely welded together the two may be. A word-meaning may crystallize in our minds a thought which has long eluded expression, but that thought is substantival in nature, and the word-meaning adjectival. The word-meaning can only describe what is meant – not *be* it. (55)

Thus Gardiner expresses the traditional view that meaning is not to be confused with the speaker's experience ("what is meant"). Elsewhere (31), he makes it clear that the "thing-meant" is "extra-verbal" but this does not imply that it is "real or materially existent"; he thus brings out the point that even when what one has in mind is an abstract idea, as in the citation from Einstein in the preceding chapter, the meaning of the word, also an abstract mental reality, is distinct from it. He evokes the relation between the two as one of "describing," i.e. a relation of depicting or representing, and so, like others, points out that "[i]t belongs to the nature of a 'word,' as that term is universally understood, to be utilizable over and over again in many different contexts and situations. This being the case, it is obvious that every word is susceptible of referring to many different particular things, to each of which it applies as a sort of common label" (38).

These linguists thus conceived of language as a representational interface between unsayable thought and sayable thought. Interesting and suggestive though their various insights are, however, none of them explored the implications of this relationship between language and thought in order to provide a setting comprehensive enough to situate meaning in all its manifestations, and particularly a given word's capacity for polysemy, "the pivot of semantic analysis" according to Ullmann (117), i.e. a crucial problem for the study of meaning in synchrony. This appears to be what led Gustaf Stern, and others, to break with the tradition we have been describing.

For Stern, meaning is not a depiction or representation of experience; rather, meaning *is* the speaker's experience. He says: "The meaning of a word – in actual speech – is identical with those elements of the user's (speaker's or hearer's) subjective apprehension of the referent denoted by the word, which he apprehends as expressed by it" (45). Since, for Stern, meaning involves no abstraction from the experience to be expressed, "[i]t is further evident that when the word *camera* is used of different cameras, the meaning changes in correlation to the change of referent" (40). By identifying meaning with the speaker's subjective experience, Stern views it as a mental reality but thereby situates it outside language in the speaker's ongoing stream of consciousness, which exists whether one talks about it or not. In this respect, he adopts a position quite at odds with the tradition.

In fact, the traditional approach to meaning we have been evoking appears to have ended with Gardiner, insofar as linguists in England are concerned. According to Nerlich, after Gardiner "we observe a stretching of the term semantics to its limits, covering everything from phonology to conversation analysis, and we observe a dissolution of meaning in the context of situation" (266–7). As a consequence, further work on lexical semantics has been based on logical, psychological, and other models. It remains, however, that the tradition, based as it is on the experience and observation of so many writers and thinkers, must reflect something of the reality of language. We have seen that their diverse insights suggest a double relationship between thought and language, but what this entails has not been explored. As a consequence, rather than neglect the tradition or dismiss it as unscientific, we should bring out the implications of this binary relationship to see what light it can throw on meaning, and particularly on the question of polysemy.

IMPLICATIONS OF THE TRADITION

To my knowledge, the linguist who has most reflected on the traditional relationship between language and thought is Guillaume, whose views provide the basis of much that follows. The realization that language is a means of expressing whatever comes into our minds, and that what language expresses is not a facsimile of what we want to express, avoids identifying meaning with our personal experience as Stern did. The idea that word meanings, as categorial representations of the experience to be expressed, mediate between experience and expressed thought entails the binary relation between thought and language seen above, and will provide the general setting for examining linguistic meaning in the following chapters.

The reciprocal causation of thought and language has many implications for such topics as the history of human understanding, the humanizing function of language, and the relationship between language and scientific curiosity.[2] The view that the system for constructing words in one's language provides the unconscious basis for developing science and for intellectual pursuits in general does not, however, lead to a sort of linguistic determinism, for the simple reason that it is thought that makes language as an instrument for its own development. "Thought is free, completely free, infinite in its actively free development,"[3] and so the mind is constantly in search of an ever more adequate means of representing its experience of the universe by using its capacity to generalize, and of course particularize. The constant aim for all languages is "to provide the mind with the permanent means of expressing itself in the moment of need."[4] What are the permanent means required to enable the mind to express itself in the moment of need?

Every language tends to make available to the speaker the means of expressing whatever comes to mind. This prompts the question: what conditions are necessary to make this possible? That is, like anyone else adopting a scientific approach, we are motivated by the desire to understand, and this leads to seeking prior factors, preconditions, the consequence of which would be what is observed. What is permanent for speakers is words,[5] which are a universal, found in every language and every act of speech. Attention is focused on the word in this way, not to the exclusion of the phrase and the sentence, but as the prior condition for producing those syntactic constructs and for explaining their meaning.

As we have seen, the traditional analysis of a word began with separating its meaning from the perceivable sign, making it a sayable unit. The next step was to separate the lexical and grammatical meanings observed in tracing the history of the Indo-European languages. This leads to discerning the relation between these two types of meaning. The declensions and the conjugations in Classical Greek and Latin show that a word's lexical meaning can be construed differently to take into account the way it is to be used in a particular sentence. That is, besides its own inherent variability, a LEXEME must be configured for whatever syntactic use it is called on to fulfill. As speakers of English, we are familiar with a similar variation in the declension insofar as number is concerned (*book/ books*), and a variation in the conjugation for tense (*I remember/I remembered*), but variability in constructing a word is far less visible in English than in the classical languages. This is why it is easy to overlook a crucial point for analysis, namely that whenever a word is required for a sentence, the speaker must construct it during the moment of speech, construing a lexeme with the particular sense called for and giving it the grammatical form required for it to function in the sentence being constructed. One linguist who did not overlook this point is Guillaume.

Imbued by the method of comparative grammar as practiced in historical linguistics by Ferdinand de Saussure and Antoine Meillet,

Guillaume decided to apply it to the speaker.[6] In so doing he reduced a vast historical time span – that between a Proto-Indo-European form and the earliest attested forms of Indo-European languages – to the present, the moment of speech, in an attempt to see if a meaning learned as part of one's mother tongue can somehow give rise to the different senses expressed by its sign. He applied this method to the article and to different grammatical morphemes in order to analyze and describe their meaning system. Here it will be applied to lexical meanings.

This important point can be made more visible in English through innovations such as *to have a think, Small is beautiful,* and *Will he medal tonight?* (a commentary heard during an Olympics). Whether such unusual uses involve the same word used differently (*to think* vs. *a think*) or different words we will examine in chapter 5, once we have the necessary parameters for dealing with the question. The point here is what this sort of innovative usage implies: namely, that we cannot consider ready-made words to constitute part of the permanent resources of a speaker's language. Rather, the fact that we can construct a word for an unusual, or even original, use in this way indicates that we have, as part of our permanent linguistic resources, the potential for constructing words. That is, what constitutes part of the mind's permanent means of expressing itself is a mental mechanism for assembling a word's components in the way required for the sentence being constructed. In short, there is no word lexicon, as this term is commonly understood, built into our language resources, but there is something far more useful – a word-constructing program or system, as well as the formative elements, the lexemes and grammatical systems, required to construct a word whenever a speaker needs it.

The awareness that we have to put sentences together while speaking or writing is of course a commonplace, but the realization that we have to construct each of the words we need during the process of speaking and writing is by no means obvious because a word emerges into consciousness only after being constructed. Outside of cases made visible through the sign by prefixes and suffixes, this word-building process has received little attention. It is, however, omnipresent in speaking; whether the sign reflects it or not, the mental components of a word must be evoked and formed appropriately for the way the word is to be used in the sentence. This proposal appears to be a necessary prerequisite for explaining what we observe of the uses of words, and has important implications for our understanding of meaning, as the rest of this study will show. More generally, it has implications for our conception of language itself.

In the latter respect, the assumption that our permanent language resources include a word-fashioning mechanism put into operation whenever someone wants to speak recalls the Saussurian static dichotomy *langue/parole*, but in operational terms. Whereas Saussure considered *la langue* to be a state of language as a potential, our approach views it as including the mechanisms that make possible the processes involved in actualizing that potential to produce the words required to constitute the resulting sentence. That is to say, these permanent means are instituted in a speaker's pre-conscious mind as a potential which can be activated at any time to produce the word required at that moment for the needs of the sentence. Saussure's terms will be Englished here by TONGUE, designating the potential instituted in the mind to produce the words for expressing the required meaning (cf. *Webster's* sense 3: "the power of communication or expression through speech");[7] and by DISCOURSE, designating language actualized in sentences, the result of assembling the words so produced into phrases in order to constitute units of expression. This makes the word the central component of language. It is the unit resulting from putting the operational resources of tongue into operation, but it serves as a building stone of discourse, an element for constructing the sentence, the unit of discourse. While the way a sentence is put together has been the object of much discussion, little has been devoted to the way a word is put together. This will be our main concern in these chapters since, as in other sciences, the task of linguistics is to shed light on that part of its object which is not accessible by direct observation, tongue, in order to explain what is observable, discourse.[8]

Viewing human language from the point of view of how a word is constructed has the advantage of providing a framework general enough for situating meaning. It is an eminently dynamic view where everything is seen in terms of the possibility of an operation, the actualizing of an operation, or the result of an operation. This background is, in fact, implicit behind the double relationship between thought and language observed in the last chapter. The thought → languaging → thought relation presupposes a potential built into language for grasping or representing pre-language thought; actualizing this capacity entails depicting the specifics of a particular experience by the abstract categories provided by one's language; the result is languaged thoughts each with its sign, a sayable unit of meaning: a word. This result is itself a potential for the ensuing operation of expression, which involves actualizing a word's potential sign in speaking or writing along with those of other such sayable units to constitute a sentence. Various bits of experience are represented, i.e. languaged, as categorial thought with a sign, and expressed in such a way that the meaning of the resulting sentence reflects as closely as possible the original experience. Like any other operations, the two involved here, representing and expressing, presuppose something that makes them possible: a mechanism, a potential. Actualizing the sign(s) is made possible by a phonological system; linking the meanings thus expressed in order to reach the intended result, the meaning expressed by the sentence, presupposes a system of syntax.

Considering the expression of meaning to be the purpose of speaking and writing brings word meaning into the limelight and raises certain questions: what in its meaning makes a word capable of depicting, as Gardiner puts it, "many different particular things, to each of which it applies as a sort of common label"? What in its meaning permits a word not only to express different senses but, for the same idea, to have different functions from one sentence to another, and this without listeners getting confused? It is within this general framework, where a result presupposes an operation producing it, and the operation a potentiality permitting it, that we will situate the question of meaning and try to explore its operativity. First, however, a question concerning the scientific status of any such attempt must be discussed.

3

Meaning: An Object of Scientific Enquiry?

> [In linguistics there are] no other observations than the sound waves ...
> Everything else is hypothesis.
>
> William Diver[1]

INTRODUCTION

We have looked at traditional views which associate language with thought so intimately that one thinks of a sort of symbiotic relationship. For some, language is a necessary precondition for thought, taken in its categorial, conceptual sense, and from this point of view it can be argued that there is no thought expressed without language (or a language surrogate such as mathematics). For others, thought, in its experiential, content-of-awareness sense, is a necessary precondition for language, and so from this point of view it can be argued that there is no language sayable without thought. This binary relationship (far from the view suggested by some scholars that would limit the word to a role of communicating ideas) gives the word a mediating role in human mentation, that of first translating the specificity of a particular experience into a conceptual mode[2] of representation and then expressing it. Taking "thought" in another sense, it has been argued that the creation of words, the very existence of human language, depends on the prior existence of the human faculty of thought.

Traditional though it may be, this mentalist view of language, which entails making meaning central to analysis, has been rejected by many linguists because they consider it to make language unamenable to scientific treatment. No alternative view to the question of meaning has, however, achieved a consensus insofar as its results or its principles of analysis are concerned. As a consequence, it will not be wasted effort to take a closer look at the reasons for rejecting the traditional view to see if they are valid. This chapter will therefore examine whether meaning as a mental entity has any claim to be considered an object of scientific enquiry.

THE CASE FOR THE PROSECUTION

Lyons (408) summarizes as follows the case against admitting meaning as traditionally understood to the status of an object of scientific enquiry: "Traditional semantics makes the existence of 'concepts' basic to the whole theoretical framework, and therefore (almost inevitably) encourages subjectivism and introspection in the investigation of meaning. To quote Haas: 'an empirical science cannot be content to rely on a procedure of people looking into their minds, each into his own.'" Taking "empirical" in the usual sense of "relying on experience and observation," the point at issue is the mode of observation, introspection, which consists of looking into one's own mind. The objection is that no other observer has access to a person's mind, and so what is observed cannot be observed by others, a necessary requirement for scientific data.

In the following passage, another scholar brings out the same objection and adds a second one: "The inner aspect [of language] – the 'content' or 'meaning' – cannot be observed except by introspection on the part of the speaker himself; it cannot be objectively recorded or described at all. Meaning cannot be dealt with, at any level of analysis, in scientific terms; and it is in any case too exclusively qualitative for statistical treatment" (T.B.W. Reid, 34). The new argument here appears to be that, being qualitative, meaning does not lend itself to measurement or to quantification even through statistics, an argument based on the assumption that the method of science can deal only with quantifiable objects.

Stern, as we have seen, appears to accept this view for the meaning of a word in usage when he defines it as the speaker's or hearer's "subjective apprehension of the referent denoted by the word." Identifying meaning expressed by a word as part of our personal experience in this way makes it as variable as each individual's momentary perception of an object like a camera. In his well-known definition, Bloomfield (141) proposes a more general meaning for words: "the *distinctive* features or *linguistic meaning* (the *semantic* features) [are those] which are common to all the situations that call forth the utterance of the linguistic form, such as the features which are common to all the objects of which English-speaking people use the word *apple*."[3] In his view, then, meaning is not one's momentary perception of a particular apple, but is the features found in all apples. Although Stern's and Bloomfield's approaches are quite distinct, they are similar in situating meaning outside language, one in the speaker's experience, the other in the extra-mental situation.

This position has certain consequences for the study of language. These are brought out by Reid in the rest of the passage just cited: "There is therefore a great deal to be said for the position taken up by those structuralists who endeavour to achieve scientific objectivity by completely disregarding the inner aspect of speech and treating their text as if it were unintelligible. If linguistics is a genuine science they are its only true exponents. If on the other hand linguistics is to be the study of language as a whole, it must abandon the claim to be a science; for few students of language would deny that meaning is an integral part of it." Since one may well question whether a discipline apt to treat only part of its object can be called "a genuine science," it would seem that linguistics without a means of treating meaning cannot be a distinct science. This may be why it is often considered a part of some other discipline such as cognitive psychology. In any case, this point of view, particularly as expressed by Diver cited above, has the merit of reminding us that the only mind-external part of language is "the sound waves," but it remains to be seen if "everything else is hypothesis," whether meaning is to be banished from the kingdom of science.

THE CASE FOR THE DEFENCE

As speakers and listeners, it is part of our awareness of language that we use words to express meaning. In view of this common experience, some linguists consider words to be "the existent unit of living speech ... a psychological reality" (Sapir, 33) and "the fundamental units of language" (Miller, 261), and believe that meaning is "the one thing that matters most in language" (Bolinger 1977, 3), "the most fundamental issue in linguistic theory" (Langacker 1987, 5). If words are a universal of language, albeit constructed differently in different languages, their existence cannot, in the name of science, be denied[4] or simply ignored, as in some theories of syntax. However, if meaning is an essential component of a word, the above claim that meaning cannot be treated scientifically must be met.

This claim is based on the fact that a meaning can be observed only in the observer's own mind, to which no other observer has access, and on the argument that this subjectivity entails the impossibility of confirming any such observation in order to establish it as a linguistic datum. As one scholar puts it: "[W]henever a scientific paper is published there is an implicit undertaking, where possible, to make the raw material available for verification. This principle is at the very foundation of scientific progress. Without independent verification, or at least the opportunity to do so, scientific results have no validity."[5]

Meaning is unquestionably a mental entity accessible only by introspection, but the entailment that it cannot be verified is open to question. In the case of other mental entities such as a dream, a feeling, or one's reaction to a piece of music, the argument appears valid, but for meaning as expressed by a sentence, the situation is quite different. The very fact that we use a sentence to communicate implies that others can understand it. That is, it implies that listeners can look into their own minds and observe the same thing, or much the same thing, as the speaker had in mind when she or he spoke. That is, the subjective observation of addressees agrees with the speaker's subjective observation because language provides the means for expressing what one has in mind in such a way that others can call it to mind as well. As a consequence, any person with sufficient competence in English can get substantially the same meaning from a sentence. A speaker's introspective observation is therefore confirmed by every person who understands, through introspection, a given sentence the same way the speaker does.

The point here is simply that the capacity of communicating the way we do by means of language indicates that the meaning of a word is shared by all speakers of the language and so must be distinguished from other mental entities in our experience (a distinction that some apparently consider to be a "false dichotomy"[6]). For example, teaching grammars often give examples such as *Kim smokes* and *Kim is smoking*, describing them as expressing 'habit' and 'ongoing activity' respectively, meanings that constitute facts to be explained in the light of the meaningful components of each sentence. That is, there is a consensus of competent observers – of people who understand what is said – concerning the meaning of these sentences. Given this consensus, the meaning of the sentences qualifies as linguistic data and so calls for an explanation within the framework of a scientific discipline. In this way, the objection based on the subjectivity of meaning and introspection as a means of observing it can be met, and it can be claimed that the observation of meaning does give valid scientific data provided there is a consensus of observers.

Granted, then, the common observation of sentence meaning, the second objection raised in the previous section can now be addressed. It was argued that, as a mental entity, meaning cannot be quantified or measured, even statistically, and that as a consequence it cannot be dealt with in a scientific manner. While the argument appears to be valid, the consequence rests on a presupposition that may be open to question. It presupposes that science can treat only what is quantifiable and measurable. If the scope of the scientific method is limited to that portion of human experience which is measurable, then meaning is not amenable to a scientific treatment. This too may be valid, but it would seem more in the spirit of science as a human venture to see if the traditional method of the physical sciences can be adapted to handle an object of common experience which, being mental, is not quantifiable and measurable as in those sciences.[7] To explore this possibility is the challenge of the present study.

THE VERDICT

The objection that meaning observed through introspection cannot provide verifiable facts is overruled. It has been successfully countered by the argument that those who introspect for the meaning of a given sentence can, and usually do, reach a consensus on what has been observed, the first requirement for data. On the other hand, even though meaning may provide facts to be explained, it remains to be shown how they can be treated in a scientific fashion, i.e. as a basis for inferring general hypotheses permitting us to understand what brings about the meaning expressed by a particular sentence. Like the object to be observed in any other scientific discipline, meaning by its very nature confronts the observer with particular problems which must be overcome to ensure a solid basis for the phase of inference. Otherwise we are left with what Aitchison calls a "hazy mush of meanings" (49).

The first problem is to delimit the meaning expressed by the sentence. An ordinary remark such as *We're nearly out of gas*[8] expresses a readily understood meaning, but it would evoke quite different reactions depending on whether the speaker and hearer are driving toward a gas station or flying over the Atlantic. Although this may prove quite difficult in some cases, it is important to distinguish what is expressed by the sentence itself, linguistically, from the effect of putting the meaning thus understood into relation with other, non-linguistic elements in the situation. Conflicting interpretations of a sentence often result from the failure to make this distinction, which will be discussed in the next chapter.

The second problem involves distinguishing the import that each component of a sentence contributes to its meaning. Experience common to all speakers indicates that the meaning of a sentence depends on the words we use, and that what distinguishes a word from other words is its meaning. As Bolinger (1963, 136) points out, "the meaning of the sentence must be discussed in terms of the meaning of the component words and traffic-rule morphemes ... word meaning has a kind of priority and to that extent is unique." Reaching a consensus on what most of the words in a sentence mean is therefore not a problem for the average speaker. For example, most people would probably agree that *throw*, as in *he threw the ball*, expresses 'to propel by the hand and arm,' or something like that. On the other hand, in *The horse threw him* or *He threw up*, one cannot describe the verb's meaning in this way, and yet the sentences are readily understood. Anyone who takes the trouble of comparing different uses may well ask what the meaning of this word is, or even whether it is the same word in all three uses. This "observation of context and abstraction away from differing contexts," as Tuggy (358) puts it, is a major difficulty, perhaps *the* major difficulty, confronting the scientific treatment of meaning, and will therefore be discussed in some detail in subsequent chapters.

Another aspect of the problem of observing meaning concerns a few "traffic-rule" words, such as *to* and *the* in *to throw the ball*, words whose meaning, like that of *throw*, is variable, but is so difficult to observe that ordinary speakers cannot attempt to paraphrase it. These are grammatical words which, because they are more abstract, require certain procedures worked out by linguists – commutation, comparing syntactic possibilities, etc. – in order to discern their import to the phrase. This too may prove quite difficult, and in fact there are cases where, unable to discern the meaning, linguists have declared certain grammatical words meaningless, a conclusion calling into question the basic idea that language is, by nature, symbolic. Since this study deals with lexical, not grammatical, semantics, we will be little concerned with such words here.[9]

A third aspect of the problem arises when what appears to be the same word acts in quite different ways in the sentence. For example, besides *to throw the ball*, we can say *a good throw*, and it seems obvious that *throw* in each case expresses the same (or at least what appears at first sight to be the same) idea. On the other hand, we cannot say **a good throw the ball* or **to good throw the ball*. Clearly there is a difference of grammatical function here which is not reflected in the sign, a difference which has led some observers to consider that *throw* is not the same word in each use, whereas others have maintained that the difference is due to some change in the meaning of the word. This problem will call for an analysis of how a word is put together (see chapter 6).

Thus, accepting meaning as an object of observation[10] entails not only isolating the meaning of a sentence, observable by all speakers, from the situation and context, but also breaking it down into its component parts, i.e. the meaning of the words involved, and then breaking down (analyzing) the meaning of a word into its formative elements. Because of these difficulties, the word as a distinct linguistic form has sometimes been ignored by linguists and considered to be simply "an item" or "an entry in the lexicon" along with other unanalyzable units such as prefixes and suffixes.[11] Any attempt to treat word meanings as data must deal with these problems because they call into question the very status of a word. Even then, however, there remains another difficulty.

For an observation to be considered a datum, it must be communicable to other observers in order to obtain a consensus, and this entails something not required of the ordinary speaker, namely describing the meaning observed. Meaning can be described only by having recourse to the meaning of other words, a procedure some would consider circular. Moreover, it is rare that one can express exactly the same meaning with a different sentence, phrase, or word. Usually, the best a linguist can do is to paraphrase, to express a meaning as close as possible to, but not identical with, the original. An approximation such as 'the fuel tank is almost empty' for the above sentence would be sufficient to suggest to someone else the meaning of the original. On the other hand, in cases requiring more precise descriptions, as when an ESL teacher is asked to distinguish between *I leave tomorrow* and *I'm leaving tomorrow*, or *three bear* and *three bears*, the difficulty involved in first discerning the sense of each sentence or phrase and then paraphrasing it to bring out the subtle nuance between the two is considerably greater.

These problems arise from meaning as an object to be observed because it is a mental reality, something that cannot be reduced to a quantifiable, measurable reality.[12] As a consequence, they cannot be solved by experimentation, a means common to the physical sciences. Establishing the validity of the meaning observed and refining one's description of it depend on accumulating numerous examples of the word or form actually found in sentences spoken or written, examples of every type of usage from the most commonplace to the rarest. Although it is always possible that some rare or new use has been overlooked, only the attempt to extend observation to all possible uses can provide a sound basis for the next phase of a scientific procedure, that of inferring what conditions made the observed uses possible. In order to proceed to that phase, however, a method of analysis appropriate to meaning is required, as we shall see in a subsequent chapter. That is, granted that data can be derived from observing meaning in one's own mind, it may be possible to find a way of inferring the conditions giving rise to that data and so provide an explanation of what has been observed. In order to do that, we will first give an idea of what is involved in generating the meaning of words.

II MAKING WORDS

4

Coming to Grips with Meaning

> Has the reader never asked himself what kind of mental fact is
> his intention of saying a thing before he has said it?
> William James

MEANING VS. MESSAGE

In the last chapter we saw that tongue, our language potential, involves a system for constructing words, a mental mechanism consisting of the means of providing both the physical part of the word, the sign, and the mental part, its import or meaning. We saw also that the role of word meaning is to help effect the transition between pre-language thought and post-language thought, between the speaker's momentary experience and the categorial, languaged version of it expressed by a sentence. Moreover, tongue provides a speaker with the permanent capacity of effecting this transition for whatever experience the speaker may have in mind to talk about. Although it is generally taken for granted, this is in fact a quite remarkable capacity that speakers have acquired, and it is thanks to the words they have learned to form that they can exercise it, as we shall see more clearly in the next chapter. William James describes this in some detail from a psychological point of view:

> Has the reader never asked himself what kind of mental fact
> is his intention of saying a thing before he has said it? It is an
> entirely definite intention, distinct from all other intentions,
> an absolutely distinct state of consciousness, therefore; and yet
> how much of it consists of definite sensorial images, either of
> words or of things? Hardly anything! Linger, and the words
> and things come into the mind; the anticipatory intention, the
> divination is there no more. But as the words that replace it

arrive, it welcomes them successively and calls them right if they agree with it, and rejects them and calls them wrong if they do not. It has therefore a nature of its own of the most positive sort, and yet what can we say about it without using words that belong to the later mental facts that replace it? (245)

Granted, then, this capacity of word meaning to mediate between the speaker's pre-language stream of consciousness – or rather that portion of it the speaker wants to talk about, what we will call here the INTENDED MESSAGE – and the meaning expressed by the sentence, it becomes clear that meaning and intended message are two distinct mental realities.[1] (After all, it is the experience we have in mind, not the meaning, that we want to communicate.) Because meaning provides a representation of the intended message, or of something in the message, it cannot be identified with that message, just as a photograph cannot be identified with the person photographed. On the other hand, just as a photograph may serve to identify the person, so the meaning of a sentence permits listeners to identify the speaker's intended message, or better, to reconstitute it as part of their own stream of consciousness. Listeners reproduce the speaker's intended message in their own minds as faithfully as they can by taking into account not only the meaning expressed by a sentence, but also messages already obtained from the preceding linguistic context, what is known of the speaker's situation, etc. Saeed (221) evokes this process when, speaking of "the linguistically coded meaning," he asks, "[W]hat do we call the result of combining it with contextual information to get the final message?"

This process of reproducing the speaker's intended message as closely as possible is generally called REFERENCE, since it aims at carrying the meaning back to what, outside language, prompted it in the first place. It remains, of course, that the message actually arrived at by a listener, the realized message, may vary, in some cases considerably, from the message the speaker intended. Understood in this way, reference is the counterpart of representation: representation is the process of translating the intended message into something linguistic – into sayable bits of meaning – whereas reference is the process of translating meaning expressed in a sentence back into something extra-linguistic – into a realized message in its context and situation.

The point of this is to show that meaning, a mental reality belonging to language, cannot be identified either with the speaker's intended message, a different mental reality, or with the addressee's realized message, another mental reality, since neither of these are part of language. As Searle (1983, 146) points out: "there is more to understanding than grasping meanings because, to put it crudely, what one understands goes beyond meaning." For both speaker and addressee the message is what the sentence refers to, the REFERENT. This is brought out quite vividly when reference is not possible, when a listener or reader cannot relate the meaning of a sentence to something outside language, as in the situation described by Gardiner, an eminent Egyptologist and linguist:

> Is it not something of a puzzle that especially in letters and in ancient documents of different kinds the meaning of the component individual sentences should often be perfectly clear, but that the reader should nevertheless be left in almost complete darkness as to what the document is really about? (11)

Presumably ignorant of who wrote an ancient document and in what situation, the reader is unable to refer the meaning expressed to its extra-linguistic referent, to the intended message, and so cannot reproduce what the writer had in mind. Even though the meaning is clear, the reader does not get the message because some knowledge of the extra-linguistic situation is lacking.[2]

We must therefore add to the sequential schema discussed in chapter 1 to bring in reference:

$$thought_1 \rightarrow languaging \rightarrow thought_2 \rightarrow referent$$

Since reference always involves a listener going beyond language-expressed thought to reconstruct the intended message a speaker had in mind before speaking, the referent is by definition an extra-linguistic mental construct, a mental referent (which of course may, once identified, be referred to something outside the mind). The above schema can be made more explicit, adopting Saeed's expression, as follows:

$$intended\ message \rightarrow languaging \rightarrow meaning\ expressed \rightarrow final\ message$$

We will not be concerned with the extra-linguistic states of mind as such – the intended message (pre-language thought) or the final message (the mental referent). Rather, we will attempt to observe the meaning expressed (languaged thought) and to understand how the speaker construes this meaning, i.e. what is involved in languaging the intended message by means of words.

With this view of meaning as mediating between two states of consciousness, namely the intended message of the speaker and the message realized by the listener (and even by the speaker in inner speech), it can be seen that the first problem mentioned above, that of delimiting the meaning expressed by the sentence, can be overcome by distinguishing what is part of language from what is not, i.e. by distinguishing meaning from message. Thus *We're nearly out of gas* expresses the same meaning whether one is in a car or a plane, but will provoke different reactions when referred to the situation the speaker has in mind. Similarly, a simple remark such as *This is very nice* expresses a fairly general meaning that can give rise to messages appropriate to the endless variety of situations *this* can refer to. Likewise, in such "indirect uses" as *Do you know the time?* various messages or "indirect meanings" such as 'please tell me the time' or 'Do you realize how late it is?' are possible (Clark, 319), depending on the situation the listener refers the sentence's meaning to. As Taylor (1992, 7) points out, "Most sentences are vague, till set in a specific context ... the different interpretations do not need to be captured in the (compositional) semantics of the expression." In the above cases one can readily distinguish between the linguistic and the non-linguistic factors involved in getting the message, and so limit the problem of observing meaning to the former, though of course there are cases where it is not so easy to discriminate between the two and the problem is more difficult to solve. The important point here: because there is no expression of meaning without a prior representing of something in the intended message, it is not the speaker's experience but its linguistic representation as expressed by the sentence that must be observed by a linguist.

POTENTIAL VS. ACTUAL

The second problem raised above, discerning the import of each component of the sentence, arises from the notion, based on common experience, that language is symbolic – that the sentences we hear, and therefore the words they are made of, express meaning.

The analysis of sentence meaning into its elements, however, encounters the problem of polysemy. To explain how a given word can, in different contexts and situations, express different senses, it is proposed that a word's meaning, like its sign, is drawn from what pre-exists as a potential in tongue. A POTENTIAL MEANING can be actualized in different ways, giving rise to ACTUAL MEANINGS or senses observable in discourse. Bolinger and Sears (109) express a similar view: "The meaning of a word is potential, like that of a dollar bill before it is involved in a transaction ... The problem of meaning is how the linguistic potential is brought in line with non-linguistic reality whenever a speaker creates an utterance." This problem will be addressed in chapter 6 when we discuss potential meanings functioning as viewing ideas. Here we will clarify the approach adopted by examining the relationship involved between meaning as a potential and meaning as an actualized sense, and contrasting it with the relationship involved in other approaches.

One approach would be to propose that a different sense makes a different word. "Each pairing of sound with sense could be said to qualify as a word ... in which case a 'word' with several senses would actually be said to be several words. This definition departs from common usage, and the term *lexical item* is sometimes used with this meaning" (Dillon, 129). This approach would conflict with the ordinary speaker's conviction that somehow it is the same word in uses such as *throw* above, a conviction based on the fact that words learned provide a means of categorizing and expressing our endlessly varied experience.

Some would view a word's meaning as a sort of painter's palette offering different senses from which the speaker chooses one. Geeraerts (255–63) takes issue with viewing of a word's meaning in this way as a set with a "fixed and restricted" number of subsets, one of which is selected in each use. He favours rather viewing "meaning as a process of sense creation," calling for an "operational definition of polysemy," a view much closer to that proposed in the present essay. Likewise, for Croft and Cruse (97–9), "neither meanings nor structural relations are specified in the lexicon, but are construed 'on-line,' in actual situations of use" to give "contextually construed meanings, or ... interpretations." On the other hand, out of context "[a]n isolated sign certainly has semantically relevant properties, semantic potential, and these properties have an influence on eventual interpretation." The idea of a semantic potential is similar to the potential meaning exploited by the speaker as proposed here, but since "words do not really have meanings, nor do sentences," the term *meaning* in Croft and Cruse appears to be limited to the addressee's interpretation of a sentence in context – what I call the message. The processes involved in construing the semantic potential of a word, its "purport," give rise to polysemy, understood as "as a matter of isolating different parts of the total meaning potential of a word in different circumstances. The process of isolating a portion of meaning potential will be viewed as the creation of a sense boundary delimiting an autonomous unit of sense" (109). That is to say, "[w]hen we retrieve a word from the mental lexicon, it does not come with a full set of ready-made sense divisions" (109). Rather, "the construal of boundaries creates pre-meanings" (103) which are "still subject to further construal" (110), presumably when the addressee integrates the word into a phrase, a sentence, and eventually a context.

The approach of Croft and Cruse, calling for mentally construing a word's lexical potential to obtain different senses, has much in common with the approach proposed here because it avoids the idea of "selecting" an already existing sense. On the other hand, having adopted the point of view of the addressee, they obtain results quite at odds with my approach. For example, they propose that *bank*, which can express unrelated meanings ('financial institution' vs. 'margin of a river'), is not two separate words, homonyms, but a single word. This is also found when senses are linked on a prototypical/peripheral dimension with homonyms "as the endpoint along the cline of relatedness" (Langacker 1991 / 2002, 268). This is no doubt the outcome of adopting the point of view of the addressee, whose first concern is to discern the meaning of a word encountered as a physical sign. Some signs, "polysemous words," are capable of expressing a series of "semantically related" senses, others, "homonymous words," of expressing quite distinct meanings (cf. Frisson, 114–16). This approach has "the major advantage ... that it frees the linguist from the obligation to search for a semantic component unifying all the different uses of a word" (Taylor 1989, 142). On the other hand, as I have pointed out elsewhere (2007b, 69), this involves a major difference in the usual understanding of what a word is: it implies that the unifying element of a word is not its meaning but its physical sign, a fundamental change in one's conception of human language.

The alternative point of view is that of the speaker, whose first concern is whether the lexeme can represent some entity or happening in the intended message in order to express it by means of its sign in the sentence. Speakers are aware of whether or not a word's lexeme can represent something in the intended message. Whether it happens to have the same sign as another lexeme (its homonym) is usually not relevant. This implies that the unifying element of a word, what makes it a unit, is its potential meaning, its lexeme, and the range of representation it permits, or in traditional terminology, its comprehension and its extension. We have seen in chapter 1 how adopting the speaker's point of view of the word permits us to discern the double relation between language and human thought. As we shall see, this entails trying to discern how a word is constructed, how the potential meaning is actualized by the speaker in one of its possible senses.

Others postulate a meaning potential. For Evans (70), "[t]hat aspect of the word's potential which is activated is a consequence, in part, of the way it is constrained by the utterance context," but he goes on to propose (76) that "any given word will provide a unique activation of part of its semantic potential on every occasion of use"; its "semantic contribution ... will vary slightly every time it is used." Allwood also appeals to meaning as a potential, but in this he includes (56) "storage of collocational relationships to other morphemes or words as well as to stored information about extralinguistic context"; in fact it is (61) "all the information (linguistic and encyclopedic) connected with a word ... which constitutes the meaning potential of a word." Including in a word's meaning all the circumstances of its past uses, or whatever the unique context calls for, would be quite the opposite of the notion of potentiality developed here, which can be compared with the ability to ride a bicycle: once acquired by a youngster it can be exploited in different ways, and by certain individuals (as in a circus) in quite exceptional ways. Only some such view of potential meaning allows for the creativity to be discussed in the next chapter and avoids the dilemma involved in "a very precarious balancing act between the maximization of polysemy, where the words themselves carry most of the polysemous workload and speakers just have to choose correctly in context, and a minimization of polysemy which leaves most of the work to the pragmatic component, that is to the interpretational work done by the speakers" (Nerlich et al., 14).[3]

The point of this brief comparison with different approaches is that a word's meaning will be considered here neither as an aggregate of more or less related parts or subsets, one of which is selected for each use, nor as setting boundaries on a portion of meaning potential, nor as an accumulation of traces of former uses. Rather it is viewed as a potential to be actualized, a potency that can be exploited in the way best representing what the speaker has in mind at that moment. Thus for the linguist – but not the ordinary speaker – observing one sense of a word entails looking for its other, related senses in order to be able to work back to a potential meaning, which can never be expressed as such in discourse and so cannot be observed. This involves employing a method similar to that of comparative-historical linguistics – observing later forms to reconstruct what prior non-attested form could have given rise to them – a method that is assumed for phonemes, which can be realized in different ways in view of the context, and that has already produced results in working back from usage to the abstract meaning potential of certain grammatical words and morphemes. However, whether we will one day be able to reconstruct the complex of characterizing traits, abstract and concrete, making up the potential of lexical words remains to be seen, particularly in view of the possible variation of a word's lexical potential between speakers – specialists vs. non-specialists, for example.[4]

Observing a lexeme's actual meanings, or senses, is not an easy job because they can be observed only in discourse, that is, once an actualized lexeme has been formed grammatically into a word and integrated through the processes of syntax into a phrase, and the phrase into a sentence. A word's import is thus combined with that of other words to contribute to the composite meaning or EXPRESSIVE EFFECT of the phrase and ultimately of the sentence, and this raises a major difficulty. One can easily confuse the expressive effect of the phrase or sentence with the sense expressed by the word, as in the example given above, where the idea of 'by the hand and arm' is included in the meaning of *throw* by a dictionary, whereas it would appear that this particular manner of throwing arises only through the expressive effect, the outcome of combining the imports of subject *he*, verb *threw*, and object *the ball*, as opposed to *He threw a fit*.

Another example of the difficulty involved in distinguishing an expressive effect from a word's import has been suggested: *rough* in *rough skin* has a tactile sense, in *a rough sea* a dynamic sense, in *a rough guess* the sense of 'approximate.' If the examination of a large number and variety of contexts confirms these and only these three senses, they will provide data for trying to "reconstruct" the potential meaning of *rough*, especially if other adjectives are found expressing parallel 'static,' 'dynamic,' and 'non-physical, mental' senses. If it expresses a metaphorical sense, as in *a rough day*, it can be treated as such (see chapter 14), but if for some speakers it simply means 'with ups and downs,' then in that context it would be another case of the mental sense. The important point in dealing with particular cases like this is to be wary of attributing a sense to the lexeme itself unless it is found in a great variety of contexts, and in parallel uses of other lexemes. Ambiguity and other tests by linguists provide clues for examining actual usage in detail, but so far they provide no criterion for recognizing polysemous uses of a lexical word. At this point in our investigation, the only firm basis for proposing polysemy is a widespread observation of the same opposition between senses. Thus the ambiguity of *I gave him a good brush* can be considered a manifestation of two related senses of 'brush,' an object and the activity it makes possible, since this condition-consequence relation has been found with a number of lexemes, as will be seen below in discussing verbs.

Taylor's observation concerning the vagueness of a sentence can be rephrased to apply to the word: until set in a specific context, most words are vague in that they express a general sort of meaning, as will be argued later. If this distinction is not made between the usually general sense a word expresses and how this sense is interpreted – its expressive effect – when combined with other components of the context to contribute to the sentence meaning, the word will be thought to express a slightly different meaning for every context it is used in, and may even be said to get its meaning from the context: "A word on its own is not meaningful; what it means depends on its context" (Mittins, 1). The different interpretations do not need to be captured in describing the semantics of the word. For example it is obvious that, in a sentence, expressions such as *open the door, open an envelope, open one's hand, open fire*, etc. would denote different activities, but this does not justify attributing these extra-linguistic activities, or even representations of them, to *open* as different actualized senses (cf. Taylor 1992, 20). Rather, the challenge is to describe a lexical import sufficiently general to permit interpretation in these different ways. Frisson (120) provides data from psychological testing that tend to confirm some such two-phased process: an "initial activation of an underspecified meaning" leading to further specification through the word's integration in the context. To be avoided is confusing the second phase, the expressive effect (further specification) resulting from grouping syntactically the imports of two or more words, with the first phase, the actualized (underspecified) meaning of one of the words. This pitfall can be avoided only by observing a word in a wide variety of uses in an attempt to filter out implications arising from the particular contexts and so isolate its own import, the actual meanings or senses it contributes to the endless variety of expressive effects in context. On the other hand, it should not be assumed, as Ruhl does (see below), that words are monosemous. Between the extremes of monosemy and the acceptance of all expressive effects, a cautious approach is called for, one admitting only widespread, systematically related variations as actualized senses, underspecified meanings contributing to the expressive effect of the phrase or clause they are integrated into.

Thus it is important to recognize that polysemy is normal in the use of a word, but it is equally important to distinguish the different senses a word expresses from the endless variation of contextual expressive effects a word contributes to. Only then can a question raised by Lyons be considered. After talking about the meaning of words, he remarks (402): "We also say that sentences have a meaning. Is 'meaning' being used here in the same sense?" The term *meaning* contributes to different expressive effects in these two expressions: "meaning of a sentence" generally calls to mind a meaning to which a number of syntactically related words contribute, i.e. an expressive effect lasting only as long as someone keeps the sentence in mind. "Meaning of a word" can designate either the permanent meaning potential constantly available to a speaker to form a word for use, or one of the actualizations of this potential in a particular use, one of a word's senses. But here, yet another distinction must be made, one dividing the meaning a word brings to the sentence, and this raises the third problem mentioned in the previous section.

LEXICAL VS. GRAMMATICAL

We saw above that a word expressing the same idea can fulfill different syntactic functions. The grammatical difference between the *throw* in *to throw a ball* and that in *a good throw* has long been attributed to a difference of meaning not of the lexical type described in dictionaries, but of the more abstract, formal type described in grammars. Medieval grammarians had a convenient way of distinguishing between these two modes of signifying: a word signifies a lexical meaning, and along with that first meaning, CONSIGNIFIES a grammatical meaning.[5] This distinction between lexical and grammatical meanings, traditional in historical grammar, is maintained here. On occasion we will resort to more technical terms and speak of the meaning or import of a word as consisting of a MATERIAL SIGNIFICATE and a FORMAL SIGNIFICATE in order to bring out that the latter, grammatical meaning, provides a category or form for the former, lexical meaning. That is, in the above phrases *throw* imports what appears to be much the same lexical meaning (material significate), but different grammatical meanings (formal significates), and it is the latter which represent the grammatical category determining the syntactic function of *throw*. Similarly, for such phrases as *an open door* and *in the open*, a reader no longer understands *open* to express an activity as in *open a door*, because its function, as indicated by its position in the phrase, here implies a different grammatical meaning.

Thus in observing the import of words, one must take into account not just their lexical meaning, or LEXEME, but also their grammatical meaning(s), or MORPHEME(S), because these too are formative elements of the word. Since polysemy is characteristic of morphemes as well as lexemes, it is necessary to compare the different senses expressed by a morpheme in order to infer the potential meaning giving rise to them. However, as indicated above by the examples *I leave tomorrow* vs. *I'm leaving tomorrow*, and *three bear* vs. *three bears*, the sense expressed by the morphemes (simple / progressive, -ø / -s) is usually discernable only after observing a large number of such uses.[6] That is, one may at first "feel" a difference of nuance between them without being able to describe it. This would require a linguist to become more acute in observing the morphemes' meaning, a requirement common to most any discipline: although at one level of perception I see the same thing as geologists, they can observe far more in a rock than I can, thanks to training. For language, this may involve ear training to enable someone to discern more readily slight variations in the physical sign, and "mind training" to enable one to become more and more sensitive to variations in the sense expressed. This enhanced appreciation of nuances of meaning is of course important for writers and students of literature, and in fact for any speaker, but particularly for linguists, because for them observed senses constitute the data base for inferring the potential giving rise to those senses.

Once discerned with sufficient clarity, each of the senses of a lexeme or morpheme must somehow be described so that other observers can corroborate it, or not. Sometimes the best that can be done in such cases is to suggest the difference one feels by contrasting two uses, thereby helping other observers – those with sufficient competence in English to feel a difference – discover the distinct nuance expressed by the respective forms (or grammatical words) in that particular context. What is often involved here is not so much paraphrasing the sense expressed, as pointing to it so that others can recognize it. This, in fact, is the role of paraphrase in any attempt to describe meaning. Since paraphrase cannot give a facsimile of the sense observed, it is a means of direction-giving to suggest to other observers what they can discern by introspecting the same example. Viewing paraphrase as a means of verifying observation in this way ensures that there is no circularity involved.

Thus there is a way of overcoming each of the problems arising from trying to observe meaning. Distinguishing the meaning expressed by a sentence from both the message delivered by preceding discourse and other factors in the situation ensures that what is properly linguistic is not being confused with what arises from outside language. Distinguishing the import of a word from what the phrase or sentence containing it expresses ensures that the word's sense is not being confused with the expressive effect of its immediate context. Distinguishing a word's lexical import from its grammatical import avoids confusing what specifies a word (its lexeme) with what categorizes it (its morphemes and part of speech). Considering paraphrase not as a means of reproducing meaning, but as a method of directing other observers' attention so that they too can observe the same meaning, respects the uniqueness of what is expressed by a given sentence while making it accessible to others. Finally, the fact that competent observers can be made more sensitive to a difference of nuance, even in cases such as the above where different morphemes express senses that are quite close, ensures that, when a consensus is reached, the senses observed provide valid data. Once these difficulties in observation have been overcome and a morpheme's or a lexeme's polysemy delimited, the possibility of inferring a meaning potential in tongue giving rise to the diverse grammatical or lexical senses observed can be explored.

PRESUPPOSITIONS

It remains to discuss one further question concerning the approach to meaning adopted here: the question of presuppositions, which is, strictly speaking, outside the field of linguistics and yet is fundamental to any approach. Any scientific venture is based on the presupposition that the object to be investigated is somehow orderly or systematic. It is this presumption of a certain coherence or order in meaning, along with the understanding of the comparative method in historical linguistics, that led to hypothesizing a potential meaning underlying and permitting the observed senses, or actualized meanings, of a morpheme and, with certain reserves (see Concluding Remarks below), a lexeme.

Thus, in line with the tradition evoked above, based on our common experience, it is assumed that meaning is a mental entity and not something in the extra-mental universe as some linguists would have it. Granted its mental status, however, we will not consider "the distinction between semantics and pragmatics (or between linguistic and extralinguistic knowledge)" to be a "false dichotomy" (Langacker 1987, 154), a position that would leave the problem of the unity of the word unsolved. The position adopted here is that "linguistic knowledge" consists of what speakers have learned of their mother tongue, what permits them to form words and communicate with others, as opposed to all the non-linguistic variables in each person's experience. That is, it is assumed that every meaning, lexical and grammatical, has been instituted as a potential in tongue by abstracting from our experience, a potential that can be actualized in different senses. In fact, except for the physical realizations of the sign, it is assumed that the whole of language is a construction of the mind, a mental construct including a system of mental mechanisms which, when activated, produces the words needed to express whatever experience the speaker has in mind and wants to talk about. As with any other such presupposition, however, the presupposition of mental mechanisms in linguistics can be considered justified only if it provides a heuristically valuable starting point to investigate "the one thing that matters most in language": meaning.

Since explaining data involves describing prior condition(s) or cause(s), it is further assumed that to explain what an addressee gets out of a sentence, we must try to describe what a speaker puts into it. Hence the speaker's point of view is adopted here. Moreover, the data must be actual uses, whether nonce or commonplace, expressing what someone has in mind, because words used for psychological testing or some other purpose may not reflect the processes involved in ordinary speech.

Hence the challenge of this essay: can the presupposition that a set of subconscious mental operations gives rise to a word in discourse lead us to a better understanding of our object of study, and help us to make sense out of meaning? To clarify this approach, we will confront it with a very different, widely accepted presupposition about words in the next chapter.

5

How *Access* "Got Verbed"[1]

INTRODUCTION

The assumption of a word-forming mechanism available to speakers during the act of language is far less well-known than an alternative, quite different assumption about words. To compare the two, examples of what, for the speaker at least, appear to be innovations in English will be examined in the light of different grammarians' comments to see if that alternative assumption can explain them. This will lead to the crucial question: "What's in a word?" Considering a traditional view of words will make the assumption developed here more explicit and provide a different basis for explaining the examples examined. Finally, I will suggest why the alternative and (in my opinion) erroneous assumption has become so widespread, and what lesson can be drawn from this.

AN ALTERNATIVE ASSUMPTION

The following citation from a study on prepositions (Tyler and Evans, 1) expresses the assumption quite clearly: "Linguists have often assumed that words constitute lexical forms that are stored in a mental dictionary or lexicon." Similarly, Aitchison's book "deals with words … it discusses the nature of the human word-store, or 'mental lexicon'" (vii), taking for granted that words are stored and not calling into question the existence of a mental lexicon. Likewise for a study on lexical semantics (Cruse, 50): "It will be assumed in this book that a (relatively) closed set of lexical units is stored in the mental lexicon, together with rules or principles of some kind which permit the production of a possibly unlimited number of new (i.e. not specifically stored) units." Another linguist (O'Grady, 8) speaks of "a lexicon that provides a list of 'formatives' (words and morphemes) and their associated properties." And Croft and Cruse (109), as we saw above, speak of "isolating different parts of the total meaning potential of a word in different circumstances ... when we retrieve a word from the mental lexicon." Although different means of construing the contextual variation may be proposed, such as "[t]he metaphor of the lexicon as a natural process of self-organization and self-regulation" (Turvey and Moreno, 9), even this operative view implies the idea that speakers store words as such: "The categories of the lexicon, like the causal categories of a self-assembling system, are known to mutate. Nouns become verbs" (28). This notion of a mental dictionary or lexicon of words is so widespread that some scholars outside of linguistics take it, not as an assumption, but as a well-established fact, as in the following passage from a study by psychologists working in neuroscience:

> A normal speaker produces about three words a second. These words are extracted from a stored mental dictionary (a *lexicon*) of somewhere between 20,000 and 50,000 words. On the average, only about one word per million is selected or pronounced incorrectly. Our remarkable ability to produce words ... (Kosslyn and Koenig, 211)

Speaking of physical systems, Turvey and Moreno (13) point out that "many necessary conditions ... are so normal, so commonplace, they get taken for granted," and so do not undergo scrutiny. This, in my opinion, is what happens to the mental system for constructing words.

One may well wonder what the assumption of words stored in a mental dictionary is based on, and the answer is not far to seek. As ordinary speakers we do not have to invent the means of expressing ourselves on the spur of the moment, as we would have to in a situation where we neither spoke nor understood the language of those around us. Rather, when we are speaking, the moment we need a word it emerges into consciousness, ready to take its place in the sentence we are constructing. This gives us the impression that all the words we have acquired are somehow ready to be used whenever we need them. What more natural, then, than the idea that our vocabulary is stocked in memory as in a personal dictionary, that words are "stored in the speaker's mental lexicon" (Taylor 2002, 74), and that we need merely "select" the ones we need for the sentence we are producing?

According to certain scholars (Tyler and Evans, 5), this assumption has been around for some time: "Starting as early as Bloomfield (1933) and rearticulated as recently as Chomsky (1995), influential linguistic theories have asserted that the lexicon is the repository for the arbitrary and the idiosyncratic." And more recently, "we can call the mental store of these words a lexicon, making an overt parallel with the lists of words and meanings published as dictionaries" (Saeed, 10). Besides suggesting where it started, these comments bring out another facet of the lexicon assumption. If we can assume that words, the constituent elements of a sentence, are learned and stored in memory as "arbitrary" items, then there is no need to analyze them, and attention can be focused on syntax. That is, besides appearing obvious, this assumption has the convenience of obviating the problem of the word. This would, in fact, appear to be the reason why "linguists are a bit uncomfortable with the idea of *words*. Words are slippery critters" (Davis, 83). Thus, as we have seen, the very term "word" is not in favour with linguists, many of whom prefer to speak of lexical items, or lexical units, or lexical entries, thereby assimilating words with prefixes, suffixes, idioms, and other "arbitrary and idiosyncratic" entities.

This mental lexicon assumption is common among linguists and, as we shall see, grammarians.[2] Before pursuing our discussion on the abstract level of assumptions and the nature of the word as a unit of language, however, it will be useful to look at some data that pose the question concretely, on the level of real examples.

NEW WORDS?

My attention was first drawn to the mental lexicon question by a commentary about a swimmer, heard during a television broadcast on the Olympics:

Will he medal tonight?

The sentence caught my attention because I understood perfectly well what was a new word for me. What intrigued me here was that I had no such word in my vocabulary, no verb *medal* I could "retrieve from my mental lexicon," and yet I had no trouble making sense of the sentence.

This triggered my interest in the phenomenon that grammarians usually call "conversion," and I started collecting other examples, getting the same reaction from some picked up by observant students, such as the following from a university publication:

> I see that kids are focused on science. They're asking science questions. They're 'sciencing' as (CETUS researcher) David Blades says.[3]

The next two examples were picked up in conversation:

> They're squirrelling stuff away.
> It ouches.[4]

And the following was found on the net:[5]

> I got totally homered this Christmas when my Dad bought me a fly fishing kit.

This one I did not understand until the link with the well-known character on television was pointed out, but then, once I understood the sentence, I had the same impression of calling to mind a new word. Like "medal," words in each of these examples seemed to run counter to the idea that my vocabulary consists of a set of words stocked in a mental dictionary.

Written texts have provided examples for me as well, and there the context helps comprehension, as in the following where "a proper name is verbed" (Crystal, 149):

> I warrant him, Petruchio is Kated.

At this point in *The Taming of the Shrew* (III, ii, 245), *Kated* is not just readily understood but bears witness to the vigour of Shakespeare's language. The same can be said of the following example from *Coriolanus* (V, i, 5–6):

> A mile before his tent fall down and knee
> The way into his mercy.

While *Kated* is a nonce formation, *knee* here is a new formation from the substantive, according to the OED.[6] Looking at things from the point of view of how the speaker / writer formed them, one gets the impression of words being created for the occasion.

A reader provides an interesting example found on a voucher from the local supermarket:

£13 discount on a £60 shop.

'Shop,' long used as a verb to represent as an event what occurs in a shop, here represents that occurrence, a transaction, as an entity. Being readily understandable, it indicates the functioning of some word-forming mechanism but poses the problem of how this can be seen as an actualization of the lexical potential 'shop.' We will return to this below when discussing the relation of the part of speech to the lexeme.

The point of these examples is that, whether or not they were just nonce uses created by the speaker on the spur of the moment, for me they were new, yet quite comprehensible. To figure out what makes this possible, I turned to Quirk et al., where a whole section (1558–63) treats such uses as examples of "conversion," i.e. "the derivational process whereby an item is adapted or converted to a new word class without the addition of an affix." This attributes to the speaker, and presumably the hearer, a mental process for deriving new words from known "items." The above verbs are called "denominals" because, except for *ouches*, they are, according to Quirk et al., derived from substantives. This grammar also gives examples of "denominal adjectives," substantives "converted" into adjectives, as in:

His accent is very Mayfair (very Harvard).

On the other hand, in more common examples such as *city life,* the pre-modifier is not treated as a denominal adjective since it cannot occur in predicate position. Huddleston and Pullum (1640) maintain that "conversion in this direction is ... very rare," that in examples such as the above and *a federal government inquiry* we do not have "nouns used as adjectives but nouns used as attributive modifiers" (537), as shown by the fact that *government* is modified by an adjective, not an adverb. It remains, of course, to explain what enables a substantive to function as an attributive modifier.[7]

Other types of "conversion" have been frequent over the centuries. Thus many denominal verbs (*to bottle, to grease, to elbow*), deverbal substantives (*a desire, a swim, a catch*), de-adjectival substantives (*a natural, a weekly, an empty*), and de-adjectival verbs (*to calm, to humble, to empty*) would hardly attract attention today as being derived from another word. Finally, there are less easily classified examples such as *ouches* above, which appears to be derived from the interjection, and less frequent cases:

It tells you about the how and the why of flight.
They downed tools in protest.

Quirk et al. (1563) consider these two uses to be derived from "closed-class words," though it is not clear why they consider *down* here a "convert" from its use as a preposition, rather than from its use as an adverb, or an adjective, or a substantive.

The point to be remembered from this rapid survey is that such uses as those above which catch our attention because of their novelty, bear witness to an innovative process "now available for extending the lexical resources of the language" (1558) and so are of interest to the linguist.[8] On the other hand, such uses are just the tip of the iceberg since the vast majority of novel uses in the past – all except nonce uses – have become part of our everyday usage. A glance in a dictionary to see how many entries are classified under two or more parts of speech will show how widespread this means of word formation has been historically, even though in general we are no longer aware when we use "converts" (such as *glance, show, even, general, convert* in this sentence). All this raises an important question. What is this process called "conversion"? How can it produce new words?

GRAMMARIANS ON "CONVERSION"

Grammars consulted characterize the process in terms of its result. Sweet, who first introduced the notion of conversion, considers (I, 38) that "the mere change of a verb into a noun can hardly be said to make a new word of it." In fact most grammarians[9] consider that *medal* is "used as" a verb in the above example, a view implying that it is really the same word, but in a different use. Other grammars speak of a word being "totally or partially converted"[10] into another part of speech. Again, the same word is found but in another part of speech. This would also seem to be the position of Quirk et al., when they speak of "the derivational process whereby an item is adapted or converted to a new word class." For such grammarians, then, it appears that the part of speech (word class) is an accidental element, something added on to, but not a constituent element of, the word, and so conversion does not produce new words.

Huddleston and Pullum (1640) adopt a different position: "We include conversion within the set of lexical word-formation processes because we see it as creating new words." The reason they give for this is clear: "we regard any difference in primary category as sufficient to establish a difference between one word and another." They recognize that a different "word class" or "primary category" – a different part of speech – is the mark of a different word.[11] That is, notwithstanding what they have in common meaning-wise, *medal* in the above example is a different word from *medal* used as a substantive, even though there is no overt indication of this difference within the word. In short, the part of speech is an essential component of a word.

Grammarians who speak of converting a word obviously take for granted that the word exists already, presumably in some sort of mental lexicon, but none of them indicate how words are converted. Huddleston and Pullum (1640) describe the process as follows: "a word is formed from a pre-existing morphological unit by simply giving it new grammatical properties." That is, recognizing the different syntactic possibilities of verbs and adjectives, they assume "the creation of the verb *humble* from the adjective *humble*." But to my knowledge, no grammarian has ever analyzed this assumed process of creation or conversion, of "simply giving new grammatical properties" to a word.

One might of course reply that the job of grammarians is to describe and not to analyze or explain, and that they have done their job when they observe *medal* or *humble* or *down* used as verbs and assume that this result, like any other result, must have been produced by some process, some "word-formation process." Granted that this lets grammarians off the hook, we turn to linguists.

LINGUISTS ON "CONVERSION"

In their introduction to *Approaches to Conversion / Zero-Derivation*, Bauer and Valera provide an invaluable survey of the question. They pose the problem of "whether conversion is best seen as a process by which lexemes are formed or whether it is best seen as a relationship between lexemes." The zero-derivation approach runs into the problem of "contrasting zeroes (and even of zeroes contrasting with a lack of a zero)." How to contrast one zero ending with another is by no means obvious, but even less obvious is contrasting it with the lack of a null ending. Seeing "conversion simply as lexical relisting ... avoids the need for zeroes ... [but] sees conversion as something outside morphology." Conversion, assuming it is a process, remains "slightly mysterious." Among other things, is it "a subtype of derivation, or a completely separate type of word-formation?" Nor is it clear "how narrowly a word-class is to be defined," whether "common and proper nouns ... animate and inanimate nouns ... countable and uncountable nouns ... concrete and abstract nouns" are to be considered distinct word-classes. As a consequence, "it seems difficult to draw any conclusion other than that there is much uncertainty about conversion and that scholars are still questioning the concept of conversion." And so "it would be extremely rewarding to be able to give principled reasons for accepting or rejecting the various options open to us" (8–15).

The notion of conversion attempts to explain the unusual or novel in usage as derived or formed from the usual, familiar use of a word. That is, certain uses of a word are so common, so widespread, they are considered to be basic to, and indeed the source of, new uses; but how one use, however "entrenched," can be converted into another remains a mystery. On the other hand, to consider every use, entrenched or not, to be the outcome of actualizing the word's lexeme and configuring it grammatically, entails viewing a new use not as derived from a known use, but as a new way of exploiting the lexical potential common to all uses. To make this more explicit and situate the type of innovative usage involved within a broader context, two questions raised by the above approaches will be addressed. One question, to be discussed in the next chapter, is the vagueness underlying the notion of "word classes" and how they relate to the lexeme. The other question, even more fundamental, involves the notion of "word" itself: what is the makeup of a word? What constitutes a word from the point of view of meaning? Without some clarification of these issues, neither what constitutes different uses of the same word nor what is involved in forming a word can be satisfactorily determined. Granted the frequency of so-called "conversion," and even of uses such as *That will involve a lot of grandfathering*, an example arising in conversation, it is important to understand conversion's relation to the process of word formation, giving rise to commonplace uses of the word. To my knowledge no analysis of how a speaker proceeds to form a word in its usual uses has yet been attempted, but without that, one cannot hope to explain how the ordinary speaker can innovate.

As mentioned above, one gets the impression that the term "conversion" is based on the (quite natural) assumption of words existing ready-made in a mental lexicon. This assumption has become so entrenched in people's minds that, outside of cases involving affixing and compounding, the very idea that a process is required to form not just a lexeme such as 'medal' as a substantive or 'humble' as an adjective or 'down' as a preposition, but any lexeme as a part of speech, has not been explored by most linguists. In "influential linguistic theories," one of the rare questionings of the makeup of a word arises toward the end of a lengthy study on morphology from a generative point of view, where the author (Spencer, 453) reaches the conclusion that "one of the key unresolved questions in morphology is 'what is a word?'" This question suggests that perhaps a word is not "arbitrary," that perhaps it is analyzable into its component parts, that perhaps this linguistic unit found in every act of language has been neglected.

Whether or not the cause of this neglect of the word is the lexicon assumption, the notion of "conversion" poses the as yet unexplained problem of how a word is recycled if it already exists ready-made in the "mental lexicon." This problem concerns not just cases such as the above examples that strike us as innovative today, but also the far more frequent cases of words which were innovative at some time in the past and today do not appear to involve anything to be explained. For example, is *empty*, commonly found in three parts of speech, to be considered a single word which is "simply given new grammatical properties" according to the needs of discourse, or three homonyms, each an entry in the mental lexicon (cf. Huddleston and Pullum, 1641)? Is conversion "best seen as a process by which lexemes are formed or … as a relationship between lexemes"? To arrive at a satisfactory explanation, we will examine the question from a more general point of view in order to analyze what sort of word-forming process would make innovation possible, as in the versatility of usage illustrated by above examples.

WHAT'S IN A WORD?

The diverse comments on conversion cited above presuppose that one component of the word, its physical sign, undergoes no change. Some linguists mention change in another component of the word, its lexical meaning. All comment on the third component, the word's "grammatical properties": "conversion" is a process that involves a word's grammatical meaning, its part of speech. That is, in the works consulted, a distinction is made, often implicitly, within the word's meaning between the lexical and the grammatical, a distinction which is by no means original with them. In his history of English grammars up to 1800, Michael (44–7) points out that medieval grammarians, building on the concept from antiquity of words as "the smallest unit of discourse," make "a threefold distinction between *vox*, the mere speech-sound; *dictio*, the word regarded as a meaningful speech-sound; *pars*, the word regarded as a syntactical unit." That is to say, the speech-sound or sign both signifies a word's lexical import, or lexeme, and, as mentioned above, "consignifies"[12] its grammatical import, or part of speech. In short, since it is the part of speech which determines a word's function in the sentence, "the syntactical function of a word is part of its meaning." Michael recounts that "[t]he Renaissance grammarians made no use of the two most important ideas about the word which were available to them: Dionysius Thrax's description of it as a minimum unit of discourse and the speculative grammarians' distinction between semantic and syntactic units." That is, the distinction between a word's lexical and grammatical meanings was no longer considered pertinent.

Grammarians' failure to take into account such a crucial distinction within the word may have been occasioned by the drastic historical reduction of visible morphology, particularly in English, or by a positivist leaning which left meaning in the shade. Although the work of nineteenth-century linguists in historical grammar always distinguished between the lexical and the grammatical on the level of the sign, this distinction on the level of the meaning within the word is often ignored or considered of no interest even today. One consequence of this is that the word itself is often neglected, notwithstanding Saussure's view that "[i]n spite of the difficulty of defining it, the word is a unit which imposes itself on the mind, something central in the mechanism of language" (154).[13]

Unfortunately, Saussure himself did not explore the subject further, considering that it would take a whole book to do so.

Words are in fact a universal in language, not just in the sense that in every language we find "minimum units of discourse," but in the stronger sense that we find words in every act of speech.[14] As we have seen, Miller calls words "the fundamental units of human language" and stresses their importance for linguists when he asks: "What is at issue in a scientific discussion of words is not so much specific words as wordiness: why are all languages wordy? Why are words a universal design feature of languages? It is words in general, not scientific words, that are scientifically important" (5). Moreover, Miller echoes the medieval grammarians when he brings out the three components of a word as follows: "Each word is the synthesis of a concept, an utterance, and a syntactic role. A person who knows a word knows what it means, knows how to pronounce it, and knows the contexts in which it can be used. These are not three independent kinds of knowledge; they are different views of a single entity" (viii). In like fashion, Wierzbicka (561) makes a clear distinction between the lexical and the grammatical when she speaks of "pre-packaged semantic bundles" in the lexicon, and "pre-packaged semantic configurations" in the grammar. Metaphors such as "pre-packaged" and "bundle" do not imply the sort of potential envisaged here, but the fact of distinguishing between lexemes and the grammatical system as two components of a speaker's linguistic resources is a crucial step. Furthermore, considering the grammatical, i.e. the part of speech, to be a "configuration" of the lexical leads to the next point I want to make.

Granted that the meaning of a word is composed of a lexical component which is signified, and a grammatical component which is consignified, the question of the relation between the two remains to be clarified. Wierzbicka appears to be implying here that the grammatical configures, or gives a certain shape or form to, the lexical. This is precisely the relation I adopt here to examine that "key unresolved question … what is a word?"[15]

As seen above, it is the relation of matter to form that holds between the two components of a word's mental import: a lexeme provides the notional content or matter that the part of speech configures or forms. This process of grammatical configuring or categorizing which provides a word with its final categorical form, its part of speech, is a mental operation that must be undertaken every time a speaker needs a word. Since in most cases a word's visible morphology in English gives no indication of its part of speech, the listener generally recognizes it thanks to its position in the phrase or sentence. This point is important, crucial even, because it implies that through the process of grammatical categorizing, the speaker of the first example above configured the lexeme 'medal' as a verb, and this determined the predicative function the word *medal* would fulfill (through the auxiliary) in the sentence, and this in turn determined its place in the sentence. But for me as listener, it was the position of the word *medal* in the sentence that indicated its function and so led me to form or configure the lexeme 'medal' as a verb in order to understand the meaning of the sentence.

That is to say, a word is not an arbitrary, unanalyzable element of language, but a unit the speaker puts together, or forms, in view of the sentence being constructed. A necessary part of this process of formation is to provide the word with a part of speech giving it certain syntactic possibilities. Otherwise all words would be, like interjections, "lacking grammatical connection." But forming a word involves more than this. Among the thousands of lexeme-sign units the average speaker has learned, the appropriate one, the lexeme best representing what the speaker wants to talk about, must also be called to mind. This other part of the word-forming process provides the lexical matter to be formed by the part of speech. Each of these operations, bringing to mind the lexeme and configuring it grammatically, calls for further analysis, in lexical semantics and grammatical semantics respectively, but this will suffice to bring out what is important for our immediate needs: meaning-wise, word-formation is a two-phase process whereby the lexical matter must be called to mind and then configured by the part of speech to produce a word's mental import – its meaning.

The importance of viewing word-formation in this way is that it replaces the static view of choosing a word listed in a mental lexicon (and "converting" it if need be) with the dynamic view of evoking an idea and grammaticizing it to produce the total meaning of a word (whose physical sign must then be actualized). This view presupposes that speakers do not possess ready-made words but something far more creative: the necessary resources of their mother tongue – the lexemes they have acquired and the grammatical systems – to produce whatever words they need at the moment of need. The advantage of this is nowhere more evident than in cases of so-called conversion because it implies that a lexeme (linked to a sign) exists in our minds with no grammatical strings attached (though its lexical matter may predispose it to be more readily formed as, say, a verb than as a substantive).[16]

WORDING

Just as we speak of "languaging" something when it is being expressed in language, and "Englishing" a text when it is being translated into English, so I may be permitted to speak of "wording" an experience when a speaker is representing it by putting it into words. In any case, this unusual term can help us keep in mind the dynamics of word-formation involved in examples discussed above, starting with *Will he medal tonight?* Having in mind one swimmer's participation in the coming competition, the commentator called on the lexeme 'medal' as the most appropriate notion to suggest a comparison with other competitors. Instead of configuring it as a substantive as in *Will he win a medal tonight?* he actualized the lexeme to express an activity necessarily linked with the metal object in the Olympics – a winning performance. As a listener confronted with *medal* in the position of an infinitive, I construed it as a verb and interpreted the lexeme as representing not the object but rather an activity linked with it, namely the activity of obtaining a medal.[17] The listener's point of view is described in Farrell (109) in like fashion: "there is a lexical semantic representation that is underspecified for the noun / verb distinction. The process meaning of the verb and the thing meaning of the noun are supplied by the verb and noun slots in which the word appears." Unfortunately, when there is no attempt to distinguish the listener's from the speaker's point of view, it seems to imply that the speaker is also in the situation of ignoring a word's part of speech until it appears in its sentence "slot." Here it is proposed that the speaker provides the part of speech as part of the word's meaning and so determines its function and the place in the sentence where it can express that function.

This example helps show not only how abstract a lexeme must be before the speaker forms it as a word and then puts it into relation with other words in the sentence, but also how the listener has to perform similar mental operations to understand the word and, ultimately, the sentence. Furthermore, the example indicates how the lexeme is formed or configured or grammaticized,[18] and that it would be misleading to speak of "conversion" here. The same can be said of the above example *They're sciencing*, where the speaker forms the lexeme as a verb to express the activity associated with, or rather inherent in, science. Again, such an unusual use (instead of the expected *doing science*) brings out how adaptable the potential lexeme 'science' is, ready to be actualized to meet the needs of the speaker in the particular sentence being constructed.

The other examples above illustrate the same word-forming process. *It ouches, squirrelling stuff away*, and even *knee the way* all call to mind a typical activity linked with the more common use of the lexeme. On the other hand, *very Mayfair* and *very Harvard* suggest a certain quality or type of accent associated with particular places. Similarly, to be able to interpret *got homered* and *Petruchio is Kated* requires a familiarity with the particular situation and the particular person designated by the corresponding proper noun. For the listener, the novelty of all these uses, and particularly the last two, involves a feeling of discovering the meaning they call to mind, and this gives a special expressive impact to them.

The remaining examples, however, involve no novelty. *To bottle, a swim*, etc. are such common uses of the lexeme that they would probably be noticed only by grammarians and linguists as word-formations introduced into usage in the past and now understood as routine configurations of the lexeme. Nevertheless, lexemes readily formed by more than one part of speech constitute a large part of our vocabulary today and so pose an even more important problem for the linguist than "conversions." The rudimentary description of the word-forming process in English presented above applies just as well to these commonplace uses as to the nonce and innovative ones. To take only one example: by postulating that the very abstract lexeme 'down' is to be configured by a part of speech each time it is used, we have a basis for explaining how it is grammaticized by any one of five systemic programs depending on what kind of a word the speaker needs for the sentence – *another down, to down a drink, a down payment, to fall down, down the drain* – and even how it can provide just a lexical component in a compound such as *to downgrade*. In *the down from geese*, however, *down* would be a homonym, that is, an identical sign signifying a quite different potential lexical meaning in tongue.

CONCLUSION

As an alternative to the assumption that words are stored in a mental lexicon of prefabricated items to be selected or retrieved when needed for constructing a sentence, I am proposing that the formative elements, lexical and grammatical, for making words are stored as potentials in the mind and that a word is (re)constructed during the moment of speech each time it is needed. Speakers combine the appropriate lexeme (the one best representing what they have in mind to express) and the appropriate part of speech (providing the required syntactic capabilities) to produce the word capable of playing the roles, lexical and grammatical, foreseen for it in the sentence under construction.[19] That is, the resources permanently available to the speaker are not words, but something far more creative, since they open the way to language development: the formative elements needed to construct words – lexemes (with their signs) and grammatical systems – as well as a word-forming mechanism to integrate them.

The assumption of a word-stocked lexicon is so widespread – to the point where, for one linguist, "the eventual result [of conversion] may be complete interchangeability of items such as substantives and verbs, which were once kept rigidly apart"[20] – probably reflects the view of the ordinary speaker, since the only experience we have of words is when they emerge into consciousness, i.e. when they are already formed. We can have no direct experience of the word-forming process, only of its result. As in other sciences, the linguist's job is to explain the observed result by what led up to it, and so a pre-conscious mental operation accomplished during the act of language is here proposed as an alternative hypothesis to the mental lexicon hypothesis with its corollary conversion hypothesis, which does not explain how speakers can come up with new words nor listeners understand such innovations.

Analyzing word-formation as a two-phase process in this way makes it easy to understand how the same lexeme can arise in grammatically different words, a widespread phenomenon, as attested by the many entries in a dictionary listed under different parts of speech. Furthermore, as we shall see in later chapters, variations such as countable and uncountable, observed within the same part of speech, do not constitute different words. Because this two-phase analysis can apply to all words in English except interjections, it constitutes an incipient theory of word-formation, something of importance for anyone who considers that the word is "something central in the mechanism of language" because words are "the fundamental units of human language." We will explore some of its implications in ensuing chapters but will not develop it further here, since that would call for an analysis of each of the parts of speech and each of their subsystems, as in my studies on the verb (2007) and the noun phrase (2009).

Our brief discussion of "conversion" helped us to focus on the problem of how a speaker can create a new word, and ended up showing that this is always a possibility since, whenever we speak, we (re)construct the words we need. Thus what is misleadingly called "conversion" is a manifestation of how we make a word, whether an innovation or not, during the act of language. It is fitting to finish with a striking example of word-making from a comic strip character.

> I like to verb words.
> Remember when "access" was a thing? Now it's something you *do*.
> It got verbed.
> Verbing weirds language.[21]

These amusing comments hint at the wording process involved in verbing 'access,' and bring out how our language resources cope with the ever-changing panorama of our consciousness – how languaging words experience.

6

Wording

INTRODUCTION

So far we have situated language, and more specifically meaning as expressed by language, the object of our study, between what precedes languaging and what follows it. What precedes languaging is pre-language thought, that portion of a speaker's ongoing experience focused on as an intended message. Languaging consists of constructing words to constitute a sentence expressing meaning. What follows speech is the realized message, the mental referent the listener has managed to piece together from the meaning expressed and its relation to the linguistic context (if any), the speaker, the situation, common knowledge, etc. What exists during the act of speech is languaged thought, the meaning expressed by words, phrases, and sentences. This differs radically from the view that word meaning is just one other component of our experience of the world, a stance which would make meaning the domain of another discipline and so, as we have seen, would free "the linguist from the obligation to search for a semantic component unifying all the different uses of a word." That view would, however, leave the linguistic problem of what constitutes the unity of a word unsolved. This predicament has led some linguists to leave aside the question of the word as a distinct linguistic form, and to talk about "items" or "entries in the lexicon," another expedient leaving the problem unsolved because the way we talk about something does not change the reality of the thing itself.

We have also seen that meaning is not to be dismissed as unmanageable by the scientific method simply because it is a strictly mental entity which, unlike the sign, can be observed only by introspection. On the contrary, the consensus of introspective observers (listeners or readers) evidenced by any act of communication makes their observations facts to be explained, i.e. data for linguists. Linguists confront certain difficulties, however, when observing meaning as data: distinguishing meaning expressed by a sentence from what context and situation contribute to the realized message; distinguishing a word's meaning import from the expressive effect of the sentence and phrase; distinguishing the lexical meaning import of a word from its grammatical meaning; and, finally, establishing a consensus, generally through paraphrase, with other observers (grammarians or linguists).

Because communication by ordinary speakers requires them to understand the meaning expressed by a sentence, it seems obvious that they become at least minimally aware of that meaning through introspection, and likewise for the lexical meaning expressed by most words. Discerning a word's abstract grammatical meaning, however, calls for techniques of observation. Similarly, observing the polysemy of lexemes and morphemes is the work of specialists (translators, grammarians, etc.) because in ordinary speech we do not compare different uses of lexemes and morphemes. It is therefore important for linguists to extend the scope of their observation (through commutation and other techniques) to the various senses expressed, in order to ensure as complete a data base as possible for the ensuing phase of inferring the conditions that have given rise to what has been observed. Thus our discussion so far has put the spotlight on words, on their lexemes and morphemes, with a view to completing our observation of what they bring to the sentence.

It has often been pointed out that in order to observe what is pertinent in any area of reality, one must have some notion, however general or vague, of what one is looking for. In the case of words, this entails having some idea of what a word consists of before scrutinizing particular words in their different uses. We have adopted the view that a word is a unit constructed from lexical and grammatical formative elements (with their signs) in the mind whenever needed for expression in a sentence. As we have seen, this helps explain the fact that at any moment words enable speakers to represent, more or less adequately, whatever experience arises in their stream of consciousness; it also allows us to see what in the makeup of words gives them both permanence and variability, both their permanent availability and their capacity to adapt to whatever the speaker has in mind – two characteristics that make language such a remarkable phenomenon. In this chapter, then, as a preliminary to examining a word's less readily observed facets of meaning, we will explore how words in a language like English can make our incessantly varying experience, unsayable in itself, sayable.

VIEWING IDEAS

Reflecting on the capacity we have of being able to speak about any experience of the world around us (or within us) that emerges into our conscious minds, Guillaume was led to view word meanings in our mother tongue as forming a sort of generalized mental counterpart of the world of experience. That is, he conceived of a person's vocabulary as a constellation of lexemes constituting an inner universe for representing our experience arising from the other universe, the one we live in. This view determines his whole approach to linguistics. As he puts it (1984, 145), "linguistics is knowledge, not of the physical universe within which man dwells and of which he is a part, but of a mental universe – tongue – that dwells within him." This mental universe is acquired by all speakers through their mother tongues, but it is not something fixed, not the same for all languages or even all speakers of the same language. Its makeup varies from one language to another, and its content within the framework of the same language varies from one speaker to another. It varies even for the same speaker over time as new lexemes are acquired. As a consequence, Guillaume (1984, 157) considers that an important part of the task of linguistics consists in "accounting for the existence in thinking man of an expanding idea-universe, destined to grow in quantity and quality, an inner universe that he alone of all thinking beings is capable of building up within himself. This idea-universe that the human mind interiorizes and infolds is tongue." In his eyes, it is necessary to postulate this mental universe as a precondition for every speaker in order to explain the ready-made ideas – lexemes – that enable us to speak of anything that comes into our minds. But permitting speech in this way is not the only role of lexemes.

For Guillaume, the abstract lexemes of our idea-universe also provide a sort of medium, or rather a series of lenses through which the mind views the input from the other universe. Thus the sensory input of some entity is focused on by the idea most affinitive to it ('bird' or 'bush' or 'bicycle,' etc.) and so the entity is perceived as an individual or specimen of a particular category. Because they provide the mind with the means of monitoring sensory input in this way, the ideas making up the mental universe of tongue he called *idées regardantes*, VIEWING IDEAS. This expression designates the same reality as what we have called potential meanings, but from a different point of view. "Viewing idea" designates the lexeme in tongue as it relates to something in our extra-linguistic experience, categorizing it and so identifying it. "Potential meaning" designates the lexeme in tongue as it relates to an act of language, giving rise to an actualized meaning or sense to be expressed by a word in discourse. This way of considering the meaning components of words led Guillaume to speak of tongue as a "viewing universe" constantly confronting the universe of our ongoing experience. He presents this way of conceiving tongue in the following passage:

> [I]n order to lighten the load of ideas carried permanently – whether there be discourse or not – the human mind has reduced tongue to viewing ideas only, and arrives at the viewed ideas whereby it depicts the real universe by applying an actualizing treatment to the viewing ideas contained in its (wholly viewing) idea-universe. (1984, 158)

Considering the content of tongue as a universe of viewing ideas led Guillaume to propose that its operativity is not limited to those moments when we engage in an act of language, when we represent and express our experience by actualizing the abstract notions it makes available. The universe of viewing ideas is operative in the mind whenever there is an experiential input. Our stream of consciousness is constantly being monitored by our viewing ideas, with the result that anything in it we focus on – whether we want to speak about it or not – is, *ipso facto*, re-cognized as belonging to a certain type, class, category, etc., i.e. identified as being somehow similar to other entities. We even have viewing ideas such as 'thingamajig' for categorizing an experiential entity which, for the moment, we cannot identify any more precisely than as something physical. Others have expressed a similar view: "the world is presented in a kaleidoscopic flux of impressions which has to be organized by our minds

– and this means largely by the linguistic systems in our minds," according to Whorf (213). Likewise, Lucy and Gaskins (487) speak of "a vision of reality as it emerges through the 'window of language.'"[1] Gethin (52) is more explicit: "The world doesn't come to us already sliced up into objects and experiences; what counts as an object is already a function of our system of representation, and how we perceive the world in our experiences is influenced by that system of representation." Likewise Taylor (1996, 47) in a more specific way: "It follows that a person has to mould his conceptualizations to match the symbolic resources made available to him by his language. English forces its speaker to make a conceptual distinction between *snails* and *slugs* ... German does not."

This makes language a sort of interface mediating between the way the universe impinges on us through our sensory input and our conscious awareness or perception of that raw experience.[2] Unless there is a momentary problem of memory (such as trying to remember the name of a specific flower) we are unaware of this "matching" between an experience and the appropriate viewing idea. However, as we have already seen, this should not be understood as a sort of linguistic determinism limiting the human capacity for categorization to what one's mother tongue permits. The potentiality of lexemes for innovation as exploited in the preceding chapter and in metaphor (see chapter 14) makes it quite plain that thought can use words as instruments to represent something new. Moreover, there are grounds for proposing just the opposite relationship: that the human capacity to generalize is a determining factor in the development of language, as we shall now see.

Because our viewing ideas are generalizations, mentally abstracted from the particularity of specific experiences, they constitute a stable universe of ideas, permanently available to confront our fluid, constantly changing experience of the universe we live in. The inconstancy and specificity of our personal experience make it incommunicable as such, whereas the stability and abstractness of word meanings make them shareable and so expressible thanks to their sign. By the same token, however, they do not portray in all its specificity a personal experience, the particularity of any intended message – whence the constant challenge to poets – but only a more or less abstract version of it (although the abstractness of scientific or philosophical discourse tends toward a faithful portrayal). This goes beyond our previous discussion of the apparent paradox involved in saying that there is no language without thought and that there is no thought without language, because it raises the question of thought as the capacity or faculty for instituting in the mind a universe of ideas. Since this question is central to an understanding of the nature of human language, before pursuing our discussion of meaning as such we shall pause for a moment to consider the binary relationship described in chapter 1 from the point of view of the human faculty of thought, and show that there is no contradiction in saying that language has made man what he is and that man has made language what it is.

THOUGHT, LANGUAGE, AND LINGUISTIC RELATIVITY

The above discussion of lexemes recalls Whorf's description (147): "this 'thought world' is the microcosm that each man carries about within himself, by which he measures and understands what he can of the macrocosm." In itself, the notion of lexemes as a means of representing a speaker's experience in order to express it obviously entails a position in the ongoing discussion of linguistic relativism, namely that language "affects the ways in which we think while we are speaking" (Slobin, 91). Furthermore, we have proposed that lexemes are viewing ideas unconsciously categorizing our flow of consciousness, thus "making sense of the world" (Györi, 85) even when we are not speaking. This raises "the general question of how language influences thought" (Lucy, ix), both our pre-language thought and our languaged thought.

There is surely no need to belabour the point if we consider the way a specialist, say a geologist or an oncologist, makes distinctions the non-specialist, with notions such as 'rock' or 'cancer,' has trouble understanding. A more developed vocabulary reflects greater scope and refinement of thought. Differences between languages such as French *faire* as opposed to *make* and *do* in English reflect differences of thought learned with the mother tongue. On the more general level of language typology, the differences in the way words are constructed in, say, English and Eskimo would seem to make this manifest. That is, even though speakers may be talking about the same external reality, their means of mentally categorizing their experience and forming the words to represent it varies. This variation in meaning expressed by words may, of course, be compensated for by other elements in the sentence.

One might also raise the complementary question of how thought influences language, how our innate faculty of thought has enabled humans to develop, generation after generation, that incomparable instrument of thought available to all human beings, their mother tongue. If, as I have maintained, words are not stored in memory as such but must be constructed from their formative elements while we are speaking or writing, this presupposes a word-forming mechanism such as the part-of-speech system in English and other Indo-European languages. The fact that languages of other types form their words in a different way would seem to indicate different word-forming systems. This opens the prospect of comparing languages on the basis of this, their most general system.[3]

The subject cannot be developed here, but this perhaps suffices to suggest another aspect of the complex relations between thought and language.[4] Language conditions our thinking by providing the means of categorizing our ongoing experience and expressing it as such, but it also provides the means of innovating, of representing new ways of thinking when the need arises. In the wider context, it is thought, as a human faculty, that conditions language. The question of linguistic relativity is perhaps best discussed in this wider context of language as a human phenomenon. This complexity is summarized by the philosopher's remark (cf. chapter 1): "Thought makes language while being made by language."

Getting back to our discussion of meaning, the proposal of an inner, man-made universe consisting of viewing ideas gives us a way to understand what provides us with the permanent means for ordering our experience of the outer universe. Since this idea-universe is unforgettably instituted in the pre-conscious mind as the mother tongue, and since each of its components is linked, directly or indirectly, to a sign, we are freed from the need to invent on the spur of the moment the means of expressing what we want to say (as when trying to communicate with someone whose language we do not speak). Furthermore, the fact that it is a universe in expansion ensures that it is capable both of categorizing any impressions arising in a speaker's experience and of providing new viewing ideas to cope with something novel or to make finer distinctions (as when we learn to recognize a particular species of bird or flower). This helps us to understand what makes a language adaptable to any intended message, an adaptability enhanced by another factor inherent in lexemes: as components of tongue they are, by reason of their generality, potentials permitting different actualizations when one wishes to speak.

LEXICAL POTENTIALS

We have been discussing lexemes in tongue as viewing ideas, and will now consider them in their other role as potential meanings, as they relate to an act of language, and not simply as a means of monitoring our stream of consciousness to make it re-cognizable. From this point of view, then, we are concerned with the way an element of experience gets languaged. An act of language being a purposive act, it can be taken for granted that, for some reason, speakers decide to talk about the experience they have in mind, or some portion of it. This initial intention to express an experiential content on which certain viewing ideas are already focused makes that experience an intended message, as we saw above, and calls for a discourse in order to express that experience. Since, however, we can express by means of language only what we have represented by means of language, our expressive intent to provide an appropriate discourse activates the system of tongue to construct a sentence, or sentences, representing the message. Thus, triggered by the expressive intent, this representational intent first entails producing the elements required to construct a sentence, i.e. the words depicting linguistically the speaker's experience. A representational intent, therefore, entails actualizing the appropriate lexemes one by one and forming each of them into the type of word required for establishing the syntactic relationships that will be needed in the intended sentence.

To attain this objective, the system of tongue provides its grammatical and lexical resources. In a language such as English, the grammatical resources, which consist of the system of the parts of speech with their various subsystems, are ready to provide a form for the lexical matter, a form enabling each word to enter into a certain syntactic relationship with other words. The lexical resources consist of the potential meanings of tongue, certain of which are already in position as viewing ideas focused on the intended message to be languaged. Carrying out the representational intent entails actualizing these viewing ideas and providing them with a grammatical form. Thus in the example *Will he medal tonight?* the viewing idea 'medal' is formed by the speaker to perform as a verb rather than as a substantive, thereby answering the expressive intent of a more vivid representation of the situation than *Will he win a medal tonight?* Since the formal significates of verbs and substantives have been examined in some detail elsewhere (cf. my recent studies on the verb and on the noun phrase), this phase of word construction will not be explored here, where our concern is primarily with the material significate, the lexeme.

As an idea viewing something in a speaker's ongoing experience, a lexeme responds to an experiential impression or set of impressions falling within its range of representation. The lexeme categorizes the impressions by viewing them within its scope, thus evoking the nature of whatever is in view. Similarly, to function as a material significate in the construction of a word, the lexeme makes available its full meaning potential, but this must be actualized in order to provide a representation of the speaker's momentary experience. Thus the hypothesis that all a word's observed senses arise from one underlying potential meaning provides both the framework required to tell us what to look for when observing different senses and a basis for trying to solve the monosemy-polysemy problem.

This hypothesis implies that the different senses of a given word are notionally linked through the same source. It further implies that words expressing senses arising from different potential meanings are different words, as is borne out by the fact that we recognize almost all words by means of a distinctive physical sign signifying a distinctive lexical potential. Even in the case of homonyms, where two words have identical signs, the conditions of normal usage usually permit a listener to access the appropriate potential meaning and so to discern which of the two words the speaker has in mind. Basically, therefore, it is not the sign but the meaning, the material significate combined with its formal significate, that constitutes the unity of a word.

This view provides a guide for approaching the crucial problem of discerning a word's import to the phrase, and eventually the sentence, but it does not suffice for the observer to discern the word's lexical import. Since a word necessarily expresses both lexical and grammatical imports, to discern either clearly involves distinguishing between them in each use. For our purposes here, this calls for a summary view of the relation between the two, but before going on to this, we must make a terminological clarification to distinguish between *lexeme* and *material significate*.

So far we have distinguished between the material and formal components of a word's meaning in terms of its lexeme signified by the root, and its part of speech morpheme(s) signified by morphological suffixes (including the zero suffix[5]) and position in the sentence.[6] This manner of designating word meaning does not fit a relatively small, but frequently used, number of words in English – grammatical words such as *this, some, do*-auxiliary, etc. Like lexical words, each of these is characterized by its material and formal components, but its material component consists of such a highly generalized notion that it is more like a morpheme than a lexeme. That is, instead of a lexeme that can be contrasted with the myriad other lexemes of the language, each of these grammatical words is opposed to the other word(s) in a little grammatical system (*this* vs. *that, some* vs. *any*, etc.) by its distinctive material significate, a highly abstract, very general import which, as in any other word, must be formed by its grammatical morpheme(s) to determine its particular role in a sentence. For this reason, I do not designate a grammatical word's material component by the term *lexeme* but by the more general expression *material significate*.

Distinguishing in discourse between lexical and grammatical words in this way should not be taken as a categorization of lexemes in tongue. We have already seen that 'down' can be actualized as the lexeme for a substantive, verb, adjective, or adverb, or as the material significate of a preposition. Likewise, *given* in *given his age* and *following* in *following the lecture the meeting was open to questions* are both prepositions.[7] It is not yet understood just how the notion in tongue is actualized in such cases as an abstract material significate in order to be routed through the morphogenetic path of a preposition, or how in cases such as *a nobody* the material significate is actualized as a lexeme to be grammaticized as a substantive.

GRAMMATICAL POTENTIALS

We have seen that a lexeme in tongue functions as a viewing idea monitoring our stream of consciousness and, when some portion of it becomes an intended message, as a potential meaning focusing on that experiential entity in order to represent it. The same can be said of a morpheme, and of the abstract material significate of a grammatical word, but with two important differences. In the first place, whereas lexemes serve both to organize experience and to represent it, the abstract viewing ideas of grammatical words serve *only* to represent experience in the making of words and sentences. As a consequence, while lexemes function as viewing ideas at all moments of conscious awareness, it would seem that morphemes and the abstract, morpheme-like material significates of grammatical words such as *this* and *that* are activated as viewing ideas only during an act of language, because their role is to serve as "traffic-rule morphemes" in Bolinger's colourful expression. That is, during the act of language, both lexical and grammatical potential meanings focus on the intended message in order to represent affinitive impressions as part of the meaning of the word, phrase, or sentence.

The second difference between the two types of material potential is that a grammatical word's significate, like a morpheme's, can be accessed only through its system. When, for example, an impression of 'spatial-position-in-relation-to-speaker' arises in the intended message, neither demonstrative is called on; instead, the speaker calls on their system, which offers only two possibilities, *this* or *that,* for representing that impression. Similarly for verb morphemes when an impression of 'temporal-position-in-relation-to-speaker' arises: the system of tense in the indicative offers the two possibilities of past and nonpast. Thus intended messages are viewed not through the abstract matter of a grammatical word or a morpheme, but through the system containing it, and the system then provides the appropriate grammatical element to represent the impression in view. This is a manifestation of the fact that tongue on its grammatical side is highly systematic as compared with its lexical side, which is less systematically organized.

This brief description of the role of grammatical potentials should not mask the fact that all words, lexical or grammatical, bring to the sentence a binary significate, material and formal. The role of the formal significate is to form or categorize the material significate so that it can fulfill the function foreseen for it in the sentence.[8] Conceiving of the relationship between the two types of significate as that between matter and form is useful because it helps explain the fact that we generally distinguish between words by what is specific to each one – its material significate – whereas we assimilate them in the same category by means of the formal significate. That is, a word's material significate is what particularizes it, whereas its formal significate is what generalizes it. Viewed in this way, the matter / form relationship has an operational dimension that underlies the process of constructing a word each time it is required in a sentence, and it is only by distinguishing the two phases of this operation that the two components of a word's import can be differentiated and observed. In short, it seems scientifically obvious that distinguishing between a word's two semantic components, its lexical meaning and its grammatical meaning, and determining how they are related are prerequisites for trying to analyze either one of them.

FORMING AND OBSERVING WORD MEANING

Forming word meaning can first be understood in the sense of constituting it, bringing together its components to provide the material + formal import of any word in a sentence. It is this combination, and neither the material import on its own nor the formal import on its own, that is understood by the ordinary speaker/listener. That is, what is accessible to ordinary means of observation is the expressive effect of a word: the amalgam of its actualized lexical sense (which may be augmented by the import of prefixes and suffixes) and the actualized grammatical sense(s) of its morpheme(s). To obtain a clear view of the contribution of either a word's material import or its formal import they must be differentiated, and this can be done by tracing the process by which they are brought together during an act of language. So here a summary of word-forming will be presented as a preliminary to examining its lexical import.

Once actuated, the representational intent triggers the operation that will actualize a lexeme viewing the intended message by first calling up the grammatical form – the part of speech – required for the lexeme to perform its syntactic role. But before the part of speech through its subsumed morphological systems can "grasp" or configure its lexical matter, the lexeme itself must be called on as an idea distinct from all other lexemes, and actualized to represent what it is focused on in the intended message. The following diagram will give a summary view of this binary operation of actualizing a particular lexeme and giving it a grammatical form:

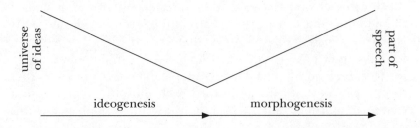

The word's idea or lexical import is actualized by the particularizing process of IDEOGENESIS and then, through the generalizing process of MORPHOGENESIS, formed by the morphological systems (e.g. gender, number, case) to receive its most general form, the part of speech (e.g. substantive). Ideogenesis tends toward what is singular, distinctive, particular; morphogenesis tends in the direction of greater scope toward what is inclusive, universal.

Guillaume insisted that these two processes constitute a single operation underlying the construction of any word's import in a part-of-speech language such as English. In one lecture he described it as "a synergy of two ideations: notional ideation and structural ideation or ideation of structure" (1998, 71) to bring out the idea that word constructing involves a real interaction between them, not a mere juxtaposition, and to stress that both processes contribute to a word's "ideation," to forming its meaning. Although the actual operation is much more complicated than the above diagram would suggest, this will suffice to bring out the important point here: namely, that a word is not a ready-made item stocked in a mental lexicon ready for use, but the outcome of an operation of construction carried out on the spur of the moment as part of a representational intent to contribute to the expression of a particular intended message.

All this is important for work in lexical semantics. In order to observe a word's lexical import in a sentence, it must be disengaged from its grammatical form, and to observe a word's grammatical import it must be disengaged from its lexical matter. On the other hand, we will see that the way a lexeme is actualized can have an effect on the way it is categorized by a given system of morphemes, and in such cases an observation of the grammatical effect can throw light on the lexical conditions producing it. In short, when attempting to observe a word's meaning, either lexical or grammatical, one should always try to distinguish it from the other component of its meaning, its immediate context within the word itself in that particular use. Without this precaution, like the precaution of distinguishing a word's meaning from the meaning of its more extended context (that of the phrase and that of the sentence), as well as the precaution of distinguishing sentence meaning from the environment (prior message if any and situation) in which it is embedded, any observation of particular uses will provide an unsure basis for generalization, and the subsequent phase of analysis will be jeopardized.

III LEXEMES OF VERBS

7

Monosemy and Polysemy

INTRODUCTION

Having set the stage in preceding chapters, we will now focus on observing meaning in the next three chapters. This is painstaking work since it calls for comparing diverse uses of particular lexemes for the senses expressed. First, however, a word of caution is appropriate. Although a word's lexical import must be accessible in ordinary discourse for anyone to understand a sentence and reconstitute the speaker's message, what ordinary speakers are not usually aware of is the variation of lexical sense a given word expresses in different uses. Certainly translators, lexicographers, and writers, to varying degrees, become aware of different senses expressed, but this is often awareness of the sense of the word in context, i.e. of the expressive effect of the phrase, or at best the word as a whole, and not of just the lexical import of the word. As we have seen, even what is normally accessible in discourse has to be decorticated, separated from the import of words around it.

As we have seen, how to deal with the problem of polysemy remains debatable, "a very precarious balancing act between the maximization of polysemy ... and a minimization of polysemy." For example, Langacker (1991, 274) "would posit numerous semantic variants of *eat*, accommodated to the nature of the food consumed and the specific activity required for ... such diverse activities as the consumption of meat, bananas, peanuts, and soup." Searle (1983, 145), after evoking *open* with different objects (*the door, her eyes, the wall, his book, the wound*) adopts the contrary position: "It seems clear to me that the word 'open' has the same literal meaning in all five of these occurrences." The problem is crucial since it calls into question the nature of the word, a universal in language.

In chapter 4 we saw the general postulate that everything in tongue – lexemes, morphemes, phonemes – exists as a potential which must be actualized to be used. That is, every lexical sense a word expresses is an actualization of its lexeme in tongue. Assuming monosemy for the potential in tongue and polysemy for the actualizations in discourse provides a basis for dealing with the problem of polysemy. It also satisfies a necessary condition for communication because it permits a listener, on hearing a given word (i.e. its sign), to access its lexical potential in tongue and actualize the sense appropriate to context and situation. To my knowledge, other approaches to meaning have not explored the problem of polysemy from this potential → actual point of view. Some linguists consider that the diverse senses expressed by a word need not be linked to a single underlying meaning but only to the same sign, and so view even homonyms as the same word. Another way of dealing with polysemy is to treat it not as a characteristic of a word, but as a result of using that word, so that a word always expresses the same meaning but is interpreted differently because of variations in the context and situation. We will now examine a study adopting the latter approach.

Few studies of particular verbs go beyond the dictionaries in examining different senses expressed in discourse. The most extensive and carefully documented one I am aware of is Ruhl 1989, which discusses four verbs, *bear, hit, kick,* and *slap,* in the light of numerous examples. Ruhl argues for their monosemy, attributing any apparent polysemy to the "pragmatic" circumstances of a particular use. Although Ruhl's theoretical approach is crucially different from the approach adopted here, his work is invaluable for the large collection of real examples arising from his basic assumption that the observation of meaning expressed in a sentence gives rise to data to be explained. His examples thus provide a testing ground for the findings of any attempt to observe lexical meaning.

TWO DIFFERENT APPROACHES

Before turning to the examples, however, it will be useful to contrast approaches in order to bring out more clearly that adopted here, and the basis for interpreting the data differently.[1] The underlying contrast is between the stances adopted. Ruhl,[2] like many other linguists (cf. 33), focuses on how the hearer (reader) interprets the sentence once it has been spoken. This leads him to include pragmatic factors as part of its full meaning (51): "General abstract meanings elude consciousness; the interpretations of the conscious mind by necessity are oriented toward reality, and thus are not purely semantic, but compounds of both semantic and pragmatic." Since extra-linguistic situations are endlessly variable, he can attribute to them any apparent polysemy of a verb not arising from other words in the sentence. He thus postulates that a verb always has the same meaning because the pragmatic factors bring in "language-external meaning" (17), "pragmatically contaminated variants" as Tuggy (344) puts it. This leads one to wonder how word meaning can exist outside language.

In the present essay, the focus is not on how the listener interprets a sentence but on how the speaker creates it. Speakers represent their intended message linguistically by means of words and express it linguistically by means of sentences. As brought out in chapter 4, it is only after understanding the meaning expressed that hearers can interpret the sentence in the light of extra-linguistic factors such as the speaking situation (including the message obtained from any preceding discourse), general knowledge, etc., in order to reconstruct the speaker's language-external intended message that triggered the act of language. In short, it appears obvious in the scientific method that one should try to analyze what a speaker puts into a sentence before trying to analyze what a hearer gets out of it.

Another contrast with Ruhl's approach lies in the manner of conceiving polysemy. Although seeking to understand why his nearly four hundred examples of the verb *bear*, taken from a great variety of sources, provide data that "*seem to be related*" (63; his italics), Ruhl rejects the "polysemic solution ... that *bear* breaks into a number of discrete semantic parts." One can only agree that polysemy would not help us understand how different senses are related if they are thought of as parts making up the whole of the verb's meaning, or as a number of subsets making up a set, as others have argued. On the other hand, if the verb's meaning is conceived as involving not a part-whole relationship but rather a potential → actual relationship, it may well provide an explanation of variation in the lexical sense expressed by the verb. And indeed, when Ruhl speaks (xi) of "a word's potential of meaning" and remarks (51) that "[t]he general abstract meaning is unconscious, providing the foundation for more specific conscious distinctions," he could well be understood to be evoking this relationship; but as just noted, he appeals to "pragmatic, language-external meaning" to account for observed variations of meaning in usage. In the approach adopted here, then, it is maintained that the "general, abstract ... unconscious" meaning is a potentiality, a potency which both ensures the unity of a lexeme in tongue and permits distinct though related senses, polysemy, when actualized for use in discourse. But this actualizing is not a matter of making "the correct choice among the meanings" (Tuggy, 358), as though meanings were "things, prepackaged chunks of information" (Geeraerts, 259) made of distinct parts; actualizing is rather "a process of sense creation" (Geeraerts, 260), of construing "'on-line,' in actual situations of use" (Croft and Cruse, 97), of exploiting the possibilities made available by the potential, of bringing to mind one of its possibilities. That is, as a permanent resource for a speaker a lexeme is monosemous, but in use, when syntactically linked to other words in specific sentences expressed in specific extra-linguistic situations, it can be polysemous.

Thus the approach adopted here allows for the interplay between meaning potential and context to explore not only how speakers/writers endow a word with the appropriate sense, but also how hearers/readers reach a word's appropriate actualized sense (cf. Tuggy, 356–60) from the potential called to mind by the sign. Moreover, it allows for a high-frequency sense that can be seen as prototypical, as well as rarely found senses, and even includes the possibility of innovating, of realizing a new sense, as seen in chapter 5. Finally, as will be seen below, postulating a monosemous meaning potential not only provides a basis for exploring the relations between the different senses of a lexeme, not in terms of rules but in terms of mental operations, but also imposes a minimalist approach to polysemy, one that can give ordinary speakers and listeners the impression of the same word in different uses (and grammarians the impression of "conversion").

With these differences of approach in mind, we will examine examples from Ruhl's data to see what they reveal about the word's lexical import. As we have already seen, and as Ruhl emphasizes throughout his study, care must be taken to distinguish the verb's actual import to the sentence from the import of adjoining adverbs, prepositional phrases, etc.

BEAR

Like Ruhl (26), we can usefully begin by reflecting on the different senses and subsenses of the verb *bear* which are paraphrased in the *OED* as follows:

I. to carry; with its transferred and figurative senses.
II. to sustain, support, uphold.
  * to sustain weight or pressure, to endure.
  ** to support, keep up, maintain.
  *** to hold up, hold, have upon it.
III. to push, thrust, press.
  * to push, press.
  ** to thrust (through) [obsolete].
  *** to press oneself; move, tend, lie in a given direction.
IV. to bring forth, produce, give birth to.

The discussion here will be organized around the four senses as paraphrased here and the relations between them, rather than, as in Ruhl, the syntactic environment of the verb.

The *OED* begins by observing an interesting relation between senses I and IV: "the senses *carry a burden*, and *bring forth fruit or offspring*, are both found in the word and its derivations in the Aryan languages generally, from the earliest period." This leads one naturally to look for some necessary link between senses I and IV to explain why the duo is so widespread. Typical examples (from Ruhl, numbered here in brackets as in Ruhl) would be:

... their sweating, straining backs bore every ounce of their supplies. [282]

for sense I, 'carry,' and

He took a wife and she bore him sons and daughters. [372]

for sense IV, 'give birth to,' but the link between the senses is not obvious. In fact, examples such as:

The earliest to bear edible fruit are bush beans. [376]
a tree bearing late pears [380]

expressing sense IV, 'produce,' appear to be closer to sense II, 'support, sustain,' as expressed in:

> ... twigs bearing April buds spin down, clipped from branches and bushes. [377]

It is not always obvious which sense is expressed. Part of the difficulty in discerning the senses here is that, according to the *OED*, the paraphrase given, *to carry*, is itself polysemous, and can express the same two senses as *bear* I and II: 'convey' (*carry* I) and 'support, sustain' (*carry* II).

Ambiguous examples provide one of the clearest ways of distinguishing different senses. Thus a phrase such as:

> oil-bearing shale [384]

could be understood either as shale holding (sense II) oil or actually producing (sense IV) oil. Ambiguity of this sort, which sometimes confronts listeners in actual usage, is usually disambiguated by more extended discourse or the extra-linguistic situation. Since speakers know what they want to say, they are never confronted by ambiguity in this way, but the fact that it can arise for listeners is a useful means of showing that a given word has the possibility of expressing different senses. To argue, as some do, that it is the context which determines the variation in sense would not explain the ambiguity of a phrase such as *oil-bearing shale*, since *bearing* could be understood in either sense here without its context, *oil* and *shale*, undergoing any change. The important point for us is that this example helps us observe two distinct senses of *bear* in the same context, an ambiguity which neatly brings out the relation between the two senses: since containing oil is obviously a prior necessity for shale to produce it, we recognize a relation of condition → consequence between them. Granted the difficulty both of distinguishing the senses represented by the verb itself before it is integrated into the phrase or sentence, and of paraphrasing them, such observations are not to be neglected.

Comparing uses in similar contexts also helps discern the relation between senses. Thus, compared with [372] above, an example such as:

> ... I think of that baby she is bearing and will give birth to. [370]

brings out a clear relation between the senses expressed: she must 'carry, convey' (sense I) the baby before she can 'give birth' (sense IV). Again a relation of necessary precondition to consequence appears to hold between the two senses.

Sense II of *bear* ('to sustain, support, uphold') comes out clearly in the following concrete examples:

> The pillars bear a heavy weight. [263]
> The old bridge can hardly bear up its own weight anymore. [98]

The 'support' sense here implies none of the movement involved in sense I, 'carry, convey,' though the relationship between the two is clear: a physical object's weight must be supported before it can be transported, as is implied in the *straining backs* example [282] above. That is, in concrete uses like this, 'bear' II appears to represent a situation (supporting) which is a necessary precondition for 'bear' I (conveying), but this does not of course imply that the latter is a necessary consequence of the former.

Observing is not so easy when *bear* expresses a more abstract sense as in:

> In my heart of hearts I bore her no ill will. [338]
> ... there are still those who bear him an abiding mistrust. [339]

The expressive effect of a sort of mental conveying to *her/him* suggests that the sense is 'bear' I. This is not the case in:

> ... the activity of the hunt had made her able to bear these past few days. [297]
> I can't bear disgrace sir. [299]

The expressive effect of 'tolerate, endure' here suggests an abstract sense of 'support,' i.e. 'bear' II. And in the following example either sense may come to mind:

> Your little sister is sick. Try to bear with her when she cries. [346]

Although what must be borne is left implicit here, the verb can be interpreted as 'support mentally what is disagreeable, tolerate,' i.e. 'bear' II. The expressive effect of the sentence may also be interpreted to suggest that the speaker has thought *bear* in an abstract 'bear' I sense, and it seems to be the *with* phrase that brings in the idea of 'accompany her,' 'go along with her, don't get angry' (cf. the change of expressive effect if the *with* phrase is replaced by *it*). That is, the verb can be analyzed as expressing either 'mentally accompany her' or its prerequisite, 'mentally support, tolerate.'

The abstract 'support' sense of *bear* just exemplified gives rise to slightly different expressive effects in:

> It bears repeating that two wrongs don't make a right. [352]
> The accident bears two explanations. [354]
> I have a list of complaints that bear airing. [361]

Ruhl (61) paraphrases such uses as 'invite, permit, need,' etc., a set of senses he considers to be arising by metonymy from the 'support' sense. Judging by the examples provided, it would seem that they involve not a separate sense of *bear* but an expressive effect resulting from combining the 'support' sense and the process involved in the direct object: inherent in the subject is something predisposing it to undergo *repeating, explanation, airing*. This comes out more clearly in examples with modal auxiliaries such as:

> ... a principle which could not bear the light of absolute honesty and intellectual integrity. [362]
> ... it is the central doctrine of Yeats's poetry, yet it cannot bear a confrontation with the dynamic world. [366]

Ruhl's paraphrase 'ability to support or withstand' describes the expressive effect here, *could* and *can* expressing 'ability,' and *bear* 'support or withstand.' The expressive effect is slightly different in:

> The answer of this witness will bear examination. [368]

Here *will* appears to express its 'future' sense and *bear* something like 'call for, invite,' or even 'hold up under.' These examples bring out the point that *bear*'s actualized 'support' sense is sufficiently general to contribute to expressive effects of a subject predisposed to undergo some process – that is, of sustaining, besides physical and mental pressure, what might be called processual pressure.

Sense II, 'sustain, support, uphold,' is thus sufficiently general to contribute to sentences portraying either physically "sustaining weight or pressure," or mentally "enduring" it, or submitting the subject to some process. It depicts situations seen as prior to those evoked by sense I, 'convey, transport,' or by sense IV, 'produce,' a close mental link that in some uses may make it difficult to distinguish sense II from these other senses. Like any other actualized sense, it is in itself very abstract and so can be discerned only by isolating its presence in various expressive effects.

There are of course a myriad of other expressive effects observed in usage, especially with *up, down, away, in, out,* and the like, as illustrated by Ruhl. It should be recalled here that an expressive effect arises from amalgamating the actualized senses of two or more words (or morphemes), and so an examination of each such element in the context would be required to analyze any expressive effect satisfactorily. This means that the results of any attempt such as the present one to examine the lexeme of a particular word must remain tentative until the investigation of other words confirms or invalidates these results. Furthermore, hesitation in attributing one or other of the actualized senses to *bear* may arise because some other word in the context is ambiguous, or it may be that *bear* itself could be understood to express different senses in a given use. As we have seen, cases where a given word is ambiguous provide evidence that its underlying potential can be actualized in these different ways. Finally, the examination of examples so far should make it clear that paraphrase cannot reproduce exactly the sense expressed and is, at best, a means of directing attention to the abstract sense the observer has understood.

The senses in group III ('push, thrust, press') are also related to 'carry' I, according to the *OED*:

> This group seems to have arisen in a transference of the sense from *carry* to an action producing the same result (i.e. the moving forward of a body) by a different application of force, that of continuous pressure. This once established, the extension of the idea to pressure of many kinds, both horizontal and vertical, followed. There thus result senses of *bear* directly contrary to each other, as when a post bears the pressure that is brought to bear on it, or a man bears up until calamity bears him down.

That the contrary expressive effects of direction in *bear up, bear down* and the like are due to the adverbs and should not be attributed to the verb is brought out by Ruhl in numerous examples such as the following:

> the wall bearing on the floor. [43]
> an arch bearing against piers. [57]

The same can be said for examples with more abstract expressive effects:

> ... the context was entirely political and bore upon the current election for governor. [55]
> The discussion bore against the bill. [59]

The interesting point in the OED citation, however, is that the sense of "continuous pressure," in whatever direction, is seen as what can produce the result of moving a body. That is, this sense III, like sense II, represents a situation prior to that of 'carry, convey,' as is brought out by the example:

> ... to bring guns to bear on a target. [82]

The 'pressure' expressed here implies an obvious result as possible – obvious for anyone who knows the function of guns. And even the target can be left implicit if the speaker assumes that it is known by the hearer, as in:

> The guns were brought to bear. [226]

This appears to be what permits the use of *bear* in:

> The lighthouse bears due north. [79]

The expressive effect of 'faces north' implies that the way the lighthouse is situated permits it to project its beam and exercise all its activity toward the north.

In some cases, the expressive effect of the sentence is one of a movement applying pressure:

> The charging horses bore down on them. [28]

In a more abstract manner, the verb may suggest applying psychological pressure.:

Kurtz bore in on her a little harder. [37]

And the use in the following example could be paraphrased by 'push left':

Bear left past the cemetery. [73]

In fact, the OED considers this an intransitive development of the 'push, press' sense. In these three examples, then, it seems that it is the verb itself expressing a 'continuous pressure' sense combined with an adverbial (*down, in, left*) indicating direction that expresses the movement.

This selection of examples from Ruhl to illustrate the main senses described in the OED gives a fairly wide view of usage. The attempt to isolate sense III of *bear* in the last examples raises the question of whether it really is distinct from sense II. That is, do the ideas of 'support' in *The pillars bear a heavy weight* and 'push, press' in *the wall bearing on the floor* arise from different senses of the verb or as an expressive effect of the verb and other elements? Since both 'support, sustain, uphold' and 'push, thrust, press' involve weight or pressure, a minimalist view would opt for a single actualized sense general enough to contribute to expressive effects of 'subject to or exerting pressure.' This is probably the better basis for further exploring data. Similarly for senses I and IV: both 'conveying' as in *bearing gifts to the newborn prince*, and 'producing' as in *a bush bearing red flowers*, presuppose supporting or sustaining the gifts and flowers. Are these two expressive effects which arise from a single actualized sense of *bear*? Again, this is a hypothesis to be kept in mind when examining further examples.

So far, then, results indicate that the potential meaning of *bear* permits different senses, at least two – 'pressure' ('support, push', etc.) and its consequence ('convey, produce') – and perhaps three, or four as the OED proposes. On this basis, how can the potential meaning of *bear* be imagined? It would, of course, be a mistake simply to take one of the actualized senses as the potential, since a potential cannot be one of its own actualizations. Moreover, unlike a grammatical word, a lexical word is not part of a small, bounded system, and so the analysis of its potential meaning necessarily involves the analysis of other potentials related to it in diverse ways. That is, before reflection on this problem can be undertaken with any hope for success, one must be in a position to distinguish 'bear' as a potential from adjoining or overlapping potentials such as 'carry,' 'support,' etc., thus calling for a prior examination of the usage of these verbs. This indicates how complex the task of analyzing even one lexeme is, but it seems to be the only way a lexeme can be approached on the basis of data, of the observed senses expressed in actual language usage.

HIT

As with *bear*, Ruhl considers *hit* to have a single general meaning, apparent variation being due to the "pragmatic continuum" of context and situation. "The supposed basic sense of 'strike'" (106), also paraphrased in the OED "To get at or reach with a blow," is expressed in:

> This time [as he was digging] Joe's spade hit the object that had been buried. [197]
> ... my right front wheel hit a pothole. [191]

Furthermore, this sense includes "to affect the conscience, feelings, comfort, prosperity, etc. of (any one) in a way analogous to physical hitting" (*OED*); i.e. the impact may be purely mental, as in:

> I was on a jet returning to New York when a thought hit me. [309]
> The poet William Cowper called Newton a 'childlike sage' for that quality, and the description perfectly hits the air of surprise at the world that Einstein carried in his face. [238]

In some uses the expressive effect involves both the physical and the non-physical:

> ... his voice hit my ears ... [208]
> The night air hit them like a clean bath. [212]
> The light hit his face. [219]

Examples such as these three suggest that the variation between literal and analogous is an expressive effect arising from the subject and object rather than from different senses of *hit* itself.

Ruhl (106) considers that the "minimal meaning" of the 'strike' sense "is approximated by the more general 'meet' or 'arrive at' or 'join' (although each gloss has misleading implications)." This 'encounter' sense, as he later paraphrases it, can be observed in such examples as:

> I hit red lights at only four of nearly two-dozen controlled intersections. [64]
> As soon as Flamand hit California he was drafted ... [72]
> The British pound sterling hit an all time low today ... [135]
> Whenever the oilmen drilled, east and west, north and south, they hit oil. [253]

Expressive effects do vary for these examples – 'encountered red lights'; 'arrived in California'; 'reached an all time low'; 'found oil' – but what is common to them all, as in the 'strike' uses, is attaining or encountering the limit set by the object of *hit*. It is even found in intransitive uses:

> When he fell, he hit hard. [W3][3]
> The grippe hit unusually severely that year. [W3]

where the limit is left implicit.

Thus the notion of 'encountering,' or more abstractly 'movement to a limit,' is sufficiently general to be applied to examples ranging from the concrete hitting of a pothole to the abstract hitting of the subconscious mind. That is, all these uses of *hit* express a process arriving at its term.

In some cases *hit* does not express the process actually reaching a limit, for example:

> The flowers of the dogwood, which are just hitting their peak ... [138]

Here the development involved in 'reaching their peak' is depicted as not completely realized in time (some blossoms have not yet opened), but this is the effect of the progressive. There is a suggestion of repetition thanks to the plural substantive in:

> ... the thud of darts hitting the board ... [194]

The 'movement to a limit' sense is expressed by *hitting* as accomplished for some darts but not for all thanks to the participle (though a more extended context might indicate a different interpretation). The same sense is grammaticized differently in the example:

> advertising techniques designed to hit the subconscious mind. [245]

This lexical representation of the occurrence is depicted by the infinitive as a possibility and not something actually accomplished, as in the preceding examples. And in:

> Motor-paced racers [bicycles] routinely hit speeds of 50 to 60 mph. [133]

this same lexical representation is expressed as an habitual event, i.e. as the predisposition of the subject to realize the event, and not as the actual realizing of it, on certain occasions. On the other hand, in *hit out at the table* (as opposed to *hit the table*) no impact or contact with the table is expressed, merely movement, as Ruhl (213) points out; but the movement is represented reaching the limit implied by *out*, presumably the full extent of a person's reach.

Thus this abstract 'movement to a limit or goal' sense underlying both the often suggested 'strike' paraphrase and Ruhl's more general 'meet, encounter' paraphrase arises with different grammatical configurations and lexical contexts and so contributes to an endless variety of expressive effects. Ruhl, however, indicates another type of use where this sense is not appropriate when he observes (104) that words sometimes convey information that is not expressed: "a stated cause can suggest an unstated effect ... an intention its realization ... or an action its purpose." The following examples illustrate this:

> Junior asks Dad if he'd like to hit the beach. [44]
> ... when the forces hit the beach. [47]

To get yourself a bucket of clams, you ought to hit the beach at low tide ... [46]

Here the message is concerned with the purpose or consequence of reaching the beach. The purposes are merely implied in the first two – swimming and invading – and made explicit in the third – clamming. Examples like these evoke not just the movement to a goal, i.e. reaching the beach, but also what that movement entails. These examples can be contrasted with:

There was a splat of ocean breakers hitting the beach ... [48]

where no such consequence is suggested, but only the impact of waves reaching the beach. This raises a question: what brings about this difference? Why is hitting the beach understood as a precondition for achieving a purpose in the previous three examples but not in this one?

For Ruhl (103) the previous three uses imply a purpose thanks to "Pragmatic Metonymy": what "the combined meanings of the words themselves ... and their possible referents suggest." That is, in an example such as:

I'm in a bar now near Columbus, Ohio, pausing before hitting the road again. [35]

road can suggest the purpose of travelling because its extra-linguistic referent is part of a travelling situation. Certainly common knowledge of roads is required to understand that the particular purpose implied is travelling and not swimming or invading, but this does not give the reader a cue that there is something implied. That is, in the sentence itself, what indicates that the speaker has some purpose in mind, and not just reaching the road? In the following example:

More and more students are hitting the road instead of the books. [36]

we again assume there is an implied purpose even though we may not be sure what it is. (Only with the message from the prior linguistic context in mind can the reader understand that students hit the road to look for jobs, not just to travel.) The point here is: what in these examples prompts us to look to something outside language – our common knowledge, the message derived from the prior context, the momentary referent – for some implied purpose or consequence? The linguistic motivation for this would appear to come from *hit* itself, from its representing not just a movement to a limit but what is entailed once the limit is attained. This would constitute a second sense of *hit*, a sense representing not the specific purpose in a given sentence but the moment for realizing whatever purpose or consequence a particular subject may have for going to the beach, getting on the road, returning to the books.

Understanding *hit* in this resultative or 'purpose' sense as expressing the phase after the limit or goal has been reached would leave the particular purpose implicit, i.e. as part of the message to be worked out by the listener, but it would also leave the listener unsatisfied until it has been worked out, as might arise with examples such as:

> But that's all you need to hit the slopes ... [91]
> I was well into my thirties before I hit the couch. [111]

Anyone not familiar with the allusions to skiing and to psychiatric treatment has the impression they do not get the message, since the speaker has, by means of *hit*, directed attention to the purpose of going to the slopes and lying on the couch. On the other hand, there is no need to work out an interpretation when the purpose is made explicit, as in:

> He hit the pillow and slept for a fragment of uneasy time. [171]
> The vagrant hit me for a dime. [326]
> At 200 feet, the pilot hits the switch to retract the wheels. [267]

The realization of the movement toward the object – 'putting his head on the pillow'; 'approaching, encountering me'; 'touching, activating the switch' – is represented as leading to the purpose phase as expressed in the latter part of the sentence.

This second sense is found in intransitive uses as well:

> In spring the peddlers hit up the coast with packs and carts. [W3]
> ... hit for the nearest lunchroom. [W3]

Here, where the notion of road or street is left implicit, the travelling is explicated by its route ("up the coast") or its goal ("the nearest lunchroom"). One gets the impression that expressions such as *hit the road, highway, trail,* etc. are so readily understood in this 'purpose' sense that merely evoking the travelling in this way suffices to orient the listener toward the message.

In some cases it is quite clear which sense of *hit* the speaker has represented, its 'movement toward a limit, encounter' sense or its 'purpose, entailment' sense:

In another instant the car hit the water and dropped immediately out of sight. [53]
Only thing to do on a day like this is hit the water. [50]

In other cases this is not so clear:

Mid-depth trolling is comfort zone trolling, and the closer we hit the level preferred by the kind of fish we seek, the better our luck will be. [56]

Although there is an obvious purpose involved here, one gets the impression that the speaker's focus is on reaching the exact depth. Similarly, the impact sense seems to come to the fore in:

The only time juries hit physicians is when they've been negligent ... [314]
Schultze hits GOP tax plan. [316]

Though a more extended context might well give another interpretation, the purpose of trials or the political comment is not brought out. In examples such as the following, however, either sense could be understood:

It's generally close to 11 when Jody hits home. [67]
I'd hit the house about four o'clock. [68]

The sense intended by the speaker might be simply 'reach home / the house' or it might entail undertaking a set of activities, as in *hit the road* above. Even if it is not clarified by the speaking situation, this ambiguity, or vagueness as in the trolling example, would hardly be noticed in the give and take of discourse because of the close condition-consequence link between the two senses.

If, in examples of *hit* in its 'movement toward a limit' sense, the limit is depicted by *it,* the listener may not be able to get the message:

> They [boats] were hitting it. [329]
> "Mike. Hit it." [330]
> ... those women are hitting it. [331]

It requires an awareness of the speaking situation or the message from previous discourse to discern the referent of *it*: here, respectively, a high speed, the ground (in a shooting episode), and a certain age. On the other hand, the referent of *it* may be clearly implied, as in:

> ... Winkler finally hit it big in Hollywood. [333]

where one understands 'achieved success in a big way.' The expressive effect of 'playing with animation' suggests a result in:

> The band was already hitting it up when we arrived. [W3]

Whether this should be attributed to *hit* in its 'purpose, entailment' sense or to *up* or to the combination of the two is not clear, and likewise in:

> ... had hit it off from the very start. [W3]

The paraphrase "to associate agreeably" suggests that this relationship was the purpose or entailment of people meeting, but until the sense of *off* is discerned more clearly it cannot be affirmed that this is due to *hit* in its 'purpose' sense. As Ruhl points out (49), isolating the sense of the verb in expressions like these calls for an analysis of the contribution of words like *up* and *off*.

Since our view of meaning implies that the same lexeme in tongue can be grammaticized in different ways, we are, unlike Ruhl, led to examine 'hit' configured as a substantive in order to see if it expresses the two senses discerned above. The main uses mentioned in W3 will give a summary idea of the situation. A common use in sports is to express not just the fact of striking an object but the result achieved by it, such as enabling a batter to reach a base in baseball. Similarly, when *a hit* designates a successful song, movie, book, etc. it represents as achieved the purpose of presentation to the public. *Hit* is paraphrased as "a blow striking an object aimed at" in:

> ... scored a hit on his first try. [W3]

It is paraphrased as "a stroke of luck" in:

> ... answered the questions correctly by a series of lucky hits. [W3]

These two paraphrases involve both the striking and its purpose, but to discern whether the 'purpose' element is contributed by *scored* and *lucky* or by *hit* (or by both), an examination of more data is required. Finally, *hit* is said to designate a "censorious, sarcastic or telling remark" in a use such as:

> ... took a sharp hit at grasping politicians. [W3]

Even without the adjective *sharp* here this expressive effect would arise, but whether it is due to *hit* evoking the purpose of the remark, or to a metaphorical use of *hit*, is not clear. Such problem cases indicate the limits of what can be safely advanced, but these preliminary observations suffice to indicate that the substantive is used to express a 'purpose' sense, and perhaps an 'impact' sense.

Our examination of usage thus leads to proposing that 'hit' as a lexeme in tongue is actualized in two different abstract senses, 'movement to(ward) a limit, strike' and 'purpose, entailment,' the phase arising after the limit is attained. Like *bear*, *hit* thus manifests polysemy in usage but the condition → consequence link between the senses observed suggests that there is a single potential in tongue giving rise to the two senses and making it possible for the reader or listener to discern what the speaker had in mind.

KICK AND SLAP

Ruhl also discusses *kick* and *slap*, distributing their uses, and those of *hit*, into three semantic domains – movement leading to contact, contact, movement effected by contact (215, 225–6) – which he depicts by the following schema:

MOVEMENT → CONTACT → MOVEMENT

Each verb has a "ground domain," its constant semantic contribution to the sentence. The other two domains result from a "metonymic potential" which "provides something cooccurrent in a situation," in which case monosemy is maintained by the claim that "though the words contribute to the meaning, the contribution is irrelevant" (219–20). Thus for *kick*, the ground domain is "move leg or foot," either literally or figuratively as in:

You have to kick rapidly when using a crawl stroke. [1]

The second domain is "shift from movement to contact," as in:

He kept watching his foot kick the suitcase. [71]

and the third domain "shift from contact to movement or change of state of something affected by contact," as in:

Halleck kicked the door shut with one heel. [100]

This threefold distinction of senses implies that movement and contact, or limit (the more abstract term), can be represented separately. This, however, does not take into account that whenever the foot or leg are concerned, any movement represented by *kick* necessarily involves a limitation imposed by the leg. Thus the swimming example evokes many short, i.e. limited, movements. This leg and foot movement is interrupted where the object imposes the endpoint or limit, as in the expressive effect of the suitcase-kicking example. Similarly, in the door-kicking example, to separate the contact from the movement it provokes does not capture the expressive effect of the sentence, since the impact is the starting point of the door's movement leading to the result, the state of being shut. Literal examples such as these, then, lend themselves to a twofold distinction of sense: movement to the limit (contact) and movement starting from the limit. Ruhl also gives examples with a figurative sense to illustrate his three domains:

As the time wore on the sea began kicking up ... [140]
But now the wind was kicking up 12-foot seas. [141]
The war in Europe was kicking prices up. [142]

One gets the impression of short movements as in the swimming example, but it is difficult to discern the exact sense of *kick* without an analysis of the input of *up*.

For *slap* Ruhl distinguishes three senses:

1. "contact," the "ground domain," as in:
   A heavy hand slapped him on the back. [253]
2. "movement before contact," as in:
   Rain slapped against the stained-glass window. [286]
3. "movement after contact," as in:
   … I put the bottle back in the drawer and slapped it shut. [334]

Again, it does not reflect the expressive effect to suggest that the first example expresses no movement, only contact, and that the other examples express movement but no contact. Rather, it better reflects what the sentences express to distinguish the last example, which focuses on the movement of the drawer provoked by the contact, from the other two examples, which evoke the movement leading to the contact. That is, as with *kick*, interpreting Ruhl's data as expressing two interconnected senses, one the consequence of the other, rather than three separate domains, corresponds more closely to the expressive effects of the sentences. Moreover, we shall see that this avoids the impasse of proposing that the "ground domain" or "lexical meaning" ('contact' for *slap*, 'move leg or foot' for *kick*) "no longer contributes any meaning" (221) when the other two domains are expressed, since the verb then supposedly gets its meaning from "pragmatic metonymy."

CONCLUSION

Because of his postulate that words are monosemous in discourse, Ruhl is led to appeal to "pragmatics, meaning supplied extralinguistically" (2002, 171) in order to explain senses other than the one considered basic, the "ground domain." But this involves putting the cart before the horse: there must be something in what the word expresses indicating that the listener is either to understand the word's lexical meaning or to look for its meaning outside language. That is, rather than propose that what a word expresses is "irrelevant," it is more satisfactory to propose there must be a variable in what a word expresses, and this amounts to proposing that a word is polysemous in usage. Besides, as Victorri and Fuchs point out (17), "a language without polysemy would be a rigid language, unable to evolve."[4]

Adopting the view that a word can express more than one sense, however, confronts us with Ruhl's pertinent query (2002, 171): "how do we select the right one when we interpret someone's use?" Implicit in this question is the problem of communication by means of language. If we accept the polysemy of words, there must be some means made available by the word and the way it is used whereby a listener can work out the appropriate sense, the sense signified by the speaker in a given sentence. We will discuss this in chapter 11, taking into account what we have seen in this chapter and what is brought to light in our examination of verbs in the next three chapters.

8

Discerning Different Senses of *See*

INTRODUCTION

In chapter 6 we saw that a word's meaning consists of a lexical import and a grammatical import, a distinction not made explicit in Ruhl's study. In order to bring into focus the actualized sense of the lexeme and nothing more, we will now turn to studies making this distinction. The difficulty involved here is considerable but perhaps not as great as Cruse suggests (5) when he remarks that "it is not possible to disentangle semantics from grammar completely. One reason for this is that many grammatical elements are themselves bearers of meaning."[1] It goes without saying that observation under such circumstances is more a matter of discernment, calling for analysis and comparison, since it usually involves more than merely ascertaining an expressive effect by introspection.

Perhaps the clearest example of this is verbs, where a variety of grammatical imports (aspect, mood, tense, etc.) expressed by different forms, both simple and compound, combines with whatever variation of senses is permitted by the lexeme in different uses. In some cases, however, this double variability encounters a constraint: a given grammatical form is not found with all the lexical senses of a word. When viewed in the light of the relation between the actualized lexeme and the grammatical categorization, such constraints do have an advantage since they offer a means of sorting out lexical senses. That is, the very fact that the progressive is unable to provide a form for certain senses of a verb's lexeme can be used to discriminate between the lexical senses involved. In this chapter, we will explore this possibility of distinguishing a verb lexeme's actualized sense by first examining the evidence resulting from a study of verbs of perception. Throughout this chapter, and in fact whenever particular examples are being discussed, it should be kept in mind that any paraphrase, at best an approximation, is intended to direct attention to the meaning expressed, not to reproduce it.

LEXICAL AND GRAMMATICAL (IN)COMPATIBILITY

The study on which this chapter is based (McGirr) was undertaken to meet a practical problem: how to explain to ESL students the constraints on the use of the progressive form with verbs of perception. In order to avoid errors at an elementary level, teaching grammars often advise students not to use the progressive form with verbs of perception. More advanced students, however, require help in discerning what the progressive expresses in its occasional use with these verbs. Here we will take examples from the McGirr study and summarize what it proposes for the different senses of *see*.

In this study the distinction between literal and analogous (figurative) senses – physical vs. mental perception – was made in order to classify different uses, but this does not provide the sort of criterion we need here, since both literal and analogous senses are found in the simple form and in the progressive. Thus for literal senses:

I see a plane.
It's so beautiful. At first you don't believe what you're seeing.[2]

And for analogous senses:

I see what you mean.
Men are seeing that the old ways of wielding power cause great stress.[3]

Moreover, most examples have mixed senses where both physical and mental perception appear to be involved:

I see another speed record was broken yesterday.[4]
At last I'm seeing the Mona Lisa. (Hatcher, 271)

Since, in such cases, there is no grammatical evidence suggesting that the ordinary speaker discriminates between literal and analogous senses, this distinction will not be useful for our purposes.

More promising is another distinction made in the above study. Almost all the examples have been classified as expressing either the process of visual perception or its result. Thus, the first example given above, illustrating one of the verb's most common uses, evokes a result of physical perception, the mental percept or image of a plane: 'I have a plane in view.' The progressive in the second example, however, evokes the operation of perception: '… you don't believe what you are in the process of perceiving.' Similarly for the following example:

> Only his eyes went suddenly beyond me to where Sherry was watching him uncertainly, and I knew he wasn't seeing me at all. (Buyssens, 33)

One might paraphrase this use as: 'he wasn't registering an image of me at all.'

Likewise for the above two examples of analogous use. The first, a common use, might be paraphrased 'I have a clear idea of what you mean' to bring out the 'resultative' sense. The second expresses something like 'Men are coming to realize that …' depicting the operation of realization being carried out by more and more men. Another example of this is:

> Perhaps part of the terror is that you feel an expanded consciousness of yourself; you are seeing yourself with a new awareness, a new clarity of perception about where you have been and where you are going.[5]

The suggestion here is that of an ongoing process: 'you are becoming more and more aware of yourself.'

The two examples above involving both physical and mental perception also illustrate the process / result distinction. The first suggests that, as a result of, say, seeing it in the newspaper, 'I am now aware that another speed record has been broken.' The second suggests that, while looking at the famous painting, 'I am gradually becoming aware of different impressions arising from it.' Another example of this 'process' sense is:

> I looked at everyone as though, in a sort of way, I were seeing them for the first time – and for the last time. (Berlands-Delepine, 225)

The process suggested here is one of 'discovering the mental implications of what is physically perceived.'

In these examples we can observe how the grammatical form of the verb helps bring out two different lexical senses expressed by *see*. The progressive provides a form for the lexeme evoking an occurrence that develops as it proceeds in time, i.e. a 'process' sense; the simple provides a form for the lexeme expressing an outcome or consequence, an occurrence that does not develop or change as it extends in time, i.e. a 'resultative' sense. It should not, however, be concluded that one can distinguish the two senses on the basis of the two grammatical forms alone. Although the progressive always takes as its lexical matter a process of some sort,[6] the simple form can take as its matter something resultative, as above, but also a process, which it depicts from beginning to end. This is particularly clear in certain uses of the past tense, as in:

Suddenly I saw the solution.

where the expressive effect is 'discovered, realized, became aware of' rather than the resulting state of 'being aware.' Likewise in the following example from a dictionary:

I saw it with my own eyes.

the focus is rather on the process as carried out by the eyes than on the result; though, of course, the existence of the result is implied. Similarly in the following example, which presumably depicts someone just regaining consciousness:

His eyes ... They were seeing ... Surely they saw. (Jespersen 1954, IV, 187)

Whereas the progressive, as always, expresses the process as incomplete, *saw* depicts it as complete: 'surely they carried out an act of perception.' On the other hand, the sense expressed by *saw* in the following example is unmistakeably 'resultative':

Though he never lost heart and was forever urging it on his sons, he saw little hope of attaining his ambition of reforming the Empire of Saud or even of recovering Riad. (Buyssens, 57)

Often, however, *saw* is ambiguous in this respect, permitting either reading, as in the following example from conversation:

He was the only one who saw the truth.

Should *saw* be understood in a 'process' sense ('came to realize') or in a 'result' sense ('was aware of')? This ambiguity, which would probably be dispelled for the listener in the light of the full context, is in no way surprising, since a complete process entails the existence of its result. In fact, the two readings of *saw* are often so closely linked that in ordinary discourse it usually matters little which of the two is understood.

Of the forty or so examples of *see* discussed in McGirr's study, all but three express either a 'process' sense or a 'result' sense. The following example, which arose in conversation, is one that does not fall into either group:

I see better with my new glasses.

See here can be paraphrased as 'can perceive,' a sense suggesting neither the result nor the actual process as realized but rather the capacity of realizing it. The other two examples, from a grammar and from conversation respectively, are:

You see whenever you open your eyes.
Every time I look at this painting, I see something new.

Here *see* evokes the process not as something going on at a given moment, but as an habitual occurrence. A habit, as opposed to a repeated event, has been shown[7] to be represented as a tendency or predisposition to carry out the process, not its actually being carried out innumerable times. These two examples, then, like the preceding one, express a process as a predisposition or capacity, i.e. as a possibility, subject to certain conditions governing its actualization. Moreover, like the 'result' sense, this 'possibility' sense is not found in the progressive form.

Thus, the constraints on the use of the progressive permit us to distinguish three senses of *see*. When formed by means of the progressive, the lexeme 'see' always has a 'process' sense. When formed by means of the simple, it most commonly has a 'resultative' sense, but sometimes a 'process' sense, and occasionally a 'possibility' sense. Do these correspond to three actualized senses of the postulated meaning potential of the lexeme 'see'? The fact that they are quite general ways of envisaging how a verb's lexeme is actualized makes this an interesting avenue to be explored, as we will see in the next section, where a wider selection of usage will be examined in the light of this threefold classification. First, however, a point concerning the relation between form and matter must be cleared up.

Previous chapters have given a general view of how the lexical and the grammatical contribute to the forming of what a word such as *see* expresses in a sentence. Unless this view is kept in mind, the above discussion could easily be misinterpreted. One might be tempted to say that the 'process' reading of 'see' is imposed by the progressive form, whereas the simple form imposes no such reading on the lexeme, leaving it open to the context or situation to determine how the verb is to be understood. This sort of marked vs. unmarked approach,[8] based on how the reader or listener reaches an interpretation, would assign the role of forming the lexeme to the progressive, but would assign no such role to the simple form, which would, in this respect at least, be a form without meaning. Moreover, this listener-based approach, in making the interpretation of the simple form dependent on the particular context and situation, would mask a generalization concerning the way time is represented in a verb and made explicit by the different uses of the simple form. Suffice it to say here that adopting a speaker-based approach, as in the last chapter, situates the problem of discerning the different senses of a lexeme in the wider perspective of the act of language, thus focusing on what necessarily precedes and conditions what the listener does. That is, to the extent that we understand how a speaker constructs a word, we will get a more coherent view not only of the role grammatical forms fulfill, but also of how words both represent the speaker's intended message and play their roles in the sentence, and this will enable us to understand better the role of the listener.

In fact, focusing in this way on how speakers actualize the potential meaning of 'see,' far from contradicting, actually presupposes what is known of the listener's role – taking into account general knowledge, the speaking situation, the linguistic context, and the grammatical form – in order to discern the lexical sense expressed and so to reconstitute the message intended by the speaker. And of course, this focus on the speaker offers a better opportunity for discerning the preconditions producing what is observed, the goal of any scientific venture. With this in mind, we will now examine the examples of *see* illustrating the different senses listed in W3, supplementing these where useful with examples from the *OED*, to see if the three actualizations discerned above thanks to McGirr's data provide an adequate means of classification.

DICTIONARY EXAMPLES

The disadvantage of dictionary examples is that, because of the limited context, many are open to more than one interpretation. On the other hand, they have the signal advantage of being accompanied by an interpretation, a paraphrase, provided by someone whose sensitivity to different nuances of meaning can be taken for granted. Our aim here is not to comment on how the different meanings listed are paraphrased (often including the meaning of other elements in the context) or on how they are grouped in the dictionary, but to see to what extent the examples can be considered manifestations of the three senses discerned in the last section: 'possibility,' 'process,' and 'result.' That is, we want to see if these three senses can be generalized throughout the range of usage covered by a dictionary. It should, however, be kept in mind that, for some speakers, the 'possibility' sense may be used only for 'habit,' since, as the *OED* suggests, 'capacity to see' is expressed rather by *can see*, i.e. by means of the auxiliary + infinitive *see* with a 'process' sense (cf. Duffley, 93–9).

We will base our survey mainly on W3 because its examples are mostly from twentieth-century texts. Paraphrases and examples from the *OED*, excluding anything dated before the nineteenth century or listed as obsolete, will be brought in to clarify usage. The simplest will be to follow the order of presentation in W3 with its nine sets of entries of *see* listed as transitive and four as intransitive, giving the best (or only) example illustrating the description.

As it stands, the first example of the first set, like the paraphrases given ("to perceive by the eye, apprehend through sight"), is ambiguous:

> ... opens his eyes to see the sunlight coming in through the window.

This could be understood either in the sense of 'to be greeted by a view of,' 'only to see,' 'and sees,' i.e. evoking the resulting percept, or in the sense of 'with the intent of perceiving,' 'in order to perceive,' i.e. evoking the process. The latter sense is illustrated by the intransitive use of *see* (paraphrased "to look about") in:

> ... stood up and fired his pistol in the air, and the naked Indians came out on the shore to see.

The former, very common, 'resultative' sense is more clearly illustrated from the *OED* by:

> Whose house is that I see?

The next example, paraphrased "to perceive as if by sight," i.e. an analogous sense, is even more ambiguous:

> It was wonderful what that boy saw who was blind.

It would most likely be understood as 'figured out,' a 'process' sense, but, given an appropriate context, might express 'had a mental image of,' 'understood,' a 'resultative' sense, as in the saying, *'I see,' said the blind man*. If, however, the writer had in mind the boy's whole life, the sense would be 'was able to figure out, could see,' i.e. a 'possibility' sense. This last sense is more clearly illustrated by the following intransitive use, paraphrased "the power of sight, have vision":

> Whereas I was blind, now I see.

As the *OED* points out, this sense, although formerly quite common, is "now commonly expressed by *can see*."

This ambiguity of interpretation, which, as mentioned above, is only to be expected granted the restricted context in dictionaries, does not interfere with our examination of usage from the point of view of what the speaker is expressing. In fact, it confirms the validity of this approach, since the speaker (or rather the writer for the examples here) intends to express one of these senses. That is, with, say, a 'possibility' sense in mind the writer cannot also have in mind a realizing of that capacity (the 'process' sense) and/or the outcome of realizing it (the 'result' sense). The reader, of course, imagining different scenarios for an example in order to interpret it, is often confronted with different possibilities, but where the context is sufficiently constraining, only one reading arises, as in:

> The supersonic streamlining of this vehicle makes it difficult to see by radar.

The paraphrase "to detect the presence of" brings out what the operation of the instrument contributes to the process of seeing.

A second set of examples in W3 begins with those expressing "to have the experience of," as in:

> Opening for a keen, practical, final year student to see dairy cattle and small-animal practice.

This example brings in the mental counterpart of physical perception, with the expressive effect of 'acquire experience of' arising from the 'process' sense of *see*. Similarly for the expressive effect described as "to learn or find by observation or experience, come to know, discover," as in:

> ... a point of view which I have since seen cause to modify.

as well as the expressive effect described as "to find out by investigation, ascertain":

> ... see if the car needs oil.

Again, the interpretation of these two examples calls for the 'process' sense of *see*.

What appears to be a figurative sense occurs in uses with an inanimate subject:

> The late glacial times saw the complete triumph of our ancestral stock.

This is described as "to give rise to, be marked by," and is similar to the use "to serve as the setting for, be the scene of, witness," as in the example:

> That house saw more worry and unhappiness.

The following examples from the *OED* also illustrate this use:

> Eighteen rivers have seen their navigation improved.
> In 1906 Cambridge saw three or four of her most learned men compete for the Greek chair.
> A bright cold morning saw us in the saddle at 6:15.

Whatever is involved in the use of *see* with an inanimate subject, each of these evokes a 'process' sense, even the last one, which could be paraphrased 'found us.'

In the third set, the first meaning described is "to form a mental picture of, visualize," as in:

> ... can still see her as she was twenty years ago.
> ... saw her in his dreams.

The first example can well be understood in the 'process' sense of forming a mental image, whereas the second suggests 'had an image of her,' a 'resultative' sense. Close to the former is "to perceive the meaning or importance of, comprehend, understand" as in:

> Because the frontier gives shape and life to our national myth, we have preferred to see its story in romantic outline.

The 'process' sense of *see* helps give rise to the idea of 'interpret its story.' In examples expressing the next meaning distinguished in this set, "to be aware of, recognize," *see* is found with both a 'process' sense evoking the recognizing, as in:

> ... planning to fire you tomorrow because you just can't see a good story.

and with a 'result' sense suggesting 'has a clear view of' as in:

> ... sees the folly of further resistance.

"To form a conception of, imagine as a possibility, suppose," the next meaning distinguished, depends on understanding *see* in a 'process' sense, as in:

> Can you see me knowing how to furnish a house?

Discerning Different Senses of *See*

The example:

> We saw, in the previous lecture, how the problem arose.

is paraphrased "to have presented for observation or consideration, be made aware of," a 'process' sense, but if the example had been *We saw ... that ...*, with the focus on what was seen, *see* would have been understood in a 'result' sense. Similarly, the interpretation of the example:

> ... see oursels [sic] as others see us.

"to look at from a particular point of view," suggests a 'process' sense (as in *we try to see, look at, ourselves*), but in another context, as in the *OED* example:

> I now see the matter in a new light.

see would be understood as 'envisage, look at' in a 'result' sense. The last meaning in this set is "to look ahead to, foresee," as in:

> ... can see the day when a college will not try to cover the whole field of liberal arts.

This suggests *see* with the 'process' sense of 'imagine, visualize, form an image of,' but might also be taken in a 'resultative' sense of 'have an image,' declaring what is foreseen.

The fourth set of meanings in W3 begins with "to direct one's attention to, put under observation, examine, scrutinize," clearly suggesting a 'process' sense, as in:

> ... want to see how he handles the problem.

Similarly for "to inspect or read understandingly (something written or printed)," as in:

> ... have you seen the story of yesterday's game?
> Let me see your pass, soldier.

Interpreted as "to read of," the example:

> I saw your appointment in the newspaper.

calls for *see* with a 'process' sense, but in an example from the OED:

> I see that something has happened.

paraphrased "I have just read (esp. in a newspaper)," we understand a 'result' sense, 'am now aware that.' Paraphrased as "to refer to," as in:

> For further information, see the documents printed in the appendix.

see evokes the process involved. Lastly in this set, *see* is paraphrased "to attend or visit as an observer or spectator" in expressions such as *see a parade, a play, the sights of the city*, where *see* has a 'process' sense. In fact it would be difficult to imagine a context where one could have a single percept, physical or mental, as a result in such cases.

The next set brings out two meanings, both clearly involving a 'process' sense of *see*, as in:

> ... would like him to have enough to see him easily to the end of his days.

The expressive effect here is paraphrased "to take care of, provide for," and the effect in the following example is paraphrased "to take care or heed, make sure":

> ... will see that he is brought up properly.

It is probably the long time span implied by each of these examples that brings out so clearly the 'process' sense.

In the sixth set of meanings, the 'resultative' sense of a formed opinion, described as "to regard as, consider, judge," is found in:

> ... did not see it right to ask for special favors.

In the example:

> ... would probably see himself shot before he told a deliberate falsehood.

a use paraphrased as "to prefer to have, allow to happen, welcome," there is, as the OED indicates, an element of 'willingness.'

Disregarding this element, which presumably comes from the auxiliary, leaves for the infinitive phrase the idea of 'view himself being shot,' implying a 'process' sense for *see*. In the use described as "to regard with approval or liking, find acceptable or attractive," as in:

> ... hope you'll be able to make her see it.

the suggestion of 'realize it' implies a 'process' sense for *see*, whereas in:

> ... can't understand what he sees in her.

the suggestion of 'what qualities he perceives in her' implies a 'result' sense.

The meanings in the seventh set all have to do with a normal consequence of actually seeing people, namely being with them, and includes the idea of achieving a purpose or aim. This calls for a 'process' sense of *see*. Thus:

> ... stopped off at the office to see his former employer.

is paraphrased as "to make a call upon, visit," and expressions such as *see a doctor* are paraphrased as "to call upon or meet with in order to obtain help or advice." Similarly, the expressive effect of the example:

> ... had been seeing each other for a year before they became engaged.

is described as "to be in the company of regularly or frequently esp. in courtship or dating," and the expressive effect of:

> The president of the bank will see you in a few minutes.

is paraphrased "to grant an interview to or accept the visit of, meet with, receive." Finally, for the example:

> ... charged that the witness had been seen by the defense.

the description "to meet with for the purpose of influencing esp. by bribery or pressure" makes the purpose of the activity explicit. One gets the impression here of a 'result' sense, the result of making perceptual contact, something similar to examples such as *hit the road* discussed in the last chapter.

The eighth set is quite similar. In the sentence:

Young men would wait to see the young ladies home.

see is paraphrased "accompany, escort." Likewise in:

... saw her onto the plane.

"to wait upon, be present with" is the paraphrase, and the example:

... saw a new edition of his book through the press.

is described "to give continued attention, assistance, or guidance to." In these examples, it is clearly the adverbial – *home, onto the plane, through the press* – which indicates to the reader that the speaker has actualized *see* in a 'resultative process' sense, since without them we would understand *see* in a 'visual image' sense, i.e. in a 'resultative state' sense.

W3's final use of *see* as a transitive verb, "to meet (a bet) in poker or to equal the bet of (a player), call," appears to be similar to the last two sets of meanings. It implies 'remaining present' (cf. *I'll stay* in the same context) as well as the purpose of staying in. Again it is a 'process' sense of *see*, expressing one player's action as a result of seeing another's bet, that enables it to contribute to this expressive effect.

The first example of intransitive uses is ambiguous:

See, the train is coming.

Interpreted as "to give or pay attention," it would appear to be an imperative use of *see*, implying a 'process' sense. But it might be taken more as a question, *Do you see?* in which case it would suggest a 'resulting image' sense of *see*. In the example:

It was so foggy that he could hardly see.

paraphrased "to apprehend objects by sight," *could* depicts the capacity and *see* the carrying out of the process of perception. Similarly when the meaning is "to perceive objects as if by sight" as in:

> ... the butterfly lightness that was teaching his fingers to see.

where *see* has its 'process' sense. When used in contexts expressing "to grasp something mentally, have insight, understand," as in:

> This fundamental bias of all thinking ... is what enables us to see, gives thought its real use.

see again makes its 'process' sense available to depict *thought* as an operation, of coming to understand, rather than as a result. Similarly in:

> When can I finish this – let me see.

the meaning described as "consider, think" implies a 'process' sense. On the other hand, when it is used as a sort of tag paraphrased as "to take note," as in:

> These aren't ordinary trout, you see.

the impression is one of appealing to what is known (cf. *you know*), a 'resultative' sense. Finally, the example:

> I can't give you an answer yet, but we shall see.

understood as "to arrive at a conclusion through observation and experience" calls for a 'process' interpretation of *see*, but it might also be construed as 'but one day we will have the answer,' implying a 'resulting state' sense. The examples in W3 where *see* occurs with an adverbial phrase (*see about it*, etc.) will not be brought in here, since they would require an analysis of their adjunct phrases in order to isolate the meaning of the verb.

CONCLUSION

Procedures of experimentation and predicting results, common in other sciences, are precluded for an act of language because, since it is a voluntary act, we cannot predict what a person will say in a specific situation of ordinary speech. The examining of data obtained from observing meaning is therefore necessarily repetitive to the point of being monotonous, since it is only by an accumulation of data that one can establish the scientific plausibility of a given hypothesis. Since *see* contributes to expressive effects as variable as the contexts in which it is found, we have tried to work back to the senses that recur frequently in our attempt to discern which senses the verb itself imports. The examples of *see* from McGirr and W3, those cited above and those not cited here, as well as pertinent examples from the *OED*, can all be seen to express one of three different senses: most commonly a visual image, i.e. a 'resulting state' sense; not infrequently a 'process' sense – a process either producing a visual image or resulting from visual contact; and occasionally a 'possibility' or 'habitual' sense. The way these senses are related as preconditions to consequence provides evidence for the hypothesis that they are different ways of actualizing the underlying potential meaning of this verb. Indeed, the very fact that some examples are ambiguous, making the reader hesitate between two (or even three) of these senses, suggests that they are possible readings of the verb's potential lexeme.

The fact that all examples of *see* examined so far can be interpreted in this threefold way raises a question: are these the only possible actualizations of the meaning potential of *see*? The distinction between literal or physical perception and analogous or mental perception (*I see what is on the table* vs. *I see what you mean*) has not been discussed because it is not observable through its grammatical consequences. The *OED* considers the analogous sense "figurative" but "with little or no consciousness of metaphor."[9] This suggests that what was presumably a metaphorical sense for 'see' historically has led to a generalization of 'see' to give a potential involving something like 'a mental image' regardless of whether it results from perception or intellection. Does this make literal and analogous senses possible actualizations, indicating a case of polysemy? Since most of the data consists of examples with mixed senses involving both physical and mental perception, it appears more likely that these are not different actualizations of the lexeme itself, but different expressive effects resulting from combining 'see' in its more general sense with other components in the sentence.

A different problem is raised by examples with an inanimate subject such as *The late glacial times saw the complete triumph of our ancestral stock* and *A bright cold morning saw us in the saddle at 6:15*. This use does not fit in with either physical or mental perception. Does it involve a metaphorical use of the verb? Or could it be a vague sort of personification of the subject?

Although such problems have yet to be resolved, it remains that the examination of examples from Ruhl and McGirr has given parallel findings. Moreover, the above interpretation of expressive effects to discern and classify the senses of *see* in W3 gave confirmation to these findings, providing a basis for examining other verbs. McGirr's study also makes it clear that the lexemes of other verbs of perception also have a 'process' sense whenever they are found in the progressive, leaving the expression of 'resulting state' and 'possibility' senses to the simple form. Rather than continue with that study, however, we will examine the uses of other verbs in an attempt to see if they confirm what has been found for verbs of perception.

9

Grammatical (In)compatibility with Other Verbs

VERBS EXPRESSING AN AFFECTIVE ATTITUDE

We will continue our examination of particular lexemes by summarizing the findings of other studies[1] of verbs rarely used in the progressive in order to discern the actualized senses they express when used in the progressive since, as with *see*, this permits us to distinguish the lexical from the grammatical import. The first group of verbs consists of *like, dislike, prefer, love, hate, despise,* and *fear,* all expressing a sort of affective attitude or mental state in ordinary uses with the simple form:

> I like the new head of department.

With the progressive, there is a different expressive effect:

> There was nothing disagreeable in Mr. Rushworth's appearance, and Sir Thomas was liking him already.

Here Sir T. is depicted as 'getting to like him,' i.e. in the process of forming his opinion or attitude. Another example of this is:

> Nan wondered how Simon's family were liking her and sensed a certain reservation about his mother.

The simple form *liked* would have evoked the resulting attitude once it had been formed. A slightly different manifestation of this 'process' sense is found in:

> What a lovely day! Are you liking the world any better?

The expressive effect here is that of changing an attitude, presumably the gloomy outlook of the day before. A similar expressive effect can be observed in:

> I'm not disliking it [India] as much as I expected.

where the process of changing to a less negative attitude is depicted. And in:

> What I was preferring was an emptiness of which I could give no intelligible account whatever.

the context indicates that the subject was in the process of choosing but had not quite made up his mind.

Love, like the other verbs in this group, expresses an attitude, as in:

> He loves his wife devotedly.

It can also express the forming of an attitude as in:

> I'm simply loving Sitrano, or is it Chitrano? My Italian's rotten.

or a change of attitude:

> She could have hit him. Yet, at the moment, she was loving him more than ever.

However, in:

> Your cousin Richard has been loving you as plainly as he could for I don't know how long.

it brings out a very different expressive effect: 'has been making his love for you as plain as possible.' This is not a forming or changing of an attitude, but rather "some activity consequent on" it, as Poutsma (1926, 342) puts it. A similar effect of 'expressing one's loving attitude' comes out clearly in:

> She was loving him into recovery.

The following example could be understood as either 'coming to love' or 'showing her love' (taking care of, caressing) in:

> She is loving him [her baby] more than ever she did before though she doesn't like to hold him like I do.

What is of interest in these examples of *love* is that they permit us to distinguish between the attitude it usually expresses and two activity senses, one leading up to that attitude and the other resulting from it.

Among verbs expressing a negative attitude, that most commonly found in the progressive is *hate*. It can contribute to the three expressive effects observed with *love*, namely, the forming of an attitude:

> I'm hating this house party.

a settled attitude:

> They hated the cold and the snow.

and an activity manifesting the attitude:

> You've seen me when I was hating something ... I was hating her.

Despise and *fear* are far less frequently found in the progressive. The following example suggests different ways of expressing, or different results of, the negative attitude:

> I had supposed him to be despising his fellow-creatures in general, but did not suspect him of descending to such malicious revenge, such injustice, such inhumanity as this.

In:

> He jerks it [her picture] out, staring at her to see if she is despising him.

there is the suggestion of a momentary reaction (perhaps to something he has just said), implying a 'process' sense of 'forming a new attitude.' This expressive effect is found with *fear* in:

> We see no evidence that people are fearing to travel by sea.

And Poutsma (1921, 89) sees the expression of an "activity consequent on [the] attitude" in:

> Was she fearing that if her poor young sister-in-law
> did die, a weight would rest on her conscience
> for all time?

The evidence arising from verbs of (dis)affection thus confirms what we found when examining verbs of perception: the progressive always calls for a 'process' sense of the lexeme and never expresses the attitude itself. Besides the activity leading up to and forming the attitude, we observe the other 'process' sense with some of them, namely an activity consequent on the attitude represented. The simple form can of course express each of these 'process' senses as well as the attitude in itself, but it is the constraint on the progressive that permits us to distinguish the two senses of the lexeme, 'activity' and 'attitude,' comparable to the distinction between 'process' and 'resulting state' found with verbs of perception. A second group of verbs examined gave comparable results.

VERBS EXPRESSING INTELLECTUAL STATES

Verbs such as *believe, doubt, remember, forget, understand, know,* and a number of others (cf. Visser 1969) in the simple form often express a mental state, as in:

> He believes ... that 'probability is the guide of life.'

Believe here, paraphrased as "to hold as true," evokes a settled state of mind. However, in:

> The Guide Chef [sic] evidently did not believe a word of it.

it evokes the mental process leading up to and resulting in the state of belief, here negated, and so is paraphrased as "to give credence to, to accept as true." This same 'process' sense is found in:

> She'd watched him as she told him to see if he was believing her.

but with the progressive the event is represented as incomplete, open to change.[2] The next example contrasts simple and progressive:

> It's no use your trying to argue me out of what I believe. I know I'm believing what it's right for me to believe.

Where the simple form expresses the 'stative' sense, the progressive brings out a 'process' sense as consequent on that state: persisting in the acquired belief, holding on to it in spite of counter-arguments. Similarly for *doubt*:

> Don't think I'm doubting your steadfastness, old man, I believe in it.

The 'process' sense of 'calling into question' contrasts with the settled state expressed by *believe*.

The mental process of recalling something to consciousness is itself unconscious and so can be known only as a complete act through its result. This is why *remember* can express either "to recall to the memory" or "to have in the memory" (Poutsma 1921, 26), and why, in the progressive, it evokes not an incomplete act of recalling something but rather an incomplete series of such acts:

> "Other clergymen," she said, "are so odd compared with ours." I could see she was remembering the whole strange world of clergymen: Mullahs, Buddhists, Orthodox, Copts, Romans, Old Catholics, Anglicans, Lutherans, Presbyterians, Rabbis ...

In the following example, the series involves all the details involved in the "thing" recalled:

> I do think it's fortunate that I've never had to give evidence in a court case. I'd just worry myself to death in case I wasn't remembering a thing just right.

Forget also evokes an incomplete series of mental acts involving different words of a language in:

> I'm forgetting my Persian.

On the other hand, in:

> You are forgetting, sir, that only Constable Dobson has actually seen the prisoner.

the suggestion is that the process of letting a single fact slip from his mind is not complete, obviously a euphemism. Rather than evoking the reality of the situation by saying *you have forgotten*, the speaker intervenes to avoid its consequences and so represents the forgetting as still going on. This is even clearer in:

> She rose, beckoning to him. He picked up the book and her bag, both of which she was forgetting, and followed her out.

Since the book and the bag were not left behind, the consequences of forgetting were avoided and so the process itself can be represented as incomplete.

According to Scheffer (74), "*understand* is rare in the progressive as it denotes a static idea, a mental or psychic state." When it is found in the progressive, as in:

> I'm understanding more about quantum mechanics as each day goes by.

according to Comrie (37), it "refers not to a state, but to a developing process, whose individual phases are essentially different from one another." Like the examples of *forget* just mentioned, *understand* is sometimes used to include the consequences of the state itself:

> Unexpectedly, I'm suddenly understanding that Smithie's dead. I haven't known it till now.

The speaker is becoming aware not of Smithie's death but of its implications.

Because "all phases of the situation *John knows where I live* are identical" (Comrie, 49), some linguists have declared that *know* is a 'stative' verb and so not used in the progressive. Although comparatively rare, uses like the following have been found:

> He had to remember that this man, helpless, an object on the operating table, was knowing the meaning of loneliness.[3]

Here the sense of 'was experiencing at that moment' evokes the process of learning that leads up to the state of knowing, the state that the simple form *know* in this sentence would have expressed as having already been acquired. A similar sense of 'getting acquainted' is expressed with regard to a person in:

> She smiled, and she felt she was knowing the panjandrum better.[4]

In the following, on the other hand, *know* expresses more than just this sense of 'becoming acquainted':

> She had a few words, very pleasant, with me, but I had a horrid feeling she was seeing right through me and knowing all about me.[5]

The expressive effect here is one of going beyond mere acquaintance to the process of discerning the different traits of another's personality.[6]

HAVE TO, SEEM, AND BE

As in the sets just examined, 'process' senses of these three verbs can be clearly distinguished in their infrequent uses with the progressive form. This can be seen for *have* in:

> As a matter fact he's having to sell his house. He's very badly off.

Here we understand not just that the subject has the obligation to sell, but that he is implementing the consequences of that state (setting a price, getting a real estate agent, and the like). Sometimes the verb evokes a series of unforeseen situations making a certain activity obligatory:

> The conversation was in French as Varenne did not speak English, and John was soon having to apologize for the corruption of his French by Italian.

This example brings out not so much the consequent activity of apologizing as the fortuitous arising of the obligation. The following example is similar:

> Power stations and gas works in Scotland are having to import thousands of tons of coal from England every week.

Here, too, the situation making the importing obligatory is seen as temporary, open to change at any moment, and so is depicted as developmental rather than stative.

Seem usually expresses the stative sense of "have a semblance or appearance" and so takes the simple form. The following example suggests a slightly different sense:

> I could explain nothing and felt that I was creating some entirely false impression. Also I knew that I was not only seeming but also feeling appallingly guilty.

The focus here is not so much on the subject's appearance itself as on the effect it is having on others, namely giving a false impression, a process open to change. Likewise, the speaker implies that the impression his appearance is making on others is false in:

> "Forgive me," Mark begged. "I must be seeming ungracious and what is more ungrateful?"

And in the following example, the speaker is not sure if the wrinkles really are more conspicuous or just appear so:

> "I've reached an age," he told his reflection, whose crow's-feet were seeming more conspicuous than usual in the clear wintry weather, "when a man becomes selfish in small matters."

The crow's-feet are making, but have not yet made, an impression on him. Although rather subtle, these distinctions of sense as compared with the simple form are real, but they would hardly be discernable to the reader without the progressive, which always expresses an event as a process open to development.

Be is perhaps the most revealing among verbs that are "more or less compatible" with the progressive not because of its infrequency (it is probably more common in the progressive than most of the verbs just examined) but because of a recent, little-known development in usage.[7] Grammars often give examples with a person as subject:

> Something – something that I suppose I may as well point out to you. Because in certain matters – in certain matters you are being a fool.

It is pointed out that this expresses a type of behaviour, usually the outcome of a personal characteristic. Similarly for examples with an adjective as complement:

> The Chief Constable was being as tactful as it was in his nature to be with Mrs. Castle.

This use is even found with a personified object as subject:

> This typewriter is being stubborn again.

The contrast between simple and progressive is clearly brought out in the following example:

> He fascinated Joyce by telling her that she was subtle, then telling her what she was being subtle about.

Where *was subtle* expresses a state, or "like parted" (Quirk et al., 198) event, *was being subtle* expresses an activity, or developmental event, the outcome of her subtlety.

What is noteworthy in the use of *be* in the progressive is that a verb dematerialized to the point of being a grammatical word can still actualize its material significate, reduced to where it represents no more than a duration, in two different ways: as an extent of time for an enduring, unchanging event or as an extent of time for a developmental event. It is significant that *be* as auxiliary of the passive voice is also found in the progressive. The fact that uses of both copula and auxiliary in the progressive arose at about the same time (earliest recorded examples from around 1800) suggests that this developmental way of actualizing the abstract material significate was first made possible at that point.

It is equally significant to observe that what appears to be a further development of the use of the progressive arose in the twentieth century. This recent innovation – the earliest example found so far dates from 1927 – still strikes some speakers as strange:[8]

> The afternoon was being golden, after all.
> The bridge party was not being a success.
> But that wasn't a novel feeling. It had come to her so often ...
> however drab her days were being.

What is novel here is the type of subject; since it is not a person, the sense expressed is no longer a type of behaviour. In fact, the noun phrase subject of each of the examples found so far represents a stretch of time or something (a bridge party) occupying a stretch of time.[9] Thanks to the progressive, the expressive effect here is that the duration is not complete and that its moment-by-moment realization could involve a change (to not *being golden*, to *being a success*, to not *being drab*). That is, the abstract material significate of *be* here is represented as developmental, as in uses where the subject depicts a person, but here it evokes the way the subject comes into being.

This use of *be* is also found with *it* as a "prop" or anticipatory subject:

> It was being a very different kind of Christmas.
> He looked with love at her blooming face: it was being a good pregnancy.
> Captain Walker got back to James Bond. "Sorry about that. It's being a busy day."

Here, the category of grammatical person enables *it* to represent the mental space occupied by the intended message, leaving the representation of what occupies that space to the noun phrase complement, which in each case involves a duration. Again the expressive effect of 'so far' indicates that *being*, through its reduced lexical import, depicts this duration as developmental, indicating the way that the *Christmas*, the *pregnancy*, the *day*, has turned out up to that point in time.

CONCLUSION

The sixteen verbs discussed in this chapter were all, like *see* in the preceding chapter, the object of studies focusing on the use of the progressive. These studies confirmed the traditional view that the use of the progressive is "associated with action or change proceeding from real or supposed activity" (Poutsma 1926, 339) and that to explain these comparatively rare uses, "one has to go in quest of the various senses and sub-senses that are tinged with a notion – however slight – of activity" (Visser 1969). Our purpose here is not to dwell on the grammatical implications of these studies but to bring out what they imply for the verb's lexeme, namely that we must distinguish between an 'activity,' 'developmental,' 'non-stative' lexical sense and a 'like parted,' 'non-changing,' 'stative' sense.

The fact that the progressive can provide a grammatical form only for lexemes actualized in a 'developmental' sense, whereas the simple form can express both this sense and their more common 'stative' sense in discourse, implies that, as a potential in tongue, the lexeme of each of these verbs makes both possible. That is, actualizing their lexical potential in order to express an event would seem to involve representing the occurrence in the intended message as either 'developmental' or 'stative' depending on the way the speaker happens to perceive it. Furthermore, the two senses are, as we have seen, closely connected. With *love*, for example, the 'developmental' sense is sometimes seen as leading up to and resulting in the 'stative' sense, sometimes as following from or due to it. The preceding chapter also brought out that the common 'stative' sense of *see* is a resulting image presupposing the 'developmental' or 'process' sense of seeing and sometimes conditioning an ensuing 'process' sense. In its 'stative' sense, 'see' can also express the existence of seeing as a potentiality (faculty of sight) or a disposition (habit). The link between 'stative' and 'developmental' senses and the fact that the simple form can express both leads to postulating a potential meaning making both possible. This provides a basis for explaining the polysemy observed in these verbs and all other verbs, since it seems that any full verb can express either a 'stative' or a 'developmental' sense. That is, this double possibility arises each time a lexeme in tongue is to be actualized as the material import of a verb.

To complete our examination of particular lexemes, it remains to observe certain verbs, not for their use in the progressive, but from a different grammatical point of view, their syntax. This is how auxiliaries are usually distinguished from full verbs in English, so in the next chapter we will explore what this distinction can tell us about the lexemes of the three verbs used as grammatical auxiliaries.

10

Do, Be, Have

INTRODUCTION

Having examined a number of verbs, including *have to* and *be*, as used in the progressive to see what that tells us of their lexical import, we will now explore the three verbs found both as auxiliaries and as full or main verbs. As in the preceding chapters, we will try to draw conclusions from comparing the different uses of each verb in discourse, but as above, this will not lead to a description of the traits characterizing the lexeme itself, a task as yet beyond the scope of our analysis.

I have elsewhere discussed (2007, 277–90) the meaning the three auxiliaries bring to the verb phrase, drawing certain grammatical conclusions. Here the aim is to see if, from the lexical point of view, auxiliary and main verb uses involve different actualizations of the same lexeme in tongue or if they involve homonyms. Unlike those linguists who consider that an auxiliary such as *do* is a meaningless word, I adopt the position that every word has some material import, however abstract,[1] resulting from its ideogenesis. I will begin by comparing three different uses of *do*, as in my 2002 article, in an attempt to show that there is a lexical link between them.

DO

Like *be* and *have*, *do* is lexically quite abstract even in its most concrete uses. It is important to understand that characterizing it in such uses as a "full" verb, rather than a main verb, is intended to compare it with its auxiliary uses. To describe its more common main verb use, Quirk et al. (135) call it "a general-purpose agentive transitive verb," as in *doing the dishes, doing the car, doing lunch, doing London*. General though it may be, its range is limited since it must be distinguished from *make*. ESL teachers are well aware of this, since they have to explain that it cannot be used for all activities – to explain why **I did a mistake* is unacceptable whereas both *I made the beds* and *I did the beds, He made a dive* and *He did a dive*, etc. are acceptable, but do not express quite the same thing. The point here is not to discuss the lexical difference between *made* and *did*, but simply to observe that in this general factotum use, *do* is more limited in the range of activities it can represent than equivalent verbs in other languages such as French or Spanish. This suggests that its representational range or extension is less than those of *faire* and *hacer*, and so its comprehension must be greater.[2]

Quirk et al. (875–9) bring out another use of main verb *do* which gives a different picture. In what is variously called its vicarious, substitute, pro-predication, pro-form, or suppletive use, *do*, often with *so*, can supplete for many other verbs:

They planned to reach the top of the mountain, but nobody knows if they did (so).
As nobody else has succeeded in solving the mystery, I shall attempt to (do so) myself.

The interesting thing here is that in this suppletive use *do* can substitute for *make*:

I was so nervous about making a mistake that I nearly did so.
She asked him to make some coffee and he did so.

These examples show that *do* in its suppletive use has a greater range of representation than in its general factotum use, and so, by implication, a lesser comprehension. That is, this observable difference between two uses of the main verb apparently arises from a difference in actualizing its lexical import. In suppletive uses, *do* appears to import fewer lexically characterizing traits than in general factotum uses. Here, then, if our analysis has not gone astray, and if the traditional relationship between CHARACTERIZING TRAITS (comprehension) and RANGE OF REPRESENTATION (extension) is valid, these two uses bring out a case of polysemy for main verb *do*.

Pursuing this observation of usage, another point made by Quirk et al. (879) is pertinent, namely that *do so* substitutes for verbs with "dynamic meaning," i.e. with a 'developmental' sense, as in the above examples and in:

I asked her to learn the poem and she did so.

The following, however, is not acceptable:

*I asked her to know the poem and she did so.

The fact that suppletive *do* cannot substitute for verbs expressing a state indicates that its range of representation, albeit greater than that of general factotum *do*, is still limited. And this is where a comparison with the auxiliary can be made:

I asked her to learn the poem and she did.
I asked her to know the poem and she did.

Did here is the auxiliary (cf. *but she didn't*), not the suppletive,[3] and as such can accommodate stative or activity verbs, a fact indicating that its range of representation is even greater than that of the suppletive. Working back to the condition permitting this observation, we can conclude that the characterizing component of auxiliary *do* is even less than that of suppletive *do*, which, as we have already seen, is less than that of general factotum *do*.

We thus end up with a comparison of the three uses on the basis of their range of representation: as a factotum verb, *do* can call to mind a certain type of activity (that activity not expressed by *make*); as a suppletive, it can call to mind any type of activity (but not states); as an auxiliary it can accommodate any happening, activity, or state. This poses the problem of the relation between the three. One can of course presume that the auxiliary is "a dummy operator" (Quirk et al., 879), i.e. a homonym with no lexical import, and so avoid the problem at least for the auxiliary, but this merely displaces the problem to a much more general level, that of the word: how can a word exist without meaning? As outlined in chapter 6, the approach adopted here postulates that the operation of ideogenesis is involved in constructing all words, and so we will try to determine the relation between the three versions of *do* in terms of that operation common to all three.

Judging by its results, the operation of actualizing the lexeme 'do' must be carried furthest for factotum usage since the lexical trait (whatever it is) distinguishing 'do' activities from 'make' activities is actualized for this use but not for the other two uses. In like fashion, the actualizing of 'do' must be carried further for suppletive usage than for auxiliary usage since the lexical trait limiting it to the expression of activities is actualized for the former but not for the latter. The notional ideation of the auxiliary must be carried just far enough to represent something common to all happenings, activities, or states.

This suggests a view of actualization delivering three different results depending on where it is intercepted in its progression, a view that can be depicted by means of figures. In the following figure, the operation is depicted by a dotted line to suggest that in tongue it is a possibility for the lexeme 'do,' available for realization whenever it is required to form a word.

When the auxiliary is called for, the operation is intercepted very early in its development, as soon as that minimum of lexical matter necessary for a word (see below for what this consists of) has been actualized, leaving the rest of the operation unrealized:

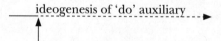

When suppletive 'do' is called for, the operation is intercepted further on in its development, once the required lexical import has been actualized, but leaving unrealized the last part of the operation:

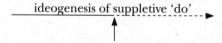

When factotum 'do' is called for, the operation is intercepted at its end, all the characterizing traits of 'do' having been actualized:

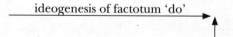

Figures such as these help to bring out the relationships involved here – the one potential in tongue giving rise to three different actualizations in discourse – but of course they are only schematic representations of the mental reality involved. In this way we can propose a solution for the problem posed by the three distinct uses of *do* which takes into account that they are closely related, a fact that would be neglected by a homonym solution. This, then, appears to be a case of polysemy, based on our underlying postulate that a formative element in tongue such as 'do' is a potential offering different possible actualizations in discourse.

HAVE

Like *do*, *have* has clearly distinguished uses as a main verb and as an auxiliary. Its most concrete sense as a main verb is probably that of 'possession,' taken in many more or less abstract ways. Outside of the sense of 'coming into possession,' it is not always clear how the various lexical distinctions listed in a dictionary relate to the 'possession' sense, but there appear to be no grounds for considering any of them to constitute a separate lexeme, a homonym. This constitutes another question calling for extensive observation of usage to distinguish the different senses of *have* itself from expressive effects depending on other elements in the context.

What is clear, however, is that auxiliary *have* brings to the verb phrase a far more abstract import than main verb *have*. As is pointed out in my 2007 study on the verb (282), "the notion of 'possession' may be evoked to suggest 'ownership' or 'holding' or some other particular manifestation, but in all cases it represents a resulting state, the outcome of a process of coming into possession of or acquiring something." Grammatical analysis shows that the auxiliary always represents a moment in the result phase of an event, a sense so general that it is found with any verb in the form of a past participle. That is to say, this extremely general, and so minimal, lexical import is already implicit in the sense of 'possession,' which is a state resulting from acquiring, obtaining, receiving, learning, or some other such process. This suggests not only that the auxiliary was developed from the main verb historically by a process of dematerialization (lexical abstraction), but also that in modern usage 'possession' and 'result phase' are two distinct actualizations of the same potential lexeme in tongue. Before this can be affirmed, however, a detailed lexical analysis of *have* must be carried out to see if other actualized senses can be identified.

BE

The situation with *be* is not as clear as with *do* and *have*, partly because it is far more abstract than either of them in its most concrete sense, that of 'existing,' as expressed in *I think, therefore I am*. Dictionary definitions of 'existing' such as "to have place in the domain of reality" (*OED*) and "to have being in space and time" (W_3) indicate how abstract the "full" sense of the verb is, but do suggest that it somehow involves the extent of something in space and its duration in time, thereby implying opposition to anything outside that extent or duration. *Be* auxiliary, like *do* and *have*, imports an extreme of lexical abstraction representing (part of) the duration involved in any event's existence, that is, the time between its beginning and its end. Grammatical analysis shows that this is its role as an auxiliary both of the progressive and of the passive.

What is not clear with *be* is its use as a copula, where it appears to be just as abstract as the auxiliary, but one hesitates to identify the two in the light of their very different roles. One wonders if, as a copula, *be* is reduced to simply providing a place in time for the person of the subject. To get a clearer view of its role of linking predicate to subject, it may well be necessary to understand better how any finite verb fulfills this role thanks to intra-verbal person – a grammatical question.

There does seem to have been an historical development here, as with *have*, but in the case of *be* it is from the already abstract sense of 'existing' to the most abstract sense possible for a verb, that of a stretch of duration. Again, until a satisfactory lexical analysis of the copula is forthcoming, the proposal that these are two actualized senses of 'be' in modern usage cannot be considered more than a hypothesis, but it can perhaps provide a framework for further reflection and research.

DO, BE, HAVE AS AUXILIARIES

Although in their most concrete senses of 'carry out, perform,' 'existing,' and 'possession' these verbs have little in common, they do share the common role of auxiliary. Each of them thus can bring to the verb phrase a sense so abstract that at least one of them is often considered a meaningless "dummy," a judgement that creates more problems than it solves. We have seen that, viewed grammatically, *have* auxiliary represents a moment in the result phase of the event expressed by the past participle, and that *be* represents a moment in (the progressive), or all of (the passive), the duration of the event expressed by the participle. *Do* auxiliary also represents a stretch of duration, namely the duration to be occupied by the event expressed by the infinitive, whether the event is realized or not. That is, without representing the event itself, all three auxiliaries represent a stretch of duration involved in or entailed by the event represented by the infinitive or participle.

This provides a view of what the three auxiliaries have in common, but since they are not interchangeable, there must be something distinguishing them. This is the relation between the moment or stretch of duration they represent and the event. *Have*'s moment of duration being in the event's result phase, it is characterized by a trait of posteriority; *be*'s moment or stretch of duration being in the event's realization phase, it is characterized by a trait of interiority; *do*'s stretch of duration being that required for the event to be realized, it is characterized by a trait of priority.[4]

Distinguishing between the three auxiliaries in this way is a consequence of examining the expressive effects of the verb phrase they contribute to, as well as comparing their different syntactic behaviours, particularly the form of the full verb they relate to. It provides further evidence that the mental import of a word is not irrelevant to its role in the sentence. On the contrary, the explanation of a word's syntax is to be found in the meaning, both grammatical and lexical, it brings to the sentence.

11

Working Out the Right Sense

INTRODUCTION

Ruhl's attempt to establish the monosemy of verbs was criticized in chapter 7 basically because language was considered uniquely from the point of view of the listener, of discourse, a view leading him to the proposal that to ensure communication a word must be monosemous, expressing the same meaning in every sentence. The other senses indicated by the data were explained as the results of pragmatic metonymy, i.e. the listener appealing to, among other things, the message resulting from referring the meaning of the sentence to its extra-linguistic setting. This would make the referent a way for the listener to understand the meaning. In fact, however, the meaning expressed is generally how the speaker orients the listener to the referent, the message. The failure to distinguish between the meaning, an intra-linguistic entity, and the message, an extra-linguistic (though intra-mental) entity to which the meaning is referred, results in confusion of this sort, blocking the progress of lexical semantics.

The only way to avoid this confusion is to view language as including not just the words and sentences we can observe, but also all the potential a speaker (and hearer) has acquired for producing (and understanding) the words and sentences constituting discourse. That is, unless one takes into account the mother tongue – language as a potential for the speaker to represent the intended message and the hearer to understand a sentence and reconstruct the speaker's message – there appears to be no possibility of establishing the monosemy underlying words, which is a necessary precondition of communication as permitted by language.

As Ruhl's data show, ordinary discourse involves a word's polysemy in usage, but it also presupposes the prior acquisition of the word by both speaker and hearer. By postulating that for the speaker this acquired meaning is an unvarying lexical potential,[1] a lexeme in tongue, the diverse senses observed in discourse can be viewed as different actualizations of that potential. That is, this potential → actual relationship between tongue and discourse provides a sufficiently wide theoretical framework to handle observed polysemy. On the other hand, the actualized senses do not correspond to the proliferation of senses listed in dictionaries, which Ruhl (1989, 3) considers "little less than chaotic." On that basis, no listener, or speaker for that matter, could work out the appropriate sense of each word during the give-and-take of spoken discourse. Even reduced to the two or three senses discerned in preceding chapters, no such list can represent the way a word's lexeme is instituted in tongue simply because no actualized sense can be part of the potential. The relationship here is not one of part and whole – the potential is not divided into actualized senses – but is rather a relationship of capacity and use, like the human hand, capable of grasping a hammer, playing the piano, and innumerable other actions. But only the actualized senses can emerge into consciousness and be observed. That is, each sense in discourse is derived from the potential by a process of actualization, and so the potential meaning must be both sufficiently general to be a constant for speaker and listener, and constituted in such a way as to make possible the various senses observed, abstract and concrete. In short, a lexeme is monosemous as a potential and polysemous as a series of representations expressed in usage. And the aim of lexical analysis is to describe a word's potential meaning in tongue and how it is actualized in order to explain the senses observed in discourse.

TAKING STOCK

As we have seen, any attempt to get a view of the potential meaning must begin with the expressive effects of sentences and phrases in order to discern the meanings expressed by a given word. One must then distinguish between the grammatical and the lexical in the meaning expressed by a word in order to observe its different lexical senses and the relations between them. Only with this in mind can one hope to imagine how these senses were derived in the moment of speech and what potential they were derived from. This is a complicated process, and so it will be useful at this point to summarize the findings for each of the verbs examined in preceding chapters.

In chapter 7 it was argued that the data for *kick* and *slap* could best be analyzed as expressing either movement to a limit (contact) or movement from a limit already reached. This corresponds better to the expressive effects than the three senses proposed by Ruhl. In fact, he represents these senses in a more abstract way as a temporal sequence (1989, 215):

MOVEMENT → CONTACT → MOVEMENT

This constitutes a significant insight because it reflects a more general relationship, one that appears to be important for understanding how a verb lexeme can be actualized. For both *kick* and *slap* there can be no contact without a prior movement establishing contact, and no subsequent movement or change of state without prior contact provoking it, the point of contact being the limit between the two movements. The following examples will recall these senses. The verbs express 'movement to the limit' in:

> ... they were standing around the back door, kicking the steps. [4]
> The old woman slapped their little haunches with her open palm. [255]

and 'movement from the limit' in:

> If I found the bottle I'd kick it deep under the snow. [97]
> I'll slap that stupid smirk right off your face. [333]

As we have seen, the uses of *hit* were also analyzed as expressing two senses, either 'movement to a limit, strike' or 'purpose, entailment.' The first is exemplified by the expressive effect 'struck the ground' in the following example:

> At this moment the volley-ball hit the ground. [175]

The second sense is brought out by the expressive effect 'get down out of danger' in:

"All of us hit the ground and stay there." [174]

This sense obviously represents what arises as a result of attaining the limit: a state (being out of danger) or a movement (cf. the *hit the road* examples).

For all three verbs, the underlying relationship between movement to the limit (L) imposed by contact and state or movement resulting from reaching the limit can be depicted in a diagram, as follows:

Since the limit is the goal of one movement and the source of the other movement or the state, the before-after sequence cannot be altered. The fact of assuming a limit common to both makes one movement a necessary prerequisite of the other. That is, the relationship condition → consequence imposes an order on the mind: to represent something as a consequence, we must depict it arising after its condition(s).

Our discussion of Ruhl's examples of the verb *bear* brought out a similar relationship between the sense 'support, press' and the sense 'convey, produce.' Here too the condition → consequence relationship was discerned. The movement involved in the idea of conveying or carrying implies supporting or pressing as a prior condition, as in concrete uses such as:

… their sweating, straining backs bore every ounce of their supplies. [282]
Buck, Lester, and Bobo whirled, grabbed Big Boy about the neck, arms and legs, bearing him to the ground. [107]

And the idea of producing presupposes the tree or soil sustaining or supporting something in:

Next year the tree will bear. [382]
This soil bears good cotton. [385]

It is important to note that the distinction between conveying and producing is made thanks to other words in the context – a person's back can convey, a tree can produce – and so this is really a distinction between expressive effects that appear to arise from a more abstract 'resultative' sense since both are understood as consequences of a necessary prior condition. This precondition is expressed by the ideas of supporting and pressing, as in:

The pillars bear a heavy weight. [263]
the wall bearing on the floor. [43]

and in more abstract uses such as:

The point at stake bears restating. [359]
The silence bore down. [321]

Again it is thanks to the sense of *bear* interacting with something in the context that each of these expressive effects is brought out (*on* and *down* implying the idea of pressing, *pillars* and *wall* suggesting the concrete idea of physical weight, etc.). This interplay of different effects implies a more abstract 'precondition' sense of *bear* allowing for each interpretation. That is, the different senses presented in the OED appear to be expressive effects reflecting two actualized senses, 'support/press as precondition' and 'convey/produce as result.' This attempt to distinguish what is variable in the context from what varies in the meaning expressed by *bear* is what led to the proposal that its polysemy is limited, in the data from Ruhl and the OED, to two actualized senses, more abstract than any of those given in the OED and as such difficult to paraphrase. Moreover, these two senses are linked to one another by a necessary before-after relationship. It remains, of course, to examine the usage of *bear* from the grammatical point of view to discern the distinction between state and activity actualizations of the lexeme.

In chapter 8 the discussion of *see* (and other verbs of perception), verbs seldom used in the progressive form, brought out these different senses. In the simple form *see* usually expresses a 'stative' sense, as in *I see a plane* (visual percept, the consequence of perceiving) and *You see whenever you open your eyes* (predisposition or capacity).

When formed by means of the progressive, the lexeme 'see' always has a 'developmental' sense, as in *His eyes ... They were seeing ... Surely they saw.* Here the simple form also has a 'developmental' sense (process of perceiving) as it does in *He saw the doctor yesterday*, parallel to *We hit the road yesterday*, where the visual and physical contacts are starting points for the respective consequences of consulting and travelling. What is interesting here is the way a condition → consequence relation holds between these different senses: capacity permitting perceiving, perceiving giving rise to a percept, percept seen as permitting an ensuing activity.

A similar patterning of uses was observed in chapter 9 with verbs of affection such as *love*. In *I'm loving it here* the verb expresses the process of forming an attitude, whereas in *He loves his wife devotedly* it expresses the resulting attitude, and in *She was loving him into recovery* the verb expresses a manifestation of the attitude. It can be seen that these uses reflect condition → consequence relations like those observed with *see*. Similarly for verbs that usually express an intellectual state, such as *believe*. In *The Guide Chef [sic] evidently did not believe a word of it* the verb expresses 'giving credence to,' the operation leading up to the state, whereas in *He believes ... that 'probability is the guide of life'* it depicts a settled state of mind, and in *I know I'm believing what it's right for me to believe, believing* suggests 'holding on to what I believe,' a 'process' sense arising from the state. Finally, with *be*, the process of coming into existence was observed in examples such as *The bridge party was not being a success*, whereas in *He fascinated Joyce by telling her that she was subtle, then telling her what she was being subtle about, was* expresses the existence of the state, and *was being* an activity consequent on that state.

The data observed for the verbs examined above thus suggests that they express different senses related to one another in a precondition → consequence sequence, even with the possibility of exploiting this relationship in a recursive fashion. Although this may give rise to senses that are often more abstract than those listed in a dictionary, and therefore more difficult to paraphrase adequately, it enables them to interact with other meanings expressed in the context to contribute to an unlimited variety of expressive effects. Furthermore, because this relationship is quite general,[2] it provides a hypothesis for observing other uses of these verbs to see if they can be analyzed in the same way. Moreover, to the extent that the senses expressed by other verbs manifest this relationship, it will provide a sound basis for reflecting on the process of actualizing the potential meaning of any verb.

NOTIONAL CHRONOLOGY

The temporal ordering of notions inherent in the causal relationship between condition (capacity, predisposition, cause, becoming, etc.) and consequence (effect, result, entailment, outcome, etc.) observed above involves a necessary sequencing, because without the prior existence of the condition, the consequence would not exist. For example, the concrete necessity of *bearing* ('supporting') some physical object before one can *bear* ('convey') it is at the basis of this mental arrangement of the two senses. That is, the very nature of the two senses links them together and requires the mind to represent them in a certain order. The expression NOTIONAL CHRONOLOGY is useful to designate what is common to this sort of before-after relationship so frequently perceived in our common experience and imposed on the mind by the notions involved.

Notional chronology, materialized by the above verbs in different condition → consequence relationships, can thus be proposed as a means of meeting what Ruhl sees as the challenge for analyzing a verb: "to understand why all the data ... *seem to be related*" (1989, 63; his italics). This appears to be a case of "regular polysemy ... governed by processes which are productive ... very much like processes of word formation" (Ravin and Leacock, 10). It has the advantage of being a relationship drawn from common experience, and so whenever some happening in the intended message strikes the speaker either as commonly giving rise to, or as being the outcome of, some state or process, the verb lexeme can be actualized to represent whichever sense is appropriate. This of course implies that the lexeme in tongue is sufficiently general to permit such actualizations.

Another advantage of this manner of conceiving how a speaker actualizes the required sense of a given verb lexeme is that notional chronology operates within the semantics of words themselves. Being the cause or result of something is part of common extra-linguistic experience, so there is no need to invent some rule that would represent the chronology involved. The impression of a conditioning factor or of a resultative element in the happening to be represented suffices to determine at what point the speaker holds up the actualization process to obtain the desired sense. Moreover, assuming a general principle of this sort in the way a verb's potential meaning is actualized would limit polysemy in discourse to a few closely linked abstract senses, and enable a speaker to exploit a new sense of a given lexeme and a hearer to understand it (as in the two possible senses of *Will he medal tonight?* – 'win a medal' or 'receive a medal').

AUXILIARY AND FULL VERB

In the previous chapter, our discussion of lexemes being actualized as the import of full verbs or auxiliaries led to the proposal that their notional ideation is a process of providing sufficient lexical matter for the use in view. The auxiliary with its very wide range of representation requires a minimum actualization of the lexeme's characterizing traits, whereas the full verb with its more restricted range calls for actualizing them to a maximum. That is, *do*, *be*, and *have* as auxiliaries represent something common to all verb lexemes, a stretch of duration, each with its characterizing position – prior, interior, and posterior, respectively – but as full verbs each imports its own characterizing traits. This appears to indicate an order in the process of lexical actualization from the most general to less general senses.

Although these three verbs do not manifest the condition-consequence relation as clearly as the other verbs we have examined, their use as auxiliaries does represent a stretch of time, a necessary trait of all lexemes formed as verbs. As such, this is also a necessary condition for their actualizations in full verb usage, and so the polysemy involved does appear to have something in common with that observed with other verbs even though it serves a grammatical rather than a lexical purpose.

STATIVE VS. DEVELOPMENTAL

Resorting to grammatical studies has permitted us to overcome one of the difficulties involved in observing a lexeme, that of isolating variations in the lexical meaning from the grammatical meaning expressed by the form of the verb. Because the progressive is not found with verbs representing a 'stative' event, we were able to distinguish between two different lexical senses expressed by verbs rarely used in the progressive. The fact that both 'developmental' (non-stative) – including accomplishment, achievement, action, activity, etc. – and 'stative' types of event can be expressed by the simple form shows that they do not arise from the grammatical form of the verb. They really are distinct lexical senses, different possible actualizations of the lexeme that the speaker forms as a verb by means of the appropriate grammatical morphemes. That is, depending on how speakers perceive an occurrence in their intended message, they will represent it either as 'developmental' or as 'stative.' The fact that these two lexical senses are available, theoretically at least, for any verb (outside of some auxiliaries) presupposes a lexical potential capable of giving rise to them.

To situate this distinction, it is useful to call to mind a characteristic of lexemes formed as substantives brought out by constraints on the use of the preposition *during*. While it is common to say *during supper, during the class, during his childhood*, we would not use the preposition with substantives such as *table, room, child*. This constraint on *during* suggests that the lexical makeup of certain substantives implies a duration, a stretch of time which is not reflected by any grammatical indication in substantives. The same can be said of the lexical makeup of verbs: all lexemes formed as verbs imply a duration, as just mentioned in the discussion of auxiliaries.

Grammatical discussions often bring in terms such as perfective, imperfective, retrospective, and the like to indicate the way a happening's duration has been represented by the grammatical forms of the verb. Such morphological representations, resulting in what is called a verb's EVENT TIME (see my 2007 study), are means of grammatically categorizing the stretch of duration already implicit in a verb's lexical makeup. This component of the lexical meaning of a verb, which has been largely taken for granted in our discussion so far, can be illustrated by *medal* in the above example. The infinitive makes us think of something to take place in time, a happening somehow associated with the object usually named by the lexeme formed as a substantive. Any happening, any process or state, implies a duration which, being part of the verb's lexical import, has to be grammaticized by tense, aspect, etc. during morphogenesis to give the verb its event time.

The lexical representation of duration is observable in any main verb through the 'stative' vs. 'developmental' distinction, a distinction which raises a question to be confronted in any attempt to explain polysemy in verbs. Although most easily recognized in discussing the use of the progressive, and so usually discussed in terms of its grammatical effects, the distinction itself is not grammatical but lexical, since it arises from the way the lexeme represents a particular happening that is focused on in the intended message. Speakers may experience a happening as either unchanging or developing during its existence, i.e. with "all phases ... identical" (Comrie, 49), "like parted" (Quirk et al., 198), or with "individual phases ... essentially different from one another" (Comrie, 37). It follows that the lexeme in tongue must be general enough to capture either impression, thus giving rise to different senses of the same verb, as brought out by the examples discussed in chapters 8 and 9.

This distinction between duration as represented lexically and event time as the grammatical configuration of this duration gives a clear view of how the two types of meaning, lexical and grammatical, mesh. Where a lexeme represents the particular impressions perceived in a specific intended message, morphemes configure the lexeme by means of the far more general categories provided by the system of the verb. Both are required to make a word capable of representing the particular experience the speaker has in mind, and of playing its part in the formal structure of the sentence.

CONCLUSION

Thus our examination of lexemes formed as verbs has brought to light three manifestations of polysemy. First, the condition → consequence type of relation between senses expressed, with its underlying notional chronology, has been found in a number of verbs and so may provide a basis, a sort of template or, better, a viewing device with which to observe the usage of other verbs in order to distinguish the actualized senses they bring to the sentence. Should this relationship turn out to be generally applicable to other verbs, it will give an indication of how the process of passing from a verb's potential lexeme to its actualized senses is effected, and so help to answer Ruhl's pertinent question, "why all the data ... *seem to be related.*"

Second, the 'developmental' vs. 'stative' opposition is another lexical distinction apparently manifested by all lexemes formed as main verbs. It involves a representation of implied duration, a generalization within the confines of the lexeme before it is formally categorized during morphogenesis, as we shall see in chapter 16.

Third, the relation between general and more particular senses observed in comparing auxiliary and full verb uses of *do, be,* and *have* suggests a process of materializing or actualizing lexical content. Whether this can be applied to other verbs remains an open question. That is, further research has yet to explore whether concrete and abstract acceptations are actualized senses or simply expressive effects arising from the conjuncture of the lexeme with other elements in the context. Nor is the related distinction between literal and metaphorical uses discussed here; it will be taken up in chapter 14 when discussing substantives.

As yet it remains to reflect on how these three manifestations of polysemy, and any others that may be found, fit together in the process of actualizing a lexeme. This is a prerequisite for attempting to describe the potential meaning of, for example, *see* – the goal of lexical analysis. Any such attempt would also call for an analysis of verbs with neighbouring lexemes such as *look* and *perceive* in order to discern what limits *see*'s range of representation,[3] and thus what distinguishes it from all the other lexemes constituting a speaker's universe of ideas in tongue.

Although the discussion of lexemes formed as verbs is far from complete, we will move on to lexemes formed as substantives in the next chapters. An examination of polysemy in the substantive will throw a new light on lexemes in tongue.

IV LEXEMES OF SUBSTANTIVES

12

Common and Proper

INTRODUCTION

In this and the next three chapters we will be examining lexemes formed as substantives in an attempt to see if certain commonly observed distinctions in discourse can throw a light on the actualization of these lexemes. As with verbs, we assume that the meaning of any word is binary, consisting of a lexical (material) and a grammatical (formal) component forming its mental content. The speaker synthesizes the two components during the moment of speech by means of a bi-phase operation whereby a lexeme is actualized and then configured grammatically. This meaning synthesis is then expressed by actualizing its physical sign. Viewing words as formed on the spur of the moment in this way entails viewing lexemes, when one is not involved in an act of language, as potentials with no grammatical strings attached. As a consequence, we will not speak of "substantive lexemes," which might imply that the part of speech is somehow inherent in the lexeme and so suggest that words are stocked as "items in a mental lexicon." Here we will speak of "lexemes formed as substantives" to imply that they might have been formed by another part of speech, or simply "lexemes of substantives" to suggest that the lexeme has been actualized and grammatically formed as a word for use as a substantive in a particular sentence.

The first distinction to be discussed, that between common and proper nouns, will be approached from the point of view of the distinction made by logicians between comprehension (= intension) and extension. Originally derived from the observation of how different but semantically related substantives can refer to the extra-mental world, this distinction will be taken not only as a basis for comparing lexemes, but also as a means of exploring the makeup of a given lexeme in an attempt to explain the differences observed.

COMPREHENSION, EXTENSION, AND REFERENCE

Lyons (454) describes this important distinction found "in traditional logic and in certain theories of semantics between the *extension* and the *intension* of a term. The extension of a term is the class of entities to which the term is applicable or refers; the intension of a term is the set of attributes which characterize an entity to which the term is correctly applied. Extension and intension vary inversely in relation to one another: the greater the extension of a term, the less its intension; and conversely." He illustrates this by means of *flower*, which "refers to more things," i.e. has a greater extension, than *tulip* because to characterize tulips calls for "a wider set of attributes than those which suffice to characterize flowers." That is, as a hyponym of *flower*, *tulip* has a greater intension (= comprehension) since it comprises not only the attributes characterizing flowers in general but also those specific to tulips.

Our discussion of this distinction here calls for a comment on appropriate terminology. A number of linguists use the term *extension* in much the same sense as logicians do, to depict the set or class of entities or things in external reality to which a word refers as a result of being used in a sentence, an acceptation which is limited to that of the reader or listener. In this essay I have been at some pains to reverse the perspective and examine how a word is constructed by speakers to represent their experience of external reality, their intended message. As a consequence, I have replaced the term *extension*, when useful, with the expression *range of representation*, in order to focus attention on how a lexeme contributes to the construction of a word: by representing something the speaker has in mind. The term *comprehension* (or *intension*) also tends to be taken in a resultative sense, so I use the expression *characterizing traits* when the focus is on actualizing the traits that characterize a given lexeme as distinct from all others.

Operationalizing comprehension and extension in this way involves viewing them as movements and the variation produced by their inverse relation as a mechanism. That is, this variation reflects not only a static relationship between words such as *flower* and *tulip*, but also an operational relationship, a mental mechanism at play in actualizing the lexeme of any given substantive or verb so as to represent something in the intended message. Thus, 'tulip' as a meaning potential consists of certain characterizing traits which determine its range of representation, and when certain impressions corresponding to these traits arise in a speaker's stream of consciousness, 'tulip' functioning as a viewing idea focuses on these impressions and so can represent them as the lexical import of a word. Once formed as a word and expressed in a sentence, *tulip* can therefore designate (refer to) what it represents in the speaker's intended message, thus permitting listeners to reconstruct what the speaker has in mind. That is, listeners in turn refer the meaning expressed by the sentence to a mental space in which they reconstruct, as best they can, the speaker's message. Once the act of language has been completed in this way, listeners can discern what the reconstructed message denotes, if anything, in the extra-mental universe.

An important distinction is involved here concerning the term *referent*, which is generally used to indicate something outside language that is focused on by the meaning of a word or sentence. On the one hand, the referent is commonly considered to be the "spatio-temporal object or event" that a word or expression "denotes" (cf. W3), i.e. something outside the mind. On the other hand, because we can talk only about what we are aware of, I have insisted that speakers always represent what they have in mind at the moment of speaking, their intended message, regardless of whether it arises from something in the external world, or from a dream, or from any other source. As a consequence, the linguistic expression of what a speaker has in mind can refer immediately only to that intended message. It is after the act of language has been completed by listeners reconstruing it in their own minds that the message itself can be referred to a referent in the extra-mental universe. That is, an expression refers immediately to its intra-mental referent, technically its DESIGNATUM, and only indirectly, once the act of speech is over, to an extra-mental referent, its DENOTATUM, if there is one. It is of course of crucial importance for a logician, judge, parent, etc. to know if something said corresponds with external reality or not, to determine its truth value. For a linguist, however, since the act of language ends with reconstruing the intended message, an expression's designatum or referent is found in the speaker's mind, or in listeners' minds once they have reconstrued the message. As a consequence, I use the terms *referent* or *designatum* to indicate what is immediately referred to, and *extra-mental referent* or *denotatum* for whatever is indirectly referred to.

CHARACTERIZING TRAITS

In chapter 4 it was maintained that the impressions arising from something in the speaker's field of consciousness call on the viewing idea, the lexeme, most in affinity with them to categorize that experiential entity on the basis of its nature, of whatever, in the eyes of the speaker, distinguishes it from entities of a different nature. Thus a lexeme's representation is not a sort of facsimile of the experiential entity but rather a generalized figuration of it. The term *nature* should be understood in the sense of whatever in the makeup or characteristics of something enables speakers to distinguish it and so to name it, though often a speaker may not grasp its makeup well enough to make it explicit. For most people, an abstract word such as *reality* calls to mind a certain notional content with little specifying detail, as compared with a concrete word such as *tulip*, which probably evokes a flower with a specific shape for many speakers. As one writer puts it: "Anyone who understands the word *cat* must have performed some type of analysis which has isolated the essential 'cattiness' involved in being a cat" (Aitchison, 43). On the other hand, for a philosopher *reality* may call to mind and make explicit certain characterizing traits other speakers are unaware of, as may *tulip* for a horticulturist.

This adaptability of words presupposes, at least for forming our first lexemes, that children acquire each one by confronting their experience of extra-mental entities with the words they hear. That is, by focusing a given word on a series of somewhat similar experiences, they are led to generalize, to abstract from the particularity of each such experience in order to institute in tongue what characterizes all of them. Since each person must undertake this process of generalization to acquire a given lexeme, there is no guarantee that the result will be identical for all speakers. On the contrary, it is only to be expected that there will be differences in the potential meanings arrived at in this way. Such differences, however, are normally not so great as to interfere with communication, and so will usually go unobserved, because the basis in our common experience of, say, tulips is never lost.

Some lexemes representing abstract notions, scientific concepts, and the like, which do not correspond to extra-mental entities accessible to our external senses, cannot be acquired by confronting experience of the external world and words heard. They can be acquired only after the means of instituting lexemes in tongue has been established by the learning of more basic, concrete lexemes.

Once established in the mind as a routine operation for expanding one's universe of viewing ideas (vocabulary), however, these means are available for instituting lexemes based not on particular experiences of the extra-mental world but on what emerges into consciousness from our mental world as feelings, imaginings, dreams, vague notions, precise concepts, and the like. Of course we can acquire a new lexeme through reading and listening, and in that case the physical sign for expressing it is also provided, but this is not necessarily the case for what arises from our own minds. Then there is the "struggle for words," to borrow Einstein's expression, suggesting that instituting some new concept in tongue as a lexeme with its potential sign is not always an easy job.

The point here is not to explore the learning process, but rather to suggest that anything emerging into an adult's conscious awareness can be categorized (more or less adequately) by a viewing idea already instituted in tongue, or can call on the means of establishing in tongue a new viewing idea. That is, our language is constructed in such a way as to confront our stream of consciousness with a universe of viewing ideas that can be expanded to keep pace with the expanding universe of our experience. Our viewing ideas are general enough to categorize diverse experiences of things perceived as having the same nature and particular enough to distinguish them from experiences of things with a different nature. Thus the set of characterizing traits comprised in the lexeme of *flower* is sufficiently particularized to distinguish what that word can designate from what *leaf* or *bud* or any other word can designate, but it remains general enough to depict what is common to *tulip, crocus,* etc. That is, 'flower' has quite a wide range of representation. By comparison, the lexeme 'tulip,' comprising more characterizing traits than 'flower,' is more particularized and so can distinguish its designatum from that of *crocus,* etc., but it is nevertheless general enough to depict any individual entity perceived as having the nature of *tulip.* Thus 'tulip' has a much narrower range of representation than 'flower' because a lexeme's range of representation and its set of characterizing traits "vary inversely in relation to one another," as Lyons puts it.

WITHIN THE LEXEME

The discussion in the last section makes us aware of the fact that the use of a word such as *tulip* not only calls to mind traits representing its designatum and distinguishing it from the designatum of *crocus,* etc., but also implies traits representing the designatum of *flower.* That is, it appears that the lexeme 'tulip,' in representing the nature of an experiential entity, depicts what contrasts it with other flowers, as well as characterizing traits common to them all. These common traits constitute the lexeme 'flower,' i.e. depict the general category that groups 'tulip' and all the other flower lexemes a speaker has learned to distinguish. Thus, to put it in technical terms, the lexical import of *tulip* involves both the distinctive or characterizing traits of the hyponym and the common traits of the hyperonym (or superordinate). This seems to imply that within 'tulip' itself there are different levels of traits, a sort of hierarchy, an inference which, if valid, would constitute an important element for investigating the makeup of the lexeme.

Before exploring this lead, however, a word of caution is in order. One of our basic postulates is that the lexical import of a word in discourse is the representation of something in the speaker's ongoing experience. In the set of impressions a speaker represents by means of 'tulip' there is nothing dividing them into those that would call for 'flower' and those calling for 'tulip': a speaker does not experience a tulip separately from a flower. That is, a speaker's experience of the object is global as is the representation of that experience, and this is why there is no expression of two parts, hyponym and hyperonym, when the word is used in a sentence. Later it will be useful to adopt a more analytical point of view and consider that a speaker represents the two. Here, however, I want to focus on how a speaker represents and expresses the nature or makeup of something without making the distinction between those two levels explicit, because our aim is to get as close as possible to the way a speaker calls on a lexeme to produce a word in ordinary usage.

This manner of conceiving a word's characterizing traits can be illustrated by further reflecting on speakers with different categorizations for the same experiential entity. Many people probably identify whales by characteristics they have in common with sharks and the like, and so consider them to be fish by nature. However, anyone with greater experience and more developed notions of whales, a marine biologist for example, would identify them by other characteristics and so consider them to be mammals by nature. That is to say, for cognoscenti, those working in a particular science, technology, trade, profession, etc., greater experience and knowledge can give rise to a more precise view of the nature of entities in their field, and this in turn can bring about a development in the lexemes involved. This permits more precise usage, understood as such by colleagues in the same field but not necessarily by those outside the field. Whether this involves a given speaker altering and refining a lexeme as originally acquired, or situating it differently within a network of lexemes, or both, is a question that remains to be explored. The point here is that a lexeme is open to development so that it can confront the widening experience of a speaker, but that this need not inhibit its use in ordinary discourse, a fact suggesting that even in cognoscenti usage the lexeme can still express the most concrete traits depicting what identifies something for ordinary speakers.

This can be illustrated by the interesting case of the relation between *dog* and *bitch*, mentioned by a reader. For speakers who make the sexual distinction in ordinary usage, *dog* can express the epicene sense 'member of the canine species,' or the 'male member of the canine species' sense, whereas *bitch* cannot express the epicene sense, only the female sense. For such speakers, the sexual trait appears to be necessary in the lexeme. This is not so obvious in the case of those who do not make the distinction in ordinary usage except by using the adjectives *male* and *female*, as with most other animal species. To explore the problem further would require discussing how it relates to the system of grammatical gender in the substantive.

So far, then, it seems that a lexeme such as 'whale' consists of traits depicting its specificity as a hyponym and traits depicting a superordinate category shared with other hyponymic lexemes. The hierarchy of categories may, of course, extend by further generalization even for ordinary speakers, as can be seen in the opposition between 'plant' and 'animal,' a fact indicating that however general a given lexeme may be – however reduced its characterizing traits and broad its range of representation – it is distinct from every other lexeme in the speaker's vocabulary.[1]

HOW WIDESPREAD?

Thus the combination of what a lexeme has in common with other lexemes and what distinguishes it from others can be observed in common nouns through the fact that both a specialist and an ordinary speaker can depict the same experiential entity by means of 'whale' even though they may represent its nature differently in some respects. This raises a problem for our theoretical approach, namely discerning how the operation of ideogenesis can give rise to lexemes of this type. Before going on to discuss that, however, a prior question should be considered: widespread though it may appear to be, can the combination of distinctive traits and common traits be found in all lexemes formed as substantives?[2] Do all lexemes fit into a hyponym-hyperonym sort of hierarchy?

Ordinary substantives such as *hammer, bus, water, sincerity* are probably understood by most speakers as naming entities to be distinguished from other entities such as those named by *saw, truck, wine, gratitude* respectively. Each of these oppositions – 'hammer' vs. 'saw,' 'bus' vs. 'truck,' 'water' vs. 'wine,' 'sincerity' vs. 'gratitude' – involves distinctive and common traits, the latter probably represented for most people by 'tool,' 'vehicle,' 'liquid,' 'virtue' respectively. But what about words such as *tool* – do they call to mind traits common to other words? If asked to define *hammer* or *saw*, a person would likely say "It's a tool used for ..." and if asked what a tool is, they might say "It's an instrument used to ..." but for *instrument* (or *implement, device*) they would possibly resort to "It's a thing for ..." Similarly, a lexeme such as 'cloud,' which does not, at first sight anyway, call to mind either hyperonym or hyponym lexemes, might be characterized as "A thing in the air composed of ..." If asked what a flower is, someone might even reply "It's a thing that develops on ..." Can we infer from this that, in ordinary (as opposed to scientific or specialist's) discourse, 'cloud' and 'flower' and 'instrument' call to mind traits in common with as general a notion as 'thing'? In fact, for the ordinary speaker 'thing' calls to mind traits so general that in discourse it can probably designate any physically observed object, and perhaps, for some, a mentally observed object such as a dream or an idea or a virtue, though it may be more common to call on the pronoun *something* to evoke less concrete entities. (It is not easy to determine even one's own common usage at this level of generality.) The point here is that the above lexemes appear to have something in common with 'thing,' or at least 'something,' and this regardless of whether or not there is a hyperonym represented by an intervening lexeme such as 'tool,' which in any case would share these 'thing' traits.

Not all substantives depicting what is physically observed, however, can be traced back to *thing* in this way. For example, *boy* usually calls to mind particular traits opposing it to *girl*, like *man* as opposed to *woman*, *uncle* to *aunt*, etc., all with common traits that can be represented by 'person' or perhaps 'human,' general notions that contrast with 'object' or 'thing,' a contrast also underlying the pronouns *someone* and *something*. This opposition foreshadows the grammatical distinction to be found in the morphogenesis of substantives and pronouns, that between 'animate' and 'inanimate' gender, the former giving rise to the further distinction between 'masculine' and 'feminine.' To get beyond this 'person' vs. 'thing' contrast by means of a notion sufficiently general to include both, words such as *being* are used, though this may well be cognoscenti usage. In any case, our point here is not to try to distinguish between the substantives expressing the most general notions, but rather to suggest that more concrete lexemes do appear to have traits in common with them, or at least, in the usage of any speaker, with *someone* and *something*.

These considerations raise the question of what, if any, common traits are shared by the lexemes of words such as *person, thing,* and *entity*. It is interesting to find that attempts in a dictionary (W3) to characterize these substantives for their most general sense do so in terms of "human being," "what exists as [X]," "the existence of something as [X]," and the like. This suggests that common to all such terms is an impression of existence or being. In fact, the word *existence* in its most abstract sense is defined as "having being ..." and *being* as "the quality or state of existing." Whether or not these abstract senses are part of the ordinary speaker's usage, it would seem that at least an impression of having existence – whether physically observed, mentally conceived, imagined, or otherwise brought to a speaker's awareness – lies behind, and is part of, whatever lexeme a substantive expresses. Considered from the point of view of how we came to form substantives in the first place, this would hardly be surprising, since one wonders how the youngest learners could have started forming basic lexemes without some impression of an extra-mental reality, of something to call to mind, to symbolize. On this basis, mature speakers of course are no longer tied to perceptual input since they have learned to represent as if it were real something arising in the imagination, and even something they know is not real. Thus it may well be that any substantive brings to the sentence a representation of its designatum as, ultimately, something that exists, whether in the mind or outside it, even if speakers do not have the means of depicting this omnipresent impression with a lexeme.

In any case, there appear to be good grounds to infer that a lexeme formed as a substantive includes both traits distinguishing it from other lexemes and traits assimilating it to other lexemes. This would explain why many lexemes appear to be related to one another in a sort of hyponym-hyperonym network on the basis of what they have in common. Any such organization would not of course be common to all speakers, since the number of, say, flower names acquired is variable from one person to another, and, as we saw when comparing cognoscenti and ordinary usage, the makeup of the lexeme itself may vary from one speaker to another. Other lexemes may simply belong to such general categories as 'thing' or 'person.' In any case, there seems also to be a trait, common to all lexemes formed as substantives, depicting the designatum as (though) existing in some way.

HOW ABOUT PROPER NOUNS?

According to certain writers, our view of common nouns cannot apply to proper nouns because they denote an individual but do not tell us anything about that individual. For them *Tokyo, Kilimanjaro, Einstein*, unlike *house* and *tiger*, do not express a class, category, or concept, and so are without linguistic meaning. They function simply as signals directing our attention to the extra-linguistic referent. Palmer (20), for example, observes that "while these [proper nouns] are used to refer to particular people, places, times, etc., it is debatable whether they have any denotation and they can hardly be said to have meaning." Jespersen (1924/1975, 64–71) takes exception to that view: "Our inquiry, therefore, has reached this conclusion, that no sharp line can be drawn between proper and common names, the difference being one of degree rather than of kind." I too take exception to it because of the principle that no word can exist without meaning.

That view seems to have arisen because, unlike common nouns, a proper noun cannot designate a concept capable of denoting an indefinite number of individuals. This is illustrated by the fact that merely reading or hearing a word such as *Tokyo* without any linguistic context suffices to call to mind a unique entity in the extra-linguistic universe. It remains, however, that such a word on its own does indicate a hyperonym, the type or class of entity the designatum belongs to. Anyone familiar with these words knows that *Tokyo* designates a city, *Kilimanjaro* a mountain, and *Einstein* a scientist, a fact indicating that, like common nouns, proper nouns do express a meaning, and moreover that a certain categorization is involved in constructing this lexical import. To confirm this view, Jespersen (1924/1975, 68) brings up the case of two people "who have nothing in common but the name" Maud. He likens it to the case of "the *temple* of worship and the *temple* of the head," but points out: "The two Mauds have really more in common than the two temples, for they are both female human beings." That is, proper nouns are meaningful, expressing both the type or category of an individual and a set of characterizing traits applying only to that individual. Because of these individualizing traits, *Maud* as the name of two people should be considered homonyms, as separate words and not as different uses of the same word.[3] This view is confirmed by the very term "proper" which, according to one dictionary (W3), tells us that these substantives distinguish "a person or a thing or a place from all others *of the same class*" (my italics). This generally accepted understanding suggests another characteristic of proper nouns, namely that they represent something as a unit, as spatially 'bounded.' That is, a proper noun's range of application is limited to one and the same individual.[4]

How can a substantive's meaning impose such an extreme restriction on its range of reference? For common nouns we have seen that there is an inverse relationship between a lexeme's set of characterizing traits and its range of representation: the greater the former, the narrower the latter. It follows that a word whose range of representation is reduced to a minimum, to a single individual, must have a set of characterizing traits that is maximized. This suggests that whereas a common noun's lexeme involves traits particular to a given type of entity but none distinguishing an individual entity within that type, a proper noun's lexical import (one hesitates to call it a lexeme) involves not only traits particular to a given type but also traits particular to a given individual entity distinguishing it from every other individual entity of that type. This overload of lexical meaning is what reduces the potentiality of a proper noun so that it cannot represent something as spatially 'unbounded,' nor as unspecified. In short, we are led to the conclusion that, far from being bereft of linguistic meaning, proper nouns bring to the sentence even more lexical import than common nouns. As Jespersen (1924/1975, 66) puts it: "In Mill's terminology, but in absolute contrast to his view, I should venture to say that proper nouns (as actually used) 'connote' the greatest number of attributes."

This, then, is the view adopted here: as compared with that of a common noun, the lexical import of a proper noun is increased to the point where its representational range is reduced to a minimum, and so it can refer to only one individual. That is to say, besides the general traits representing the nature of its designatum ("a person or a thing or a place"), a proper noun expresses sufficient particularizing traits to characterize its designatum as a specific individual. Because it always expresses the same lexical meaning, a proper noun on its own, without determiner or adjective, can constitute a noun phrase and, outside of any linguistic context at all, can call to mind its designatum. But if they always express the same actualized lexical meaning in discourse, can proper nouns be said to arise from a lexical potential in tongue? Although, as we shall see in the next chapter, the substantives in expressions such as *an Einstein* or *the Tokyo I knew* are not used as proper nouns, this possibility of varying their lexical import does permit a common noun use, as Jespersen (67) points out, and so indicates an underlying lexical potential. Moreover, there is certainly a possible variation in meaning from one speaker to another with proper nouns, as between someone whose knowledge of, say, Tokyo is derived from newspapers and someone who has visited it, or better still lived there. The better one knows that city, the more particularizing traits its name calls to mind. It is as though 'Tokyo,' maximized as a set of characterizing traits for all speakers to ensure its minimal extensity, remains a lexical potential open to accommodating the growing experience of each speaker. This sort of variation, seen above in common nouns as between ordinary speakers and cognoscenti, helps bring out how lexical potentials fulfill their representing role by adapting to the experience of the speaker.

The final point here is to bring out the variation observed in the lexical imports of substantives. We saw that for common nouns a lexeme such as 'thing' or 'entity,' or 'being' in more intellectual usage, consists of only the most common traits depicting a very general class or category, as compared with 'tiger' and other such lexemes with their particularizing traits representing a particular nature as a limited category while implying a more general category. Now we have seen that the lexical meaning of proper nouns (*Einstein, Tokyo, Kilimanjaro*) consists of singularizing traits representing a specific entity as a hyponym, since it implies a particular type or category as a hyperonym (scientist, city, mountain), and even a more general category (person, place, thing). That is, according to the set of characterizing traits comprising its lexical potential, a substantive arises in discourse either as a common noun capable of representing a type of entity of a certain nature, or as a proper noun restricted to representing one individual entity of a certain nature. The point I am making here is that a proper noun and a common noun each represents something by its nature, but differs in the degree to which its characterizing traits delimit its range, at least in non-metaphorical usage.

CONCLUSION

Our discussion has led to distinguishing nouns on the basis of their lexemes: where proper nouns incorporate enough traits to characterize a particular individual as distinct from all others, common nouns incorporate enough traits to characterize a particular nature, differentiating it from all others. This in turn led to the proposal that the hyperonym-hyponym organization observed with many substantives suggests that a lexeme comprises general traits as well as particularizing traits, and even individualizing traits in the case of proper nouns. However, this hierarchical organization cannot be assumed to be identical for all speakers, since nothing permits us to assume that all speakers learn a lexeme and institute it in tongue in exactly the same way. Moreover, a certain variability between speakers in the makeup of a given lexeme allows for particular speakers to develop a lexeme's potential in order to represent new areas of their own experience, but the extent of such variation remains limited by the requirements of communication.

The institution of any set of traits in tongue as a lexeme is further constrained by the needs of representation. This was brought out by the fact that although all lexemes cannot be assumed to be part of a particular hierarchical network in tongue, when formed as substantives they do appear to depict either something or someone, though for some speakers these overriding categories may not be represented by an abstract lexeme such as 'entity' or 'being' or 'existent.' Whether related directly or through intermediate categories to overriding categories, the most general lexemes for any speaker obviously cannot themselves be subject to a more general one. It remains, however, that a speaker's most abstract lexemes, whatever they may be, are actualized, like more concrete lexemes, as either 'unbounded' or 'bounded,' two ways of representing extension in space. Since this appears to reflect a component common to all lexemes formed as substantives, we will examine it in the next chapter.

13

'Unbounded' and 'Bounded'

INTRODUCTION

In this chapter we turn to a component in the lexemes of all substantives with grammatical results, a component that has long been observed. For example, when Jespersen (1954 II, 114–15) remarks that besides "countables" there are "a great many words which represent 'uncountables', that is, which do not call up the idea of any definite thing, having a certain shape or precise limits," he is making a lexical distinction. He illustrates this distinction between "mass-words and thing-words" mainly on the basis of their grammatical number: whether or not they take 'plural' -s, the indefinite article, *each* and *every*, etc. Similarly, "both for semantic and grammatical reasons," Quirk et al. (245) distinguish "count" and "noncount" as different subclasses. In this way grammarians generally allot substantives to two different classes or subclasses, but without bringing out the relation involved between the lexical representation and the grammatical behaviour as discussed here.

To clarify this, we will examine the distinction to see if it is a case of lexical polysemy, approaching the problem from the general point of view of the word outlined in chapters 5 and 6. There it was pointed out that words do not exist as ready-made items in a preconscious lexicon, but must be made to order each time we speak. It was shown that constructing a word during the moment of speech from its formative elements in tongue involves generating its mental import or meaning, its PSYCHOGENESIS (and by implication its sign, its SEMIOGENESIS).[1] As we have seen, a word's psychogenesis develops in two phases and results in the lexeme being "packaged" as a part of speech with its functional possibilities for the sentence.

Without this view of a word, one would have no clear idea of the way its lexical import, arising from ideogenesis, can condition its grammatical import, arising in morphogenesis.

Before exploring this relation further, however, we must clarify a question of terminology. Christophersen (25–6) points out that the term "mass-words," first used for concrete substantives signifying a substance (*wood, water*, etc.), is hardly appropriate for those signifying abstract notions such as 'sincerity.' He proposed "continuate-words," a term which has the advantage for analysis of indicating the way something is represented, rather than what is represented, but it has the disadvantage of including most singular substantives such as *a book*, which also depict a continuum in space. For this reason the term "unbounded" is adopted here. Similarly, for Jespersen's "thing-words" Christophersen proposed "unit-words" to indicate that the designatum is represented as a self-contained unit. This term, however, hardly applies to a use such as *Jill has a good knowledge of Greek*, which does not call to mind the notion of a self-contained unit but rather a delimited amount. For this reason, the more general term "bounded" is adopted here.

Because these terms designate how the lexeme is actualized, they are preferred to "non-count" ("uncountable") and "count" ("countable"), terms which, because they designate a frequent expressive effect arising from the lexical representation and the system of number, sometimes lead to confusion. For example, Huddleston and Pullum (339) consider *knowledge* in the above example to be "non-count," even though it is used with the indefinite article "to individuate a subamount of knowledge." They argue that "this individuation does not yield an entity conceptualised as belonging to a class of entities of the same kind" and so is not countable or pluralizable. Here it would be clearer to describe *knowledge* from the lexical point of view as actualized in a 'bounded' sense in order to contribute a 'singular' notion to obtain a 'subamount' expressive effect, as made explicit by the noun phrase. The relationship between the lexical and the grammatical is frequently neglected in this way, and so we will begin by recalling this crucial distinction.

SIGNIFYING AND CONSIGNIFYING

To examine the relation between the 'unbounded' vs. 'bounded' way of representing a notion and its grammatical consequences in the noun phrase, it is important to keep in mind the two phases of producing a word's meaning import, since failure to do so would jeopardize any attempt to get beyond the observations of expressive effects in discourse. Thus most grammarians, failing to distinguish between the lexical and the grammatical, classify an 'unbounded' substantive as "singular," i.e. without the -*s* inflexion, but do not explain why it does not express the grammatical notion of 'singular.' The only grammarian who has evoked this problem is, to my knowledge, Jespersen (1954 II, 72–3): "Next, we have what are here called mass-words ... Here such notions as singular and plural are strictly speaking inapplicable." This would seem to suggest that the system of grammatical number does not apply to all substantives – hardly an acceptable conclusion. It therefore invites anyone with a systemic view of grammar to examine how these two types of -ø substantive, the lexically 'unbounded' and the grammatically 'singular,' are related. Among linguists, W. Reid (80) does adopt a systemic view, maintaining that there is an essential link between inflexion and grammatical meaning and so a -ø substantive always signifies 'singular,' but that in "mass substantive" usage a -ø substantive is "employed *faute de mieux* to communicate messages for which it is not ideally suited." Langacker (1991, 76–81), adopting a very different approach, dissociates inflexion and grammatical meaning when he maintains that, like an 'unbounded' substantive, a 'plural' substantive in ordinary usage "designates a mass (unbounded region) consisting of indefinitely many instances" and that syntactically they "behave alike in numerous respects." As a consequence, "a singular substantive and its corresponding plural represent distinct categories" since "plurals themselves fall under the mass-substantive category." To conclude that the 'plural' substantive is "a subclass of mass substantives" follows from limiting the evidence to similarities in syntactic behaviour and expressive effect but disregarding the morphological evidence, i.e. ignoring what the -ø and -*s* inflexions tell us about a word's grammatical meaning as opposed to its lexical meaning. Elsewhere (1982; 2009, 68–125) I have described the system of grammatical number in English and the polysemy of its two constituent morphemes, -ø and –*s*, and illustrated their actualized senses. If the distinction between what a word signifies (lexical "boundedness") and what it consignifies (by grammatical morphology) is kept in mind, this will clarify how -*s* substantives can give rise to expressive effects of either a 'bounded' or an "unbounded region."

More pertinent to our concern here is to take into account the fact that -ø inflexion can express other senses besides 'singular,' because this brings out its relation with 'unbounded' lexemes and shows how 'unbounded' notions are configured grammatically by -ø. That is, one can begin to probe, for example, the link indicated by -ø inflexion between *He is in hospital* vs. *He is in the hospital*. Comparing the two reveals that in the former phrase, *hospital* represents its designatum as 'unbounded,' i.e. as "not inherently bounded" in space, whereas in the latter it represents its designatum as 'bounded,' as an "individuated" entity, "atomic in the sense that [it] cannot be divided into smaller parts of the same kind as the whole," as Huddleston and Pullum (335) put it. On the other hand, both of these noun phrases represent something occupying a space, whether bounded or not, a space which is undivided, continuate; this is what the -ø inflexion quantifies in the two expressions. As a grammatical form configuring the 'bounded' notion expressed by *the hospital*, -ø here represents a minimal, i.e. indivisible, continuate space, and so the phrase expresses an object, a building; as a grammatical form configuring the 'unbounded' notion expressed by *in hospital*, -ø represents it occupying a non-minimal, continuate space, and so the phrase expresses the function or nature of the activity the speaker has in mind, which could be exercised in any hospital.

Sorting out the respective roles of the lexical and the grammatical in this way shows that a noun phrase expresses an individuated 'singular' sense because the substantive's -ø inflexion represents a continuate space as minimal for a 'bounded' notion, whereas another noun phrase expresses a spatially undefined, 'non-singular' sense because its substantive's -ø inflexion depicts a continuate space as non-minimal for an 'unbounded' notion. In short, -ø inflexion is not restricted to representing 'singular,' but can also represent a greater-than-minimal space, depending on the notion it configures. Thus a lexeme depicted as 'unbounded' can be given a maximum extent by the -ø morpheme to express a 'generic' sense (*Light travels faster than sound*) or an intermediate extent to express a 'vague amount' sense (*I need light*), but not a minimum quantity, a 'singular' sense, since this requires a 'bounded' representation (*I see a light*). A lexeme depicted as 'bounded' can be multiplied by the -s morpheme to give a 'plural, more than one' sense or even an 'all, generic' sense. Recognizing this grammatical polysemy is important for discerning the relation between -ø and -s inflexions and the system of grammatical number containing both (and why we occasionally find 'plural' substantives with -ø inflexion and 'singular' substantives with -s inflexion, uses that cannot be gone into here). Only if we have a clear understanding of the senses expressed by the number morphemes can we discern the contribution of the lexeme and explain the expressive effects combining the two formative elements.

This discussion of the grammatical system will not be pursued here, since enough has been said to bring out that Jespersen was quite justified in pointing out that a substantive expressing an 'unbounded' notion cannot be considered a 'singular.' On the other hand, granted the polysemy of -ø inflexion, it can be seen that the system of number still applies to 'unbounded' notions. The important point for us here is that distinguishing between a word's lexical and grammatical imports in this way will help us focus on the lexeme and avoid attributing to it what is expressed by the number morphemes.

With this distinction in mind, we can see how the lexical conditions the grammatical in the constructing of a word: either an 'unbounded' or a 'bounded' lexical representation of something can be configured by -ø inflexion, whereas a 'bounded' representation of the notion appears to be a prerequisite for a substantive with -s inflexion. In this respect, it should be recognized that the 'bounded' representation of a notion does not always result in such clear-cut entities as *the hospital* or even *an idea*. In *a good knowledge*, as we have seen, the delimitation is sufficient to suggest a "subamount" but does not permit pluralizing. Similarly, for 'bounded' notions in examples such as *the waters of the Nile* and *the sands of the desert*, "there is no suggestion of definite parts, and the plural seems to suggest indefinite extension or repetition" (Sweet, 47). Whatever quantum of water or sand is extended or repeated is vague indeed. Such examples suggest that the term 'bounded' must be understood to include notions representing even the most vaguely delimited entities, entities which are certainly not countable. Although their expressive effect is difficult to paraphrase satisfactorily, the last three examples do show that 'unbounded' and 'bounded' representations correspond to impressions, sometimes quite subtle, arising from the speaker's intended message and so permit the speaker to exploit a given lexeme in different ways. And this brings us to the question of determining the status of these two ways of expressing substantive lexemes, after which we will look at the relation between them.

WORD CLASSES OR POLYSEMY?

It is not uncommon, as we have seen, for grammarians to speak of the 'unbounded' vs. 'bounded' distinction in terms of mass- or thing-words, non-count or count substantives, uncountable or countable lexical items, and the like; all these expressions focus on the expressive effect or even the extra-linguistic reality, not on the means of representing the lexeme. This usually results in grammarians dividing substantives into two types or classes, with all the problems that arise "when noncount substantives are used as count substantives or vice versa" (Quirk et al., 1563–4). To account for these problems, operations of transfer, conversion, or reclassification are assumed to take place, but since no more is said about such operations they do little to advance our understanding of usage. Allan, on the other hand, assumes that "countability is not in fact a characteristic of nouns per se, but of NP's" (541), a point of view corresponding to that of the listener / reader, but not that of the speaker / writer, who must construct the noun phrase, starting with the substantive.

Christophersen (27) also speaks of two types of substantive, but remarks that they "are not absolute groups but only represent different modes of apprehension." Huddleston and Pullum (334) are more explicit. They consider the "count vs non-count distinction," as in *another chocolate* and *some more chocolate*, to be different "senses of a single lexical item. *Chocolate* exhibits polysemy: it has more than one sense." Although they "regard this as a case of polysemy, not homonymy," all they do to explain how *chocolate* can express different senses without being "distinct lexical items," i.e. homonyms, is to observe that "there is a clear relation between the two meanings." This recalls Ruhl's remark (63) concerning verbs – "The challenge is to understand why all the data ... *seem to be related*" – and poses the real problem here: what is this relation that enables *chocolate* to express different senses yet be understood as the same word? What do these senses have in common, and what distinguishes them?

Like Huddleston and Pullum, we will consider that the 'unbounded' vs. 'bounded' distinction is a case of polysemy, but will examine it from an operational point of view, that of the speaker (intended message → languaging → meaning expressed), to explain how it is that the same lexeme can express the two senses. As in the examination of verbs, we will adopt the general assumption concerning the act of speech that a word must be constructed from its formative elements by the speaker each time it is required for a sentence. Like all other formative elements in tongue, the lexeme 'chocolate' is a potential for viewing and representing certain impressions arising in the speaker's momentary experience. To represent these impressions, the lexeme is actualized in a 'bounded' sense to construct the phrase *another chocolate*; to represent the slightly different impressions involved, the lexeme is actualized in an 'unbounded' sense in order to construct the phrase *some more chocolate*. Thus the same set of impressions for characterizing the nature of what is being spoken of can be represented as either spatially bounded or not, depicted as either an "individuated entity" or a substance, depending on the particular experience to be expressed. In short, the meaning potential of the lexeme in tongue provides the possibility for giving rise to either actualization in discourse.

In this way, by distinguishing between the unchanging lexical potential in tongue and what is involved in actualizing it for discourse, we can understand why speakers have the impression of using the same word even though they use it now in a 'bounded' sense, now in an 'unbounded' sense. Considering a lexeme in tongue such as 'chocolate' as a viewing idea ready to represent the nature of the experiential entity it focuses on, helps us understand how it can respond in two spatially different ways to the changing panorama of a speaker's experience, as in *There is more chocolate in this chocolate*. It also allows for the fact that certain lexemes such as 'water,' 'knowledge,' and 'magic' are, by the very nature of their impressive makeup, predisposed to an 'unbounded' actualization and so will be found rarely, if ever, actualized as 'bounded' substantives, whereas for others such as 'boy,' 'car,' and 'idea' it is just the opposite. On the other hand, one should not limit their possibilities, since even lexemes like these may be found in uses such as:

... masters of poems and small magics, who could make ... spells and runes. [W3]
"It's not brutality," murmured little Hartopp ... "It's boy, only boy."[2]

It seems, therefore, that both 'unbounded' and 'bounded' representations are possibilities for all lexemes that can be formed as substantives, even if one of these possibilities may not have been exploited so far.

When we postulate the possibility of the lexeme's being actualized in either sense, it follows that, as a potential in tongue prior to entering an act of languaging some experience, the lexeme is not classified for either. This eliminates one problematic issue since it obviates any need to establish classes of "lexical items" on the basis of "countability" in a pre-conscious "lexicon," as many are prone to do, being unaware that speaking involves psychogenesis, constructing on the spur of the moment from its formative elements the mental import of any word we want to use. That is, viewing the 'unbounded' vs. 'bounded' dichotomy as a consequence of actualizing a lexeme in different ways makes it unnecessary, as we saw in chapter 5, to suppose a complicated set of operations whereby substantives are somehow declassified, transferred, or converted from one class to another in order to account for the facts of usage.

What the two senses have in common, then, is that both are possible spatial actualizations of a given lexeme. That is, a lexeme in tongue is capable of representing anything spatial, whether bounded or not, whose nature is perceived as corresponding to that depicted by the lexeme. It remains to examine what produces this difference between the two senses.

THE RELATION BETWEEN 'UNBOUNDED' AND 'BOUNDED'

The various grammatical means of bringing out the two lexical senses make it quite clear that what distinguishes them is whether or not the designatum is represented with some limitation or boundary. Something perceived as a mass or substance (e.g. *There's coffee on the table*) involves no such delimitation, whereas the same substance perceived as a thing or entity does involve delimitation (e.g. *There's a coffee on the table*). Such common observations of usage are invaluable as a starting point to indicate how different experiences of something with the same nature are represented by a lexeme, but they do not make explicit why these two senses are so widespread, why they appear to be possible ways of actualizing any lexeme. That is, the fact that the two senses can be found with (theoretically) any lexeme formed as a substantive suggests that there is something common to all such lexemes, something that can be actualized in these two ways. The terms "unbounded" and "bounded" have been adopted to help focus on this common element by designating how it is represented.

What is implied by all the terms used for these two senses of a lexeme – mass, non-count, or unbounded vs. thing, count, unit, or bounded – is a notion of space. Because space is so general a parameter of our experience, we are often unaware that whatever substantives represent has been conceptualized as occupying space, physical or mental. That is, even notions such as 'idea' must be thought of spatially.[3] This can be most readily shown by the fact that all lexemes formed as substantives have been configured for number during their morphogenesis, and as we shall see, it is this spatial parameter already represented in actualizing the lexeme that grammatical number configures. It has often been remarked that an 'unbounded' notion is not pluralizable, implying thereby that grammatical number is conditioned by this spatial dimension of a lexeme, by the way it is actualized. The point here is that for any lexeme to be formed as a substantive it must represent something as occupying space, and this includes lexemes representing abstract and immaterial entities, and even those representing time ('hour,' 'week,' etc.).

Thus there are good grounds for proposing that there is a spatial trait in every lexeme called on to provide the material import of a substantive, and that actualizing the lexeme involves characterizing this spatial parameter. This calls for opposed ways of representing the spatial parameter, hence the 'bounded' vs. 'unbounded' dichotomy, which corresponds to the lexeme's experiential correlate perceived as occupying a space either without or with limits (coffee spilt on the table vs. a cupful). The lexeme's potential for representing some entity in conformity with these two ways of perceiving space is a fact of tongue; in discourse only one of them is found actually represented in any given use. Between the fact of tongue and the fact of discourse, the process of actualizing the lexeme in order to represent the experiential entity realizes one or the other possibility. And as in all representational processes made possible by an opposition in tongue, the two possibilities arise in a certain order because any opposition presupposes two mutually exclusive positions within a common parameter.

The relation between the two possibilities in the process of actualization is not difficult to find. The very notion of delimiting presupposes something to delimit. Representing space without limits therefore appears to be a necessary precondition for representing space with limits. It follows that the process of actualizing the lexeme along its spatial dimension offers initially the possibility of a spatially unconfined representation, and subsequently the possibility of a spatially confined representation. In short, there appears to be an order in notional chronology between the two spatial senses so that the possibility of an 'unbounded' representation of space precedes that of a 'bounded' representation in the operation. It is this relation between two ways of representing space that gives the impression that the two senses of the lexeme are "closely related."

We have discussed a parallel opposition between two different senses of lexemes formed as verbs. Just as it is not possible to actualize a lexeme to be configured as a substantive without depicting it as either 'unbounded' or 'bounded,' so it is not possible to actualize a lexeme to be configured as a verb without depicting it as either 'stative' or 'developmental.' Why these constraints? The implications of this question concerning the relation between the lexical and the grammatical will be discussed in the final chapter. In the meantime, we will turn to another question arising directly from the lexeme, that of metaphor.

14

Metaphor

INTRODUCTION

Up to this point we have discussed variations in the sense of a lexeme that give rise to grammatical consequences in the word or its syntax. That is, any listener recognizing a word as a substantive knows that the speaker has given its lexeme either an 'unbounded' or a 'bounded' sense (as opposed to recognizing it as a verb with either a 'stative' or a 'developmental' sense) because this distinction is always part of the actualized lexeme of a substantive in English. Unlike the distinction between a common noun lexeme and a proper noun lexeme, this is a lexical distinction within a given lexeme to indicate the way a particular entity has been represented by the speaker. Moreover, since it is found in all lexemes formed as substantives, this distinction brings out a component common to all, a spatial trait which, as we shall see in the next chapter, permits the lexeme to be generalized during morphogenesis, thus categorizing it grammatically like all other lexemes formed as a substantive. In this way, we can understand how the lexical meshes with the grammatical to produce a space word, a systemic construct expressing the particularity of an individual lexeme set in a spatial universe.

Thus our discussion of substantives indicates that a particular lexical potential is actualized both with its own characterizing traits (some of which may be found in other lexemes, as in its hyperonym) and, as in all other lexemes to be formed as a substantive, with a spatial trait that gives rise to an observable variation in the actualized lexeme. This, however, is not sufficient for us to reach our objective of describing the makeup of the potential itself. In an attempt to find more indications in usage, we turn in this chapter to metaphor, restricting our comments to substantives, where the relationship between characterizing traits and range of representation (extension) is readily observable. It is hoped this exploratory venture will provide a basis for examining metaphorical usage of verbs and adjectives, a task that cannot be undertaken here.

Metaphor involves a very different sort of lexical variation, a variation that appears to be possible for most, if not all, lexemes formed as substantives. It is hoped that exploring metaphor from the point of view of a lexical potential will throw further light on the nature of a lexeme, because, unlike the variations already examined, the variation between literal and metaphorical senses cannot be observed through its grammatical consequences but only through the sense it expresses, a sense designating something outside the lexeme's usual field of representation. And yet the metaphorical sense expressed by a given substantive appears to be so closely linked to its lexeme that various studies have shown that substantives whose lexemes have something in common can express similar metaphorical senses. These findings will not be explored here since our aim, as always, is to discern what permits a speaker to obtain a metaphorical sense from most any lexeme.

SITUATING THE QUESTION

The considerable literature devoted to metaphors from antiquity to the present cannot be taken into account here, since it is for the most part concerned with the effect of metaphor in poetry and other literary works. Lyons (406), for example, points out that "the Greeks introduced a number of principles to account for the extension of a word's range of meaning beyond its 'true' or 'original' meaning. The most important of these principles was *metaphor* ('transfer') based on the 'natural' connexion between the primary referent and the secondary referent to which the word was applied." To consider metaphor from the point of view of the referent, or as "one of man's most fruitful potentialities" because it "alone furnishes an escape" from "the realm of the real, of what is already there,"[1] focuses on what metaphor can do, a necessary preliminary. But to limit discussion to its diverse effects in this way would divert us from our object here, which is to discern what in the lexical makeup of a word permits it to achieve such effects. Moreover, in our discussion the term 'metaphor' will be used only in a restricted sense, and will not include various figures of speech. This will permit us to focus on the problem as expressed by Beardsley (cited in Ortony, 34): "The problem is to understand how that radical shift of intension comes about; how we know that the modifier is to be taken metaphorically; and how we construe or explicate its meaning correctly." It is only after we understand how the speaker brings it about that we can explain how the listener construes the radical shift correctly, how "a listener/reader can go behind the literal meaning and construe the speaker/writer's intended meaning" (Taylor 1987, 131).

Thus our concern here will be that aspect of metaphor which is most challenging for a linguist: to explain how a speaker can use a word in a quite unpredictable sense, as in *She speaks poniards*. This unpredictability has suggested to some authors that metaphorical usage is a phenomenon arising outside language, a nonlinguistic phenomenon of no concern to linguists.[2] Others have maintained that metaphor calls on some special process arising either in the lexicon or in the syntax, a process we are little used to. Yet others such as J.M. Murry (cited in Hawkes, 67) consider that "metaphor is as ultimate as speech itself," and thus basic to language, and particularly to the historical development of lexemes giving rise to change of meaning. Some would analyze metaphor from the point of view of substituting one word's meaning for another, whereas others, going beyond the word, analyze it from the point of view of interaction between the meaning of the sentence and the word (cf. Ricoeur 1975), or even between meaning and the extra-linguistic referent. In general, such varied treatments approach metaphor from the point of view of the reader or listener and so will contribute little here, since our discussion will, as usual, approach metaphor from the point of view of the speaker. That is, in trying to discern how the speaker produces a metaphorical sense in discourse, we will hypothesize that it is somehow made possible by the potentiality of the lexeme in tongue.

Although the literature on metaphor will not be taken into account here, the very fact of its existence is of considerable importance for two reasons. In the first place, it indicates a widespread consensus that the distinction between the normal or literal senses of a lexeme and its metaphorical sense(s) is a fact of discourse, verifiable by any competent observer.[3] This is all the more important because there is no semiological evidence of metaphor, no morphological or syntactic indication that a distinctive lexical sense is being expressed. To realize that a speaker is expressing a metaphorical sense, the listener must of course be familiar with the word's lexeme, and then, as we shall see, must cast around in the context and situation to find some indication of the sense intended. The point is that nothing in the syntax or in the word itself signals "metaphorical sense" – another confirmation of the idea that a consensus concerning the observation of meaning expressed provides data.

The second reason is that, in treatments of metaphor, it is traditionally assumed that a metaphorical sense is a variant of the literal sense of a word and is somehow derived from it. This too is significant because it implies the hypothesis on which our discussion is based, namely that metaphor is another case of polysemy; that is, if the lexical component of a word exists as a potential in tongue ready to be used, then it appears that metaphor involves a particular manner of actualizing that potential. In preceding chapters, the same approach to polysemy avoided all the complications of classifying and declassifying substantives and verbs, and here it opens an avenue of reflection that avoids the predicament of those who propose that the meaning of a metaphor is derived by interaction with the sentence meaning or the referent.[4] Appealing to sentence meaning or referent in this way has probably been suggested by what any reader or listener does to interpret a word or sentence, but adopting that as an explanation would put speakers in an impossible cart-before-horse situation: they would have to construct a sentence and even refer it to their extra-linguistic experience before they could understand their own meaning as expressed by the words they had used to construct the sentence. We will therefore proceed on the assumption that metaphor does involve the speaker actualizing lexemes in either literal or metaphorical senses, to see if it throws any new light on how we use words in these two ways.

Keeping this hypothesis in mind, we will begin by evoking certain observations of usage, in particular discussing the listener in a situation that is no doubt familiar to most people – how to make sense of a new metaphor, one that at first sight is opaque. In the light of a listener's efforts to understand, we will then attempt to infer what is involved in the speaker's pre-conscious operation of actualizing the lexeme in a metaphorical sense. Only then will it be useful to turn to the basic issue involved here, to show how a word can designate something outside its own range of representation, how a metaphor can give rise to a "radical shift of intension"; to what another author calls "an erroneous statement" (cited in Sacks, 162); to what Ricoeur (250) considers, in Ryle's expression, a "category mistake." These views arise because of the traditional view that the limits of a lexeme's range of representation, its extension, are determined by its characterizing traits, its comprehension, whereas in metaphorical use a word is said of something beyond the limits of its range of representation, an extrapolation at the root of the term *metaphor* itself. Can these traditional views of a word's literal and metaphorical uses be reconciled?

MAKING SENSE OF A METAPHOR

Approaching a metaphor from the point of view of how a listener or reader makes sense of it has the advantage of bringing out a number of problematic issues. Although some metaphors are novel to the point of being esoteric, others such as *the cradle of the nation* or *the sunset of life* are transparent and suggestive, and yet others such as *the foot of the mountain* or *the leg of the table* are commonplace to the point of being stereotyped and may no longer be considered a metaphor by some. Is it really the same phenomenon in all such cases? Another fact to be explained is the ambiguity of many metaphors. Thus the example *The mind is a dovecote* first suggested to me that the writer was thinking of the mind as a series of little compartments, whereas the author discussing the example interpreted it as the mind being a place where ideas come and go. What makes it possible for a metaphorical use to give rise to different expressive effects for different readers, and even for the same person at different readings? As mentioned above, metaphor also raises a problem from the diachronic point of view. It is well known that the general or abstract meaning of many words today is the result of a metaphorical use now lost sight of, and even that "language is fossil poetry" (Emerson, cited in Bartlett, 498). How can this be explained?

Since "the metaphor poses a problem that each reader must solve for himself" (Bontekoe, 65), I will begin with a metaphor I had trouble interpreting to bring out something concerning the process involved. During a conversation some years ago (cf. my 1992 article) I failed to understand the expression *a teflon adolescent* and spent some time trying to figure it out. My failure to understand was due to the fact that I did not know how the notion expressed by *teflon* could be applied in this use to qualify the notion 'adolescent.' It seemed that *teflon* was not properly used, or rather that the meaning it brought into the phrase had nothing to do with what it was supposed to describe, its support 'adolescent.' Making sense out of the noun phrase thus consisted of trying to see what element or trait in the meaning of *teflon* could provide an import applicable to the meaning of *adolescent*. The interesting thing was that I had a vague, barely conscious feeling of projecting the different characteristics of *teflon* onto the notion of *adolescent* in order to find which of them could relate to it. Or as one writer (cited in Ortony, 190) approaching things from a psychological point of view puts it: "It appears that people interpret metaphors by scanning the feature space [of 'teflon' here] and selecting the features of the referent that are applicable to the subject [here 'adolescent'] ... the nature of this process is left to be explained." That is, it was as though, keeping the idea of *adolescent* clearly in view, I were scanning it through the idea of *teflon*, viewing it in the light of the various traits making up *teflon*'s lexical import. I was not looking for a formal, syntactic link between the two words (this adjectival link was obvious) but rather a material, lexical link between the two ideas on the level of the traits involved. Although not successful,[5] this scanning of one idea through another reminded me of the notion of viewing ideas discussed in a previous chapter, something we will return to in a moment.

A similar case of frustrating incomprehension arose when I first read the expression *a goosefeather sea* in a poem by Dylan Thomas. With the two notions in mind, one supposed to provide an import of meaning, the other its SUPPORT, I was unable to establish the link and carry out the operation of INCIDENCE of one to the other. This situation might be represented as in the following figure, where the incidence of the adjective's meaning-import to its support of meaning is depicted by a dotted arrow to suggest that it is prospective, not having been carried out yet.

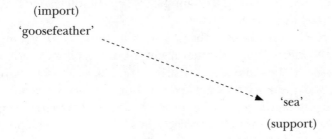

I had the impression that attempting to effect the prospective incidence here involved going over the various traits called to mind by 'goosefeather' to find at least one that could characterize something in 'sea' and so permit the transport of the import to the support, thereby constituting the noun phrase as a lexical unit. Once again it was like trying to focus one idea on another. When at last the image of white-tipped feathers occurred to me and was projected onto 'sea' to suggest whitecaps, the incidence was carried out and I understood.

The advantage of showing that a reader or listener may not understand a metaphor even though there is no problem understanding either the words or the syntax is to direct attention to the process involved at a moment when the mechanism of metaphor is momentarily blocked. We can now attempt to work back from what we do when confronted with a metaphorical use to what the speaker does to produce it, from the effect to the condition permitting it. In this way, we can perhaps obtain a better understanding of both the mechanism making metaphor possible and its various manifestations in discourse.

METAPHOR – A SCANNING IDEA?

Granted the number and variety of problems raised by metaphor, any indication of the processes involved is worth exploring. Since the notion of mental scanning seemed to describe quite adequately the way one goes about seeking an interpretation for difficult metaphors, it provided a starting point for reflecting on how the metaphorical use of a word is produced. The idea of a reader mentally looking at one lexeme, 'sea,' through the lens of another lexeme, 'goosefeather,' until some common trait comes into view recalled the expression "viewing idea." As was seen in chapter 4, this expression was used to characterize lexemes as instituted permanently in tongue, something worth recalling here since it will lead to the heart of our problem.

A typical substantive such as *house* will serve as an example to recall the idea of how lexemes monitor our ongoing experience. If we consider the number and diversity of distinct objects in our everyday experience that the lexeme 'house' is able to represent in ordinary literal usage, we can get some idea of its remarkable power of representation, as well as its capacity to categorize perceptions we do not intend to talk about. Normally acquired when one is young as a potential meaning in tongue, 'house' permits speakers to depict not only the objects of experience from their youth but also all the objects or sets of objects which will make up part of their later experience, however different they may be, provided they are judged by the speaker to be of the same nature. Furthermore, this same lexeme enables us to call to mind the very idea of 'house,' the concept, without having any particular house in view, and it can even be formed as an adjective or a verb.

Although the process of representation never emerges into consciousness, one can get a hint of its existence in cases where we hesitate in naming some object of experience as a result of failing to discern its nature clearly: *house* or *shed, briefcase* or *suitcase, fruit* or *vegetable*. In situations such as these, where the process of representation is momentarily frustrated by the failure to identify the nature of something in our immediate experience, we seem to view that entity or substance with different lexemes, or better, through different lexemes, trying to find a correspondence, an affinity between the lexeme and the experiential being. It is as though speakers were confronting impressions arising from the object of experience they want to talk about with the characterizing traits that make up the two lexemes 'house' and 'shed' in tongue, as if they were viewing the object of experience with the help of each lexeme to see which one best provides its correlate and thus permits the appropriate linguistic representation of the object. It is this way of imagining the interplay between a set of impressions in a speaker's ongoing experience and a lexeme in tongue that led to describing the latter as a viewing idea classifying the impressions even when there is no intent to represent and express them in speech.

The important point here is that a potential lexeme should not be conceived of as a ready-made representation all set to be lined up with other such representations in the sentence. Rather it is a means of depicting certain groupings of impressions in our experience which vary more or less appreciably but which are all perceived as entities of the same nature. That is to say, lexemes in tongue are ideas, each involving traits operating like a set of lenses, through which we monitor our experience of the moment. When something in our live experience, focused on in this way, becomes part of an intended message, the object of an expressive intent, this leads to representing its experiential impressions by activating correlative traits in the viewing idea–lexeme such as 'house' to produce the actualized meaning, the viewed idea that can be observed as the lexical sense expressed by a word in discourse. This way of considering the lexeme 'house' – as a means of focusing on and then representing something in the universe of our ongoing experience – can obviously be extended to the other lexemes in tongue, each of which can thus tell us of the speaker's intended message.

The above remarks suggest that something similar occurs when readers and listeners try to understand a metaphor. It is as if they used the lexemes 'teflon' and 'goosefeather' as ideas, as lenses, to scan 'adolescent' and 'sea.' That is, having in mind the meaning of *adolescent*, the listener focuses the meaning of *teflon* on it until some similarity is perceived – in this case the non-stick quality of teflon and the indifference to advice often associated with teenagers – and actualizes the corresponding trait(s). Likewise, by scanning the import called to mind by *sea* through the import of *goosefeather*, the reader discerns some like characteristic and actualizes 'goosefeather' to express it. The same approach would apply to metaphors such as *the sunset of life*, where 'sunset' ascribes traits such as 'serene ending' to 'life,' though in such common, readily understood metaphors the scanning process would not emerge into consciousness. Thus, it would appear that the viewing function of a lexeme can be used by listeners to scan the import of another word, which they already have in mind, in order to find a correspondence between the two notional imports. This even applies when the other word is not expressed, as in *She speaks poniards*. What 'poniards,' as direct object, characterizes is something necessarily implied by the verb *speaks*, i.e. words, but it attributes certain qualities to the words *she speaks*.[6]

If this manner of conceiving how we get to understand a metaphor is valid, it constitutes a significant step, since it links metaphor with something postulated as common to all lexemes: their viewing or scanning function. However, what is scanned in these examples is the meaning of another word or phrase as understood by the listener, not the intended message as experienced by the speaker, because our discussion has been concerned with how a metaphor is interpreted. We will therefore turn to the speaker to see if this way of looking at metaphor sheds any light on how a metaphor is created.

NON-METAPHORICAL USAGE

It is assumed, then, that lexemes in tongue constitute a "universe of viewing ideas" which allows us to focus on the complex of impressions making up our stream of consciousness at any moment, and that the intention to talk about something therein triggers the process of representing it by means of its corresponding viewing idea. This viewing idea, or lexeme, once actualized and given a grammatical form by morphogenesis, constitutes the mental import of a word, which will express the lexeme as a viewed idea, the linguistic representation of that experiential "something." The viewed idea a word expresses, its lexical import in discourse, may of course vary from one use to another according to the intended message, thus giving rise to polysemy. Our problem at this point is to explore how the actualizing of a metaphorical sense differs from the actualizing of literal, nonmetaphorical senses.

Perhaps the best way to approach this issue is from the very general point of view evoked by the term 'metaphor' itself: that is, the idea of a word's notion being carried or transferred to designate something of which it does not represent the nature. This is best brought out by concrete substantives such as *poniard* and *tiger*, which, when used literally, designate something according to its nature. In a metaphorical use such as *She speaks poniards*, the substantive *poniards* does not represent the nature of its designatum, i.e. the words and sentences she speaks, but rather certain characteristics of them such as hostility and aggressiveness. Similarly, in *Put a tiger in your tank*, it is not the nature of an animal but the power generally associated with it that is understood. This transfer from expressing what something is to expressing what it is like appears to be quite general in metaphorical usage, and it is in reflecting on the conditions leading up to these very different interpretations in discourse that we can perhaps discern the two different ways of actualizing the lexeme.

As was seen in chapter 12, it is commonly pointed out that in nonmetaphorical uses lexemes such as the above represent the class of individual entities which is itself a hyponym implying a superordinate class or type. That is, 'tiger,' 'poniard,' and 'house' can each designate an unlimited number of perceived or imagined individual entities as belonging to the same type or sort (having the same characterizing traits identifying its nature), while situating its type in a more general one, such as animal, weapon, building, each of which may in turn belong to an even more general class. This sort of hyponym-hyperonym organization appears to provide the categorizing import enabling many lexemes both to serve as a viewing idea by identifying an experiential being as belonging to a certain type, and, when called on to participate in the psychogenesis of a word, to represent that being by depicting its nature. It may well be this succession of notional categorizings, leading from the experience of a particular individual to representing its type or hyponym (such as tiger) distinct from all others, to representing a hyperonym (such as animal), to representing the most general category (such as thing or being), that permits the lexeme to be used in a literal sense. Although perhaps not applicable to all lexemes, as we have seen, to the extent that hyponym classification of this sort is applicable this hypothesis would thus provide the precondition for a notion in tongue both to serve as a viewing idea identifying something in the intended message and to provide the lexical import of a word depicting the nature of its designatum. The particular sense of the lexeme along with other components in the sentence, such as adjectives and determiners in the noun phrase or adverbs and direct objects in the verb phrase, would of course help particularize this abstract import so as to reflect more adequately the intended message.

This exploratory hypothesis of literal usage arises from the traditional way of explaining the hyponym-hyperonym organization of lexemes and, as we have seen, allows for variation in the way individual speakers conceive the nature of something. Understood in this way, a lexeme can adapt to our way of viewing and of representing something, even if our view develops as a result of further experience, provided we have the impression of something of the same nature.

METAPHORICAL USAGE

Since it is a lexeme's set of characterizing traits in tongue that predetermines its range of representation, the problem posed by metaphor is to explain how a given lexeme is actualized to permit the exceptional use outside this range; we want "to understand how that radical shift of intension comes about." In literal usage a substantive's lexeme expresses an entity's nature by means of a characterizing import, as we have just seen. What differs in metaphorical usage is that it expresses not the set of characterizing traits defining a particular nature, but only certain prominent characteristics of the set, those corresponding to striking impressions arising in the speaker's momentary experience, and so the lexeme can be applied to something of a different nature, something outside its usual range of representation.[7] How does this way of actualizing a lexeme come about?

We will begin, as in the case of literal uses, by examining that moment preceding the triggering of the word-forming mechanism, when the lexeme is exercising its function as a viewing idea. Since *poniards* and *tiger* in our two examples do not call to mind the nature defining the classes of their respective designata, it seems obvious that the speaker's or writer's aim was not to identify something but simply to characterize it. That is, when focusing on the intended messages that were to give rise to the two uses, the viewing ideas 'poniard' and 'tiger' did not provide their usual categorizing frames to indicate the type or nature of the entity they were focused on; rather they reflected certain striking impressions that those entities gave rise to in the speaker's experience – the hostility and aggressiveness of words in the case of 'poniards,' the power of fuel in the case of 'tiger.' This indicates that these lexemes in tongue offer the possibility of being actualized literally to give a hyponym view (if one perceives the weapon or the animal), or metaphorically, with a more impressionistic view, if some characteristic(s) of the perceived entity (the words or the fuel) strikes the speaker as similar to some well-known characteristic(s) of the weapon or the animal. It is these two possibilities of representing an entity that permit the speaker to depict either what it is or what it is like.

The particular impressions giving rise to a metaphor may vary with the same word. For example, *bird* can be used to designate a "guided missile" (W3), thanks no doubt to the impression of 'flying' common to the two. It can also designate a person perceived as exceptional in some way: *a queer bird, a clever old bird*. This may be suggested by the way a solitary bird often flits by, surprising us, or perhaps by the idea of a rare specimen bird-watchers commonly seek. In neither of these cases does it express the nature, an object and a person respectively, of its designatum. *Bird* can also be used to express "dismissal from employment," as in *I've got to get busy if I don't want to get the bird* (W3), a use I am not familiar with. The interesting thing in this example is to discern the trait(s) in the lexeme 'bird' solicited by a particularly striking impression in the speaker's idea of being dismissed – perhaps 'being chased away.'

Through metaphor, then, the usual hyponym effect, telling what something is, appears to be excluded, but in the above examples, *poniards* and *tiger* and *bird* do represent something as an entity or being (and not as an event). That is, in metaphorical usage such words "represent not only [their] characteristics but also some being as a support of these attributes" (Konrad, 88n). Thus a minimally classifying component limiting the range of representation – representing something as an entity – does seem to be involved here, but this component may not be developed to the point of representing the type or hyponym represented in literal usage. This minimally classifying component appears to be required for the lexeme to attribute certain prominent characteristics to some spatial entity outside the range of entities the lexeme designates in literal uses. We will return to this point in a later chapter.

Hyponym lexemes such as 'poniard,' 'tiger,' and 'bird' bring out this effect of similitude underlying metaphor most clearly, but the same sort of effect whereby the substantive designates something outside its literal range is also observed in a lexeme such as 'cloud' with no obvious hyperonym other than 'something.' To speak of someone as *in the clouds* or *under a cloud* does not call to mind the atmospheric entity itself, but only a mental state or social situation with certain of that entity's characteristics. Here too, some, but not all, of the lexeme's characterizing traits are actualized. Similarly, in *Time is an ever-rolling stream,* there is a relation of similitude, but not in *Oil is jobs* or *Time is money.* Here there is a relation of condition-consequence between subject and predicate.

Proper nouns present a parallel picture. In ordinary literal usage, as we have seen, actualizing their lexical potential involves traits characterizing not only a nature (person, place, or thing) but also a specific entity or individual as distinct from all others of the same nature. However, in an expression such as *an Einstein* the substantive categorizes its designatum as a human person, i.e. represents its nature and thus limits its range of representation. It also represents certain well-known characteristics of the person usually designated, but attributes them to some other individual. It thus appears that other characterizing traits required to specify the proper person are not called to mind. That is, in such uses only certain of the proper noun's characterizing traits are actualized and, as a consequence, can be attributed to an individual outside the minimal range of the proper noun. Although not always considered to be used metaphorically in expressions like the above, *Einstein* does manifest the same two properties observed above with *poniards, tiger,* and *bird,* namely expressing only striking characteristics and attributing them to an entity not otherwise within the lexeme's range of reference.

Thus proper nouns, like common nouns, can be used to designate an entity outside their representational range when their lexical matter is actualized to produce a version lacking certain traits, a dematerialized version, or more precisely, a version incompletely materialized. It is interesting to note that, as evidence that proper nouns are not meaningless, Jespersen (1924/1975, 67) comments on them in this use in substantially the same way: "out of the complex of qualities characteristic of the bearer of the name concerned ... one is selected as the best known, and used to characterize some other being or thing possessed of the same quality. But this is exactly the same process that we see so very often in common names, as ... when some politician is called an old *fox*." He assimilates this use of proper nouns to the metaphorical use of common nouns.

Thus it appears that for both common and proper nouns, the characterizing traits of their lexeme can be actualized either partially for a metaphorical use or fully for a literal use. In the next chapter, we will try to discern how these two possibilities are exploited to obtain such different results in discourse.

V THE GRAMMATICAL CONNECTION

15

Making Lexemes into Nouns

INTRODUCTION

Examining lexemes from the point of view of how their characterizing traits condition their range of representation has shown that, in ordinary non-metaphorical uses, common nouns bring to the sentence a representation characterizing the nature of an entity as perceived in the experience of the speaker. In many cases, that entity is depicted with certain identifying traits as a hyponym implying traits of a more general hyperonym, which can itself be represented by another lexeme. Some substantives may not have this hyponym effect, but they do imply a very general lexeme such as 'thing' or at least a vague, abstract notion such as 'something' or 'someone.' The characterizing traits of a lexeme may vary to some extent from one speaker to another. In scientific, philosophical, or other cognoscenti usage, it seems that the characterizing traits tend to be construed more analytically so that the speaker represents the experiential entity in a more abstract manner, but whatever the type of usage, the lexeme of a common noun represents an entity's nature as seen by the individual speaker. Since proper nouns always designate the same experiential entity, this minimal range of representation, granted the inverse relation involved, presupposes that proper nouns have a maximized set of characterizing traits permitting them to represent the particular individual and its nature (person, place, thing). In short, a lexeme's characterizing traits (comprehension) determine its range of representation (extension) in both common and proper nouns.

This does not appear to be the case in metaphor, where, as the notion of "transfer" so often evoked indicates, a common noun expresses certain prominent traits to characterize some entity of a different nature, an entity not within the lexeme's range of representation in literal uses. These traits do, however, imply a more general range, one extending to the entity represented in the metaphorical use and any other entities that manifest those characteristics, because here too the inverse relation between characterizing traits and range of representation comes into play. Similarly for proper nouns: when used improperly (if one can put it this way) to designate an individual outside their minimal range of representation, there is the same incomplete actualization of characterizing traits and the consequent extension of representational range, giving the same effect of transfer as in metaphorical usage of common nouns. In both literal and metaphorical usage, then, a substantive lexeme implies a range within which it represents one or more entities as a support for the characterizing traits it expresses.

Thus a substantive, whether common or proper, expresses traits characterizing the nature of the experiential entity represented – certain traits distinguishing it from, and other traits shared with, entities of a different nature. Furthermore, variation in the characterizing traits appears to be the factor differentiating the two types of substantive. A lexeme instituted in tongue as a set of traits capable of characterizing a type of entity by representing its nature will provide the lexical import of a common noun; a lexeme instituted as a set of traits capable of characterizing a specific entity and its nature will give rise to a proper noun. This leads to proposing two types of lexeme in tongue and raises the problem of how the process of ideogenesis can accommodate them.

A given lexeme of either type permits different uses, metaphorical and literal, and this appears to arise from a possible variation in actualizing its characterizing traits. Actualizing a lexeme's characterizing traits only partially in a given use gives a lexical import with a wider range of representation than is usually found with that lexeme and permits a metaphorical use expressing certain characteristics of the entity it represents, whereas actualizing its traits fully limits the lexeme to a literal use expressing the nature of the entity it represents. This poses another problem: how can a stable lexical potential be actualized to give rise to these different results in discourse?

We will approach these problems by adopting the same analytical technique used previously. That is, we will first examine the relation between the differences observed in each case – between common and proper nouns, between literal and metaphorical usage – and then attempt to operationalize it, i.e. infer the relative positions where each of the results is obtained in the process involved. The need to operationalize the data in this way arises from our initial assumption that, like everything else in tongue, a lexeme is a potential which must be actualized in order to be formed as part of a word to be used in discourse. It follows that distinctions of a given word's sense observed in discourse must arise from different ways of actualizing its lexeme. We will begin by looking at the two functions of a lexeme more closely than we did above.

VIEWING AND REPRESENTING

We have seen that a lexeme's set of characterizing traits includes traits distinctive of the nature of the entity represented, some of which are traits it has in common with other lexemes. On the level of perception, we distinguish an entity by grouping diverse sensory impressions, some of which are distinctive of the sort of entity perceived – say the colour, size, and cry of a crow for many people. The impressions permitting a speaker to distinguish a crow from other sorts of birds can be represented by specific traits along with traits it shares with other sorts of birds, all instituted in the lexeme. Since not all sensory impressions are distinctive, and since even those that are may vary somewhat, the distinguishing traits constitute an abstraction with regard to the complex of impressions making up our actual experience of the entity. As a consequence, the lexeme cannot represent and express the full complexity of the way we experience it; but on the other hand, being more abstract, it can represent quite different entities insofar as non-distinctive impressions are concerned. Furthermore, since what is distinctive may vary from one speaker to another, the characterizing traits of a lexeme may also vary (a variation between speakers that can be quite considerable for lexemes such as 'justice' which are not abstracted directly from sensory impressions).

Our diverse sensory impressions are not experienced simply as disparate intrusions on our state of consciousness (as when one is half awake) but as a percept, in the sense of "the meaningful impression of an object obtained by use of the senses" (W3). That is, before any representation by means of language can take place, sensory impressions are grouped into a percept, an experiential entity, thanks to a lexeme functioning not as a potential meaning but as a viewing idea. This grouping takes place when certain sensory impressions activate corresponding characterizing traits in the set of traits making up a viewing idea. In this way, the turbulence of sensory or other impressions arising into consciousness is reduced to a certain order by the unconscious intervention of our lexemes, which group them into an experienced entity (or quality or happening, etc.) and characterize its nature. Thus when used as the lexical import of a common noun, a lexeme expresses the nature of an entity, not an individual entity as such (though determiners and other elements in the noun phrase may help to specify some individual). The point here is that as a potential meaning, the lexeme is called on to represent the percept during an act of language, and this involves calling on the whole set of characterizing traits in order to obtain an abstract representation of the experiential entity's nature or type. This can be illustrated most clearly when there is only one such impression giving rise to the percept. For example, on hearing a cawing one might say *I hear a crow*, the lexeme expressing not merely the sound heard nor even the particular entity making that sound but the nature of that entity.

The two functions of a lexeme, viewing and representing, are brought out here. As a viewing idea, a lexeme groups sensory input (cawing) into a percept, an experiential entity, whose nature can then be represented by the potential meaning if one decides to speak of it. Considered as viewing ideas only, lexemes in the idea-universe of tongue are used for grouping sensory impressions into percepts; when we want to speak, the mind calls on a lexeme to represent the entity as experienced by actualizing the lexeme actually viewing it. Distinguishing between these two functions of viewing and representing is important because it permits us to discern two operations here: that of integrating sensory impressions, or a single impression, into a "meaningful impression" or percept corresponding to the lexeme, and that of actualizing the lexeme's potential to represent this percept. Our concern here is to see if these two functions, considered as two operations wherein one necessarily precedes the other, can help us discern the difference between proper noun and common noun lexemes, and the difference between literal and metaphorical usage of the same lexeme.

COMMON AND PROPER LEXEMES

As seen above, a proper noun lexeme has the capacity of representing both the nature of a specific entity and its particularizing characteristics, whereas a common noun lexeme cannot represent characteristics specifying an individual entity, but only characteristics specifying its nature, thus classifying it with other entities. Different lexemes can represent classes varying in range: most obviously, a hyponym such as 'crow' as opposed to its hyperonym 'bird,' whose range contains that of 'crow.' In chapter 11 it was brought out that a hyperonym such as 'bird' is itself a hyponym of 'animal,' and so on to a speaker's most general lexemes, such as 'thing,' 'entity,' 'being,' or 'person' for a human being. Does this reflect the way lexemes are organized in our universe of ideas?

To the extent that these considerations are generally valid for lexemes to be formed as substantives, it would suggest a sort of particularizing process in activating a lexeme as a viewing idea to confront something in our ongoing experience. Thus any speaker can classify a specific entity as a bird, but not all speakers have the lexeme required to particularize the experience still further by identifying it as, say, a chickadee or a nuthatch. Since 'crow' or 'chickadee' or 'nuthatch' is not a hyperonym for any other lexeme, at least in non-cognoscenti usage, this would appear to be as far as the process of particularization can be carried for common nouns. However, for proper nouns, as we have seen, the particularizing process, carried beyond what is required to identify a specific nature, accumulates enough characterizing traits to identify a specific individual.

Operationalizing observed differences between lexemes functioning as viewing ideas by comparing their degree of particularization has permitted us to understand what common and proper nouns have in common and what distinguishes them. The lexeme of every noun, made up of general traits and particularizing traits, is particularized to the point of being distinct from all other lexemes. On the other hand, where the process of particularization enables a lexeme to identify an entity by its nature, it gives rise to a common noun, but when carried to an extreme to enable a lexeme to identify an individual, it gives rise to a proper noun.

Hypothesizing the operation in this way is of course based on the traditional inverse relation between the distinctive material input of a lexeme and its representational range. To what extent it will prove valid, granted that categorizing may vary from one lexeme to another and from one speaker to another, can only be shown by detailed studies. The hypothesis does, however, bring out how common nouns of different degrees of generality and proper nouns can all be produced by the same underlying process. As such, the hypothesis raises the question of how a given lexeme, a specific representational potential, can be actualized to express different senses. That is, we have now to examine not the relation between different lexemes functioning as viewing ideas but the relation between different uses of the same lexeme in words with a grammatical function – the question of polysemy. We will begin with the most readily observed type of polysemy.

POLYSEMY: LITERAL VS. METAPHORICAL USES

Here we will be concerned with how a lexical potential, called to mind by a particularizing process to identify something, can be actualized to express such different senses in a sentence. We have already seen that a substantive used metaphorically expresses certain characterizing traits in common with its literal uses but predicates them of something outside its lexeme's range of representation. This will require us to examine how the ideogenesis of a lexeme can find a support not within its potential.

In discussing the viewing function of a lexeme, we saw that a single impression arising in our experience (cawing) suffices to activate a corresponding characterizing trait in a lexeme, which in turn, through its association with other traits, activates the lexeme itself (*I hear a crow*). In such cases, the lexeme viewing that impression is led to view it not just as a sound but as a percept, as an experiential entity of a certain nature. When, however, some striking impression (or impressions) in our experience (hostility, aggressiveness) activates a characterizing trait (or traits) in a lexeme ('poniard') but none of the other characterizing traits of the lexeme correspond to other impressions in that experiential situation, the lexeme as a whole is not activated to integrate the impression(s) into a percept, into an entity of a certain nature. If called to mind to participate in forming a substantive, that lexeme then exercises its representational function by depicting the striking impression(s) but not the nature of the entity giving rise to it. The material import of the lexeme thus consists only of the trait(s) activated by those impressions, traits characterizing a spatial entity whose nature remains unidentified by the substantive. The substantive represents "not only [these] characteristics but also some being as a support of these attributes" as Konrad puts it.

In the case of proper nouns, as well, the lexeme can represent some striking impression and none of the other particular impressions characterizing the person, place, or thing in literal uses. As a result, *another Shakespeare* can refer to any person considered to be a literary genius. Like common nouns, a proper noun used metaphorically is out of bounds, so to speak, but its range is more limited. *Shakespeare* here can depict another person but not a place or thing in the intended message: it represents the nature of the experiential being (a human) as well as the striking impression characterizing it. This of course raises the question of metonymy, as in *reading Shakespeare*, a question that has not yet been broached from the theoretical point of view adopted here. Might such an example be considered as involving a relation of entailment, a necessary link, like those observed in our above examination of *bear* and other verbs?[1]

Because a substantive in metaphorical uses has a reduced lexical import, it has a wider representational range than in literal uses. As a consequence, it may be said of anything giving rise to the same impression(s). This is the reason why, bereft of many of its characterizing traits in a metaphorical use, the lexeme of a common noun is incapable of representing the specific nature of the entity it represents. For the same reason, a proper noun in a similar use cannot on its own represent a specific person. Here again the inverse relation between characterizing traits and representational range comes into play. This comes out most clearly in proper nouns. In literal uses, all the characterizing traits of 'Shakespeare' (as understood by the particular speaker) are actualized to represent the proper individual but the individualizing traits are not actualized when the same word represents another individual, as suggested in the following figure:

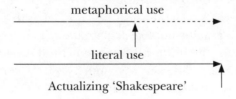

Similarly for common nouns: in literal uses to represent the nature of its referent, all the characterizing traits of 'poniard' are actualized, but in metaphorical uses to represent something outside this range, only certain prominent traits are actualized to characterize an entity otherwise unspecified, as suggested in the following figure:

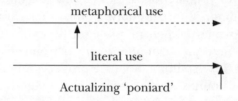

Actualizing 'poniard'

Viewing metaphor as the result of an incomplete actualization of a lexeme's characterizing traits in this way helps explain the impression of scanning when confronted with a momentarily opaque use, as mentioned in the last chapter. As listeners or readers, we try to discern through clues in the context which traits the speaker has actualized. It also allows for different interpretations of a metaphor, particularly in literary texts where one reader may actualize traits other than those actualized by others, or even by the writer. Since it is up to the listener/reader to work this out – to discern what *poniards* attributes to words and sentences – this gives rise to an element of freshness, of discovering a new relationship, in new metaphors. Each of these situations brings out the main point here, namely that metaphor results from an early interception giving an incomplete actualization of its lexeme and resulting in a partial representation of the experiential entity.

This view also helps us to understand why metaphor is generally considered to involve a transfer, or as we have seen, "an erroneous statement," "a category mistake." Such descriptions depict impressions arising for the listener/reader who compares a word in its two types of use. Furthermore, we can now see how the "radical shift of intension" is brought about during the process of generating a word's meaning. In fact, since it arises in the normal process of a speaker constructing a word, metaphor may be exploited with any word whose lexeme allows for an incomplete actualization. This view of metaphor opens the way for the historical development of meaning giving rise to words expressing different and more abstract concepts, and so helps explain why J.M. Murry considered that "metaphor is as ultimate as speech itself." Moreover, because a metaphor calls for an incomplete version of the lexeme, it is understandable that our most abstract words afford little or no possibility for it. If *thing*, for example, is "applicable to ... anything whose existence is inferred from its signs, its effects and the like" (*Webster's Dictionary of Synonyms*, s.v.), its lexeme in tongue would appear to be reduced to a minimum.[2]

These considerations bring out the adaptability of the lexeme when exercising its representational function in contributing to the forming of a word. It always portrays linguistically the impression(s) that activated it as a viewing idea by actualizing the corresponding trait(s), but can leave unactualized its other particularizing traits, thus permitting it to represent something outside its usual range of representation. In this way metaphor shows that a lexeme is actualized by responding first of all to the dominating impressions received from an experiential entity, and so brings out how effective an instrument of representation a lexeme is. Viewed in this way, metaphor also shows how a single meaning potential can be actualized to express different senses in discourse: a clear manifestation of polysemy. This brings us to the question of another widespread variation in sense discussed above: the possibility of a lexeme formed as a substantive to express an 'unbounded' or a 'bounded' sense, and the relation between the two.

POLYSEMY: SPATIALIZING THE LEXEME

Whether the process of actualizing a lexeme's characterizing traits is intercepted at its end to give rise to the literal use of a substantive, or at an earlier point to permit a metaphorical use, the result is a grouping of the actualized traits into what is variously called the lexical meaning (import, sense, content, notion, idea, concept, etc.) expressed by a predicative word. Every notion is imported into a sentence to be said about something, its support. In the case of an adjective, an adverb, or a finite verb, the lexical import has external incidence, i.e. is said about the import of another component of the sentence, as is made clear by syntactic means. A substantive, self-sufficient in this respect, has internal incidence, i.e. is said about itself, since its import brings in its own support. This is where the 'unbounded' vs. 'bounded' opposition comes in.

Although this opposition is called on to represent particular experiential impressions arising in a specific intended message (e.g. *coffee* vs. *a coffee*), its result can be discerned in every use of every substantive. It would therefore seem to reflect something quite general – so general, in fact, that one hesitates to include it among characterizing traits distinguishing particular lexemes. In chapter 13 we saw that what is involved here is representing an extent in space, either without limits or with limits. It was also pointed out that this would be a fitting way to prepare a support for a substantive's lexeme, a support to be configured by the substantive's grammatical subsystems providing spatial categorizations during the word's morphogenesis. Albeit general, boundedness involves a lexical opposition and so must arise during the ideogenesis of a substantive's lexeme. This poses the question of how this spatial component relates to the particular characterizing traits of a substantive's lexeme.

Although the characterizing traits of a lexeme particularize it in the sense of distinguishing it from all other lexemes, in themselves they represent something general, the nature of something in the intended message, "the essential 'cattiness' involved in being a cat." This very general view a lexeme provides of its designatum gives it a range of representation including a great variety of entities all of the same nature. In chapter 11 we saw that the lexeme of every substantive, concrete and abstract, appears to depict its designatum as something in space, an entity. This led to considering the 'unbounded' vs. 'bounded' opposition as expressing a spatial trait found in the lexical import of every substantive in English but representing what is specific to each substantive. That is, it now appears that this trait represents, not space in general, the container of all entities, but a specific space, that occupied by the particular entity.

Thus the 'unbounded' / 'bounded' opposition expresses the common spatial trait representing the space occupied by an entity in the intended message. This of course is an abstraction since, in our experience, no entity can be separate from the space it occupies, and yet as represented no entity is without the 'unbounded' / 'bounded' trait. Not only does the spatial trait provide the lexeme with a characteristic it shares with the lexemes of all other substantives, it also provides the lexeme with a linguistic support: it represents as its support the space occupied by the entity within the lexeme's representational range. That is, the lexical import provides its own support and so is said about itself. This even applies to abstract substantives such as *thought* vs. *a thought*, or as we saw in *a good knowledge of Greek*, lexemes whose designata do not occupy a physical space. Here, too, the spatial trait indicates that the lexeme is represented with a spatial support. And in the case of a metaphor, where the substantive does not express the nature of some entity but only certain of its characteristics, and so can refer to something outside its scope in literal usage, the lexeme brings in a spatial trait, indicating that it has a spatial support.

Here, then, it is being proposed that the ideogenesis of a substantive's lexeme involves spatializing its characterizing import, representing its inherent space as a support, either 'unbounded' or 'bounded.' As mentioned above, this process, observable only by its result, offers a double possibility for spatializing a lexeme, implying a sequence: an extent without limits is a precondition for limits to be represented. From this we can infer that when the lexeme is actualized with characterizing traits calling for no limits, the spatializing is intercepted before its term and it is the 'unbounded' space represented up to that point that provides the support. When limits are prefigured in the characterizing traits, we infer that the spatializing proceeds to its conclusion and a 'bounded' space is represented as a support for the lexeme. This is why lexemes with 'unbounded' spatial supports so frequently give rise to expressive effects of vagueness or mass, whereas with 'bounded' spaces as supports they give unit or count effects.

Thus spatializing involves representing the space occupied by the experiential entity as a support prefigured by the characterizing traits and therefore within the representational range of the lexeme. Actualizing one or other of the two possibilities is a question of how the characterizing import prefigures its support and not of how much space is involved, this being the role of the system of number. Number categorizes the lexical import by treating its spatial support. As a consequence, whether the support is 'bounded' or 'unbounded' entails certain constraints observable in the substantive's morphogenesis. As grammarians have often pointed out for number, substantives in the 'singular,' a sense presupposing a spatially limited support, always express a 'bounded' sense. Similarly for gender: because 'animate' gender (masculine or feminine) presupposes a 'bounded' sense, substantives expressing an 'unbounded' notion are found only with 'inanimate' gender, as exemplified by the example mentioned above *"It's not brutality,"* murmured little Hartopp ... *"It's boy, only boy."* Here *boy* is 'inanimate' in gender because it expresses something like 'boyish nature,' an 'unbounded' sense. Such facts indicate how the ideogenesis of a lexeme can condition its subsequent morphogenesis, leading to the substantive, the part of speech situating a word's lexeme in the universe of space.

This presupposes that, at the outset, the word's ideogenesis is oriented toward providing the material import for a space word, a substantive. We will return to this initial orientation of word formation in the next chapter, but it will clarify things if we first treat a question concerning the substantive and the adjective.

THE ADJECTIVE AS A NOUN

We have taken for granted that the meaning of every word is brought into a sentence to be said about something, that "every lexeme is an import of meaning that must find a support" (Guillaume 1990, 122). The lexeme of a substantive finds its support within what it signifies. Thus even if it signifies something temporal (*a moment, the past*), something abstract (*a principle, the species*), a process (*a think*), or whatever (*fear, my dream, beauty*), its characterizing traits are spatialized, thus providing their own support, as we have just seen. An adjective, on the other hand, finds its support not within what it signifies, but outside that – within what a substantive signifies. Here the question to be examined in the light of our analysis is why an adjective, unlike an adverb, is restricted to finding a support for its lexical import in that of a substantive.

As pointed out in chapter 5, grammarians describe the use of *small* in the well-known book title *Small Is Beautiful* as "conversion" of an adjective to be "used as" a substantive and explain this as "simply giving new grammatical properties" to *small*. We will try to discern what property distinguishes the two, and thus how the forming of an adjective differs from that of a substantive, by approaching the question from the point of view of the process involved in the speaker actualizing a lexeme. There appears to be little difference between the characterizing traits of 'small' in the above use, and its traits when used as an adjective. What does differ, however, can be brought out by approaching such nominal uses from the point of view of spatializing the lexeme. The fact that grammarians do not discuss adjective lexemes in terms of the 'unbounded' vs. 'bounded' opposition[3] is significant because in this example 'small' is actualized to express an 'unbounded' notion. This would suggest that the spatializing of lexemes formed as substantives, as described in the preceding section, is carried out when 'small' is formed to function as a substantive. There is, in fact, something in this use of 'small' that is common to every substantive, namely that it provides an internal spatial support for its own characterizing import: it expresses the vague, 'unbounded' idea of 'anything small.' That is, the lexeme 'small' is not "converted" or "given new grammatical properties" in the above example,[4] but is formed as a substantive during the act of writing.

At first sight, this might seem to entail that when 'small' or any other lexeme is formed as an adjective there is no spatializing process involved in its ideogenesis. As we shall see below, this argument may well apply to adverbs, which can relate to a support of most any type, but the fact that adjectives are constrained to find their support in the spatialized lexeme of a substantive suggests they have an inherent affinity with the substantive. That is, an adjective's lack of an internal spatial support is not merely an absence, but appears to be somehow built into an adjectivized lexeme as a specific syntactic relation to be accomplished, a capacity to be exploited when it takes its place in the noun phrase being constructed. This, in fact, is made manifest by the agreement of adjectives in languages such as French.

To suggest how this capacity can be represented within the lexeme, how 'small' can be construed as an adjective with the capacity to be predicated of whatever external spatial support the speaker provides for it in a substantive (but not in a verb, an adverb, etc.), we can return to the above discussion of how the lexeme's integrated generalization provides a spatial support for a substantive. Rather than assuming that there is no such spatializing process involved in adjectives, we will suppose that this internal generalizing process is part of actualizing 'small' to be an adjective, but that it is intercepted the moment it starts. That would leave the rest of the space-depicting process to be actualized in discourse by its external incidence. This would make the adjective's characterizing import dependent on an external spatial import for its support, a support to be found outside the adjective only in a substantive (or a pronoun).

If the analysis up to this point is valid, it helps explain why, unlike an adverb, an adjective is formed to find its support in a word with an actualized spatial support, a substantive. It also helps us understand how so many lexemes usually formed as adjectives can be readily formed as substantives in English. This would entail realizing their spatializing process and intercepting it either, as in the case of 'small' above, at some mid-point to give an 'unbounded' support within the lexeme, or, as in the case of 'an empty,' 'an intellectual,' and many others (cf. Huddleston and Pullum, 1642), at its final instant to give a 'bounded' support. On the other hand, the lexeme 'fun,' which is usually formed as a substantive, can be adjectivized, as in *a very fun person* (1643), by intercepting its internal spatializing the moment it starts.

Thus, I am proposing that when a speaker actualizes a lexeme to be formed as an adjective, the process of representing a spatial support seen above for the substantive must be undertaken but intercepted at its beginning, before it depicts enough space to provide a support, thus leaving its spatial support prospective. This would restrict the adjective to finding a support in a substantive, but give it the capacity to be incident to any substantive (provided there is some affinity between their characterizing imports, of course). This amounts to proposing the same spatializing process for the lexical phase of all nouns, whether adjectives or substantives, distinguishing between them by the point where the spatializing process is intercepted: at the beginning for an adjective, in the middle for an 'unbounded' substantive, and at the end for a 'bounded' substantive, as suggested by the following figure.

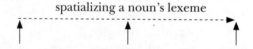

Our exploratory discussion thus results in a view reminiscent of the traditional manner of designating these parts of speech as 'adjective noun' and 'substantive noun,' designations originally based on their common declensions. Besides helping us understand why they had common declensions, the view that the same spatial trait, more or less actualized, provides the link between the lexical and grammatical imports in both word types permits us to explain how so many lexemes can be readily actualized in both these syntactic roles. Further discussion of this capacity of lexemes will be undertaken in the next chapter, where we bring in our findings of lexemes formed as verbs.

CONCLUSION

Starting from common observations of substantives in discourse, we have attempted to analyze their lexemes in tongue as potentials making the observed variations possible. The distinction between metaphorical and literal senses was analyzed as the result of actualizing the characterizing traits of a lexeme differently, either partially or fully, and so was proposed as a manifestation of polysemy. The distinction between 'unbounded' and 'bounded' senses was analyzed as arising from actualizing the spatial trait common to all lexemes formed as substantives differently, represented either without or with limits, and so was proposed as another case of polysemy. The distinction between forming a lexeme now as a substantive, now as an adjective, was analyzed as a third way of actualizing a lexeme's spatial component and so is proposed as another case of lexical polysemy, even though it results in a different part of speech because the spatial component is not developed enough in the adjective to provide a support for its lexeme. Each of these distinctions, and particularly the last one, indicates the degree of potentiality of any lexeme in tongue if it allows for such different possibilities of actualization. These three cases of polysemy are to be contrasted with the distinction between common and proper nouns, which was analyzed as arising from lexemes of different types in tongue and so is not a case of polysemy.

To the extent that these proposals are valid, we can conclude that a lexeme in tongue is made up of a particularizing component, or set of characterizing traits, that is variously actualizable. However, no lexeme's characterizing component has yet been analyzed, and so the question remains open as to whether some of the different senses dictionaries attribute to a substantive or adjective are also manifestations of polysemy, or whether they are all expressive effects, i.e. the outcome of combining a word's actualized lexical import with its own grammatical import, and with those of other words in the noun phrase and in the sentence, and with impressions arising in the speaking situation. Although the spatial trait is found in all substantives and adjectives, one hesitates to attribute it to the lexeme in tongue, since many lexemes are readily used as verbs as well. In the next chapter, where these findings on substantives and adjectives are compared with those from chapters 7 to 11 on verbs, we will see that, as a potential, the lexeme is even more abstract than envisaged so far.

16

Space Words, Time Words, and Adverbs

LEXEME AND PART OF SPEECH

We have seen (chapters 4–6) that we construct words only when we need them, that is, only when we want to say something about what we have in mind. This entails the intention to construct a discourse, a sentence (in the broad sense) or sentences that will express our intended message. This expressive intent entails the intention to represent our message by an appropriate word or words capable of forming the required sentence. The important point for our discussion here is that the constructing of a word is preceded by, prompted by, the intention to construct a sentence in which the word will play a syntactic role. The function that a word is to fulfill in the projected sentence is already foreseen when the actualization of its lexeme is undertaken to represent something in the intended message. That is, the word-forming mechanism starts by evoking the part-of-speech system as a whole, and then, in the light of the role foreseen for a particular word in the projected sentence, activating a particular part of speech and putting it on standby, so to speak, until the lexeme is actualized and ready to be configured by its formative subsystems.

Any act of speech involves an encounter between our acquired tongue and a momentary experience, some extra-linguistic content of consciousness we want to express by means of language. In English and other part-of-speech languages "like Sanskrit, which already weave into the unity of the word its relations to the sentence" (Humboldt, 128), this encounter involves representing components of the intended message to form words and giving them the capacity to fulfill their function in the projected sentence. That is, lexeme and part of speech are both present from the beginning of the word-forming process, the lexeme as the viewing idea already focused on something in the intended message, and the part-of-speech system activated and kept on standby as the first step in forming a word representing that something. Both, however, must be adapted to the particularities of that intended message: the viewing idea called to mind provides a lexical potential that must be actualized during ideogenesis to represent the experienced entity in view, and the subsystems of the particular part of speech must be exploited during morphogenesis to configure that actualized lexeme for its role in the sentence. These two components of a word's mental import are discernible in the sentence, but to understand the essential relation between them, they must be examined separately and the complicated process of word-forming described.

In this study we have examined the lexical components of verbs and substantives separately because of the very different sentence functions they are called on to play. Here we will compare the findings to see what light they throw on the lexeme as a potential in tongue prior to any grammatical configuration.

SPACE WORDS AND TIME WORDS

There is a striking parallel between lexical components of verbs and substantives: in each case the lexeme has two possible actualizations, 'developmental' or 'stative' for verbs and 'unbounded' or 'bounded' for substantives. In substantives, as we have seen, this double possibility manifests an underlying generalization in actualizing a lexeme whereby a spatial trait is abstracted from the traits characterizing the particular entity to provide a support for them. In verbs this double possibility also manifests an underlying generalization, but here what is abstracted from the traits characterizing the particular happening is a temporal trait: the duration involved in any happening. Furthermore, as in substantives, this temporal trait providing a generalization within the lexeme is taken up, along with its characterizing traits, by morphogenesis and configured as an event by the subsystems of the verb conjugation to give the lexeme a part of speech and situate the event in the universe of time. We see here the basis for calling verbs time words, as opposed to which substantives can be considered space words. It remains, of course, that verbs also have a spatial trait, represented by their grammatical person, enabling them to seek an external spatial support in their subject.

This parallel between the two types of word implies a similarity insofar as their lexemes are concerned. In both cases, the lexeme consists of traits with the particularizing role of characterizing something, an entity or happening, as well as a generalizing trait preparing it for further generalization during morphogenesis. Thus, if what was proposed above proves valid, then for a lexeme to be formed as a noun (substantive or adjective) or as a verb, its actualization must have as support a spatial or temporal trait, which is configured during the word's morphogenesis. Furthermore, the discussion of "conversion" in chapter 5, which brought out how readily many lexemes can be formed by different parts of speech ('empty' for example can be formed as a substantive, an adjective, or a verb) leads to the conclusion that the lexeme in tongue has the potential for being formed by any of them. That is, a lexeme as a viewing idea is a set of traits but no specific grammatical vocation. However, when called upon to represent something in the intended message, a lexeme must be actualized as part of a word, a word whose function in the projected sentence is foreseen, i.e. whose part of speech with its subsystems is already activated and ready to configure the lexeme, either spatially or temporally. It is in view of this projected function that a lexeme is actualized with its generalizing trait.

To complete this exploratory survey of how the lexical relates to the grammatical during the word-forming process, it remains to mention the fourth predicative part of speech: the adverb.[1]

THE ADVERB

Like the adjective, the adverb is a word with external incidence, a type of word whose capacity for establishing syntactic relations requires it to find a support outside its own field of representation. Unlike the adjective, however, an adverb cannot make its lexical import incident to that of a substantive. This fact implies that there is no generalizing process of abstracting a spatial support, even incipient (as in the case of the adjective), in the ideogenesis of an adverb's lexeme. An adverb can be incident to a verb, but this cannot be taken as indicating that the internal generalizing of its lexeme is a process of abstracting a temporal support, as in a verb's lexeme, because an adverb can also be incident to an adjective. Although the particular characterizing traits of any given adverb will limit its range of usage, adverbs can also find a support in another adverb and in various other sentence components. This complexity of usage, which makes the adverb "the most nebulous and puzzling of the traditional word classes" (Quirk et al., 438), is analyzed in great detail in Guimier's study, which includes valuable discussions of the adverb's place among the parts of speech. From a lexical point of view, all this would seem to suggest an ideogenesis allowing for more syntactic possibilities than any of the other predicative parts of speech, and so raises the question of what is involved in actualizing the lexeme of an adverb. What sort of internal generalization underlies the adverb's characterizing traits to provide a link with its morphogenesis?

Besides their syntactic versatility, adverbs differ from the other predicative parts of speech in having no declension or conjugation. This suggests that the adverb has no subsystems in its morphogenesis, that its lexical import has direct access to the part of speech and requires no morphological support to complete its generalization. That is, if, without any intervening categorizing subsystems (like aspect, tense, etc. for a verb), a lexeme can be formed as an adverb and made incident to an adjective lexeme, or to a verb lexeme, or to another adverb lexeme, etc., then the adverb's lexeme must be sufficient in itself to permit these possibilities. Not having an internal support (like the substantive), an adverb must seek an external support, but not having a built-in orientation for its own external incidence (like an adjective or a verb), it can bring to the sentence only what is inherent in every lexeme: the need to be said about something.

How should this be conceived? As a component of the lexeme requiring it to be said about something else in the sentence? Compared with interjections such as *Wow!* which cannot be said about anything in the sentence but only about the intended message, adverbs do have the capacity to seek a support in the sentence. Compared with adjectives, adverbs bring in no predetermination of the nature of their support. As a consequence, the adverb can exercise this capacity only by joining in the support-seeking of another word, phrase, etc., by being incident to an adjective, a verb, etc. which is itself in the process of finding an external support. Does this entail proposing a sort of support-seeking trait for an adverb lexeme, calling for its syntactic incidence to some other meaning in the sentence – or to the sentence meaning itself? Only a meticulous examination of the diverse types and uses of adverbs as described in Guimier's study will permit us to discern what types of polysemy they manifest and thus provide a basis for inferring the sort of generalizing trait inherent in their lexeme.

THE LEXICAL AND THE GRAMMATICAL IN A WORD

These considerations bring us to the point where the lexeme, whatever the part of speech it is observed in, is seen to exist in tongue as a potential in itself before being grammaticized for use in a sentence, before any prospective part of speech provides a blueprint, so to speak, for integrating it into a word. What then gives a lexeme its unity and makes it a distinct entity in tongue? To situate this question, key in lexical semantics, we will summarize the general relation between the lexical and the grammatical within the word.

We have seen that it is a commonplace that every word is formed to be said about something, or in analytical terms, that "every lexeme is an import of meaning which must find itself a support." This requirement of finding a support is thus inherent in the very makeup of the lexeme itself. A lexeme's support may be found within the word's ideogenesis through a generalizing spatial trait; it may be found within the word's ideogenesis through a generalizing temporal trait, calling for a spatial support outside the word; the support may be partially determined within the word but the actual support found outside it; or the support may be found through the incidence of another word or phrase to its support. This is what orients the lexeme toward one of the generalizing systems in tongue – substantive, verb, adjective, or adverb respectively. This manner of conceiving the two-phase operation of producing a lexical word involves actualizing the lexeme through ideogenesis and grammatically configuring it through morphogenesis until it is provided with the part of speech enabling it to perform the syntactic function foreseen for it in the sentence. What is involved here is Guillaume's general theory of the word in part-of-speech languages, a subject that cannot be developed here.[2] For our purposes, the important point is the way the lexical import signified by a word relates to the grammatical import it consignifies – the way the actualized lexeme, through its generalizing trait, is oriented toward the support it is to characterize.

The attempt to explore the lexical import of the predicative parts of speech has taken us from substantives predicating their lexeme of their own support, to adjectives predicating their lexeme of a support in a substantive (or pronoun), to finite verbs predicating their lexeme of a support in time and subsequently of a support in a noun phrase subject, and finally to adverbs predicating their lexeme of practically any word seeking a support in the sentence. This does not of course take in the non-predicative parts of speech, grammatical words such as auxiliaries and pronouns, because their makeup does not include lexemes but rather far more abstract material imports organized in systems. Nor does it answer the key question raised above concerning the makeup of a lexeme in tongue.

VI CONCLUDING REMARKS

Conclusion

In trying to make sense out of meaning, we began by situating the question as seen by linguists and other writers, and then turned to examining it from a scientific point of view, arguing that, though introspective, the observation of meaning expressed by sentences, phrases, or even words permits communication. Since communication presupposes a consensus of qualified observers, the meaning observed can be considered data. Assuming there to be an order or system behind what has been observed (the second necessary condition for adopting a scientific approach), and considering that "unless we already have some hypothesis in mind, we are unable to know which portions of our 'observation' are relevant and which are not," we turned to Guillaume's theory of how a word is constructed during the act of language in order to distinguish between its lexical and grammatical imports and to bring out that these components exist as potentials, ready to be actualized whenever required to form a word.

This involved analyzing the act of language as beginning with speakers' expressive intent, their desire to express in a sentence or sentences some experiential content already monitored by appropriate lexemes acting as viewing ideas. Since language can express only what it has represented, the expressive intent gives rise to the intention to represent that intended message by means of words. This representational intent triggers an appeal to the formal system of systems in tongue to provide the part of speech for each lexeme in order to produce, one by one, the required words, those capable of representing and expressing the particular intended message and of functioning syntactically as the projected sentence requires of them. Provided the sentence is understood, this permits listeners to reconstruct (more or less faithfully) what the speaker had in mind, i.e. refer the sentence to its designatum. It is this overall understanding of the act of language that provided the general, hypothetical viewpoint from which to consider apparent polysemy in the data.

The observations of lexemes drawn from detailed studies of some twenty different verbs provided data posing the problem. From the point of view of the speaker, who forms the word and constructs the sentence (and not the listener, who analyzes the word and reconstructs the sentence), our examination of the data led to two proposals. All these lexemes have the possibility of being actualized as either 'stative' or 'developmental,' and since this view concords with that often put forward in other studies of the verb in English, it was proposed these two senses are a manifestation of lexical polysemy. Also observed in these verbs was the expression of different senses notionally linked by a condition-consequence relationship, a finding that arose frequently enough in the data for it to be proposed as another case of lexical polysemy but that has yet to be explored in the usage of other lexemes formed as verbs to validate this proposal.

Turning to substantives, three generally accepted, non-grammatical distinctions observed in usage provided the data. Considered in the light of the traditional comprehension vs. extension relationship, the difference between common and proper nouns was seen to be the outcome of different lexemes instituted in tongue and so not to be a manifestation of polysemy. The distinction between 'unbounded' and 'bounded' senses, which is common to all lexemes formed as substantives but is not attributed to any grammatical category, was proposed as a manifestation of lexical polysemy. A third general distinction in the meaning expressed by lexemes is that between literal and metaphorical senses, a distinction not limited to substantives. This was proposed as another manifestation of lexical polysemy, since only an incomplete actualization of characterizing traits can account for the way metaphor permits a lexeme to designate something outside its range of representation as observed in literal uses.

Our findings of course invite further study to see if these proposals are valid. No attempt has been made to examine metaphor in other parts of speech or on the level of the noun phrase, nor have uses involving metonymy been analyzed. Furthermore, it is important to undertake the detailed study of verbs other than those discussed here to check the findings presented. By starting with the various senses attributed to a word in dictionaries, one can attempt to distinguish expressive effects combining other imports in the context from different actualized senses of the lexeme itself which would be a manifestation of polysemy. One important aspect of this for substantives will be to determine whether distinctions between 'general' and 'particular,' or 'abstract' and 'concrete,' arise from the lexeme as different senses and not from the phrase or sentence as different expressive effects.[1]

To complete this study, and to explain the parallel dichotomies between substantive and verb, we explored briefly the relation between actualizing a lexeme and grammaticizing it, the two phases required to form a word's import. It was proposed that the 'unbounded' vs. 'bounded' dichotomy expresses a trait found in all substantive lexemes, giving the lexeme a spatial support which permits it to be taken up and configured by the subsystems of gender, number, and case, making it a substantive. It was also proposed that a lexeme with the same generalizing trait, but not actualized enough to provide an internal support, is formed as an adjective, a word that seeks a support in a substantive's lexeme. Moreover, the widely observed 'stative' vs. 'developmental' dichotomy in verbs was also considered a manifestation of a generalizing trait giving the lexeme a temporal support that prepared for its configuring by the subsystems aspect, tense, etc. leading to the part of speech 'verb.' The adverb's lexeme, which has no internal support, either prospective or actualized, for its incidence, appears to configure a lexeme with no internal generalizing trait except the potential common to all lexemes, that of seeking a support it can be predicated of. In discourse this enables the adverb to find a support in the ongoing incidence of some other sentence component. In this way, taking into account the grammatical consequences of forming the lexeme can throw some light on the lexeme itself. Some of these proposals may throw light on the word-forming system itself, the most general system of a language, which ensures that every word says something about something, about some support.[2]

Since this has been an exploratory study, most of the proposals made must be considered tentative. To the extent that they prove valid, they will throw some light on the lexeme. It goes without saying that any further study that confirms, rectifies, or replaces them with more adequate explanations will contribute to progress in the field of lexical semantics, and particularly with regard to the crucial problem of polysemy. This essay does, however, provide some confirmation of the basic assumption that a word's formative elements are permanent potentials available to the speaker, and that the word itself must be (re)constructed each time it is required in a sentence. This assumption has permitted us to explain how the same lexeme can give rise to different lexical senses and to opposed versions in substantives and verbs, how it can be grammaticized by different parts of speech, how it can be used creatively in a new word or in metaphor to express an unforeseen relationship – all this without an appeal to hypothesized rules which can so easily be reified.

For subsequent work in lexical semantics it is worth emphasizing two important conditions brought out in this essay. It is essential to have a clear concept of that much-neglected linguistic universal, the word – an analysis or theory of a word that distinguishes between its two meaning components, the lexical and the grammatical, and describes the operation combining them to form the word's meaning. Without this, there can be no distinct view of a word's lexical import and how it contributes to the syntactic construction of the sentence. Secondly, distinctions in sense must be widely attested, either by grammars ('mass' vs. 'count,' so-called "conversion," etc.), or by detailed study of particular lexemes in numerous real examples of usage. Only a widespread consensus of competent observers can give data arising from introspection the desired scientific validity.

It remains that describing the set of characterizing traits constituting a lexical potential in tongue has not been achieved. According to Guillaume (1992, 198), this is an impossible task: "On the material [lexical] level of tongue, it is absolutely impossible to get an exact view of the fundamental and in a way essential sense of a word." Is this a reaction occasioned by frustrated attempts to analyze the lexeme, or a realization that he is confronted with the ultimate constituent of his object of enquiry, recalling that of certain researchers in the physical sciences? Whatever the case, much remains to be done in our attempts to make sense out of meaning.

Glossary

ACTUAL MEANING or SENSE: one of the possible representations a LEXEME or MORPHEME can express in DISCOURSE. (See also POTENTIAL MEANING)

CHARACTERIZING TRAITS: the set of attributes, characteristics, or features included or comprehended in the word's lexical meaning. (= comprehension)

CONSIGNIFY: to signify a word's grammatical meaning when combined with its lexical meaning.

DENOTATUM: the spatio-temporal (extra-mental) event or entity denoted by a word or expression. (See also DESIGNATUM)

DESIGNATUM: the experiential (mental) entity in the INTENDED MESSAGE referred to by a word or expression. (= REFERENT)

DISCOURSE: the actual speech or texts a speaker or writer produces. (See also TONGUE)

EVENT TIME: a happening's duration as represented by the grammatical forms of the verb.

EXPRESSIVE EFFECT: the synthesis of two or more ACTUAL MEANINGS in discourse.

FORMAL SIGNIFICATE: the grammatical form a word brings to the sentence. (See also MATERIAL SIGNIFICATE)

IDEOGENESIS: the mental process of actualizing a word's MATERIAL SIGNIFICATE. (See also MORPHOGENESIS)

IMPORT: the meaning a word, phrase, or clause brings to the sentence. (See also SUPPORT)

INCIDENCE: the process of transporting an import of meaning to a support within language.

INTENDED MESSAGE: a content of consciousness (feeling, percept, thought, dream, etc.) that one wants to express by means of language.

LEXEME: the lexical meaning (MATERIAL SIGNIFICATE) imported by certain words (substantives, adjectives, adverbs, verbs) to be formed by their grammatical meaning. (See also FORMAL SIGNIFICATE)

MATERIAL SIGNIFICATE: the lexical or abstract systemic sense a word brings to the sentence. (See also FORMAL SIGNIFICATE)

MORPHEME: a unit of grammatical meaning that provides a generalizing form for a word's lexical meaning.

MORPHOGENESIS: the mental process whereby the MORPHEMES constituting a word's FORMAL SIGNIFICATE categorize its MATERIAL SIGNIFICATE. (See also IDEOGENESIS)

NOTIONAL CHRONOLOGY: the inherent temporal priority of notions such as 'cause,' 'condition,' etc. with regard to 'effect,' 'consequence,' etc.: an order imposed by common experience.

POTENTIAL MEANING or SIGNIFICATE: a sign's constant mental counterpart in TONGUE permitting the actualization of various senses in DISCOURSE. (See also ACTUAL MEANING)

PSYCHOGENESIS: the mental operations involved in forming the meaning of a word, both lexical and grammatical.

RANGE OF REPRESENTATION: the range of entities, events, qualities, etc. in the INTENDED MESSAGE a LEXEME can represent. (See also CHARACTERIZING TRAITS)

REFERENCE: referring the meaning expressed to its extra-linguistic DESIGNATUM in the speaker's INTENDED MESSAGE.

REFERENT: the INTENDED MESSAGE (or something in it) designated by the meaning of a word, phrase, or sentence. (= DESIGNATUM)

SEMIOGENESIS: the process of actualizing a word's sign during the act of expression. (See also PSYCHOGENESIS)

SUPPORT: that which an IMPORT of meaning characterizes by being made incident to it.

TONGUE: the pre-conscious part of our language permitting us to produce whatever words and sentences we need. (See also DISCOURSE)

VIEWING IDEA: a POTENTIAL MEANING in TONGUE confronting the universe of our ongoing experience, organizing it into percepts.

Notes

INTRODUCTION

1 This is implied by claims that mental phenomena "are features of the brain" (Searle 1984, 19) or that "states of mind begin physically, and physical they remain" (Damasio, 15, note).
2 Words introduced in small caps are used in a technical sense and are listed in the Glossary.
3 Cf. Artigas, 27–57.
4 Jacob, 29 (my translation).
5 Fowler, 95.

CHAPTER ONE

1 Dawson, 77.
2 Cited in Waldron, 74.
3 Ibid., 74.
4 Ibid., 148.
5 Orwell, 265.
6 Ibid., 49.
7 Dalrymple.
8 Cited by Dilworth, x.
9 *Four Quartets*.
10 Frye, 1124.
11 Cited in Bartlett's *Familiar Quotations*, 749n19.
12 Tennyson, 226.
13 Note that *sentence* is used here to designate "real pieces of speech" or writing, not "abstract grammatical elements" as in other approaches to semantics (cf. Saeed, 14).

14 See my *Language in the Mind*, ch. 15, for a more detailed discussion.
15 We will not adopt the point of view of Frye and others that the underlying physiological processes are part of thought.
16 Among these categories are the parts of speech in English, but this is not intended to imply that they are necessarily found in all languages.
17 Cited in Guillaume 1984, 145.

CHAPTER TWO

1 Cited in Waldron, 184. Cf. Humboldt, xix.
2 See the 1984 translation (138–65) for various texts of Guillaume touching on these topics.
3 Guillaume 1987, 14.
4 Guillaume 2005, 17. All citations from Guillaume, except those from 1984, are my translations.
5 Strictly speaking, the more general term *vocable* (a sayable bit of meaning) should be used here rather than the term *word*, which implies both lexical and grammatical meaning. Since our concern is with English, however, there is no need to consider minimal units constructed according to a different typology.
6 The opening sentence of Guillaume's first major publication reads: "The present work is an attempt to apply the comparative method to the formal part of languages," i.e. to the abstract meanings of the articles in Modern French. Valin 1996 describes this major innovation in some detail.
7 In order to distinguish our permanent language resources from *speech* or *discourse*, the term *tongue*, as commonly used in the expression *the mother tongue*, is adopted here to avoid the less adequate *language as a potential*.
8 This view of words is developed more fully in chapters 2 and 3 of my *Language in the Mind*.

CHAPTER THREE

1 Cited in Hirtle 1995b, 154.
2 "Conceptual" is used here not in the broad sense sometimes found of 'anything mental,' but in the more restricted sense of 'resulting from a generalizing mental operation.'
3 Cf. Koerner, 158–60, for a discussion of Bloomfield's "fervent rejection of 'mentalistic' explanations."
4 "The word is not a reality of general linguistics." Cf. Mounin, 222.
5 Sykes, 165.

6 "The distinction between semantics and pragmatics (or between linguistic and extra-linguistic knowledge) is largely artifactual, and the only viable conception of linguistic semantics is one that avoids such false dichotomies and is consequently encyclopedic in nature." Langacker 1987, 154.

7 One is reminded here of Polanyi's plea (46) for "revising the claims of science itself. The first task must be to emancipate the biological sciences, including psychology, from the scourge of physicalism; the absurdities now imposed on the sciences of life must be eliminated. The task is difficult for it calls in question an ideal of impersonal objectivity on which alone we feel it sage to rely. Yet this absurd ideal must be discarded."

8 *Petrol* for the British.

9 For *to* + infinitive, see Duffley's study. For *the*, see my study on the noun phrase.

10 Since ordinary discourse presupposes at least minimal awareness of the meaning expressed, we have assumed that anyone who understands the language can observe by introspection the meaning expressed by most sentences and even by most words. As just mentioned, however, the meaning expressed by words such as *to* and *a* is inaccessible to introspective observation in this way. It therefore calls for techniques such as commutation with similar words, such as *at* and *the*, or, where possible, the omission of the word, techniques permitting one to contrast the meanings of minimally different phrases in an attempt to isolate the import of the word in question. Similarly for the grammatical meaning of any word: other than perhaps the substantive's *-s* when it expresses 'plural' and the verb's *-ed* when it expresses 'past,' this formal import of a word does not emerge clearly into consciousness for the ordinary speaker, presumably because the grammatical means of forming a word and a phrase are so highly systematized that their function, usually indicated by position, is an entailment of their grammatical import.

11 In this respect, it is instructive to consult the index of many contemporary works in linguistics for references to "word."

12 See Geeraerts 1983 for an overview of such problems.

CHAPTER FOUR

1 Some linguists do not make this distinction. Cf. Jackendoff, 16–18.

2 It may be this which led Tuggy to argue that "[c]ontext underdetermines meanings" (359).

3 Here the authors presumably have in mind "speakers" in their role as listeners.

4 This no doubt calls to mind the well-known example of *game* discussed by Wittgenstein. His conclusion provides a linguist with the starting point for exploring other variants of the lexeme not only as a substantive, but also as an adjective and even a verb.
5 Cf. Michael, 14, 44–7.
6 See Hirtle and Curat 1986 and my 2009 study respectively.

CHAPTER FIVE

1 Much of this chapter is drawn from a paper given at LACUS 35. See 2009b online reference.
2 A notable exception is the work of Wierzbicka, whose "semantic primitives" are intended as a "natural semantic metalanguge" applicable to all languages. See Goddard, 324–53, for a convenient survey.
3 *UVIC Torch*, Autumn 2006, 24.
4 When I suggested this might well have been a child speaking, one scholar, married to a phonetician, pointed out that her seven-year-old daughter once said: "Oh Dad, stop phoneticianing."
5 http://www.urbandictionary.com/define.php?term=homered.
6 See Crystal, 148–9, for other examples from Shakespeare.
7 This example involves the question of case in the noun phrase, as discussed in my 2009 study. The same line of argument would suggest that *government* in *a strictly government enquiry* is an adjective. Likewise, the argument that *city* in the example given is not an adjective because it would not occur in predicate position is not conclusive: the same argument would apply to adjectives such as *only* in *an only child* and *main* in *the main road*. The question of why certain adjectives are limited to use within a noun phrase calls for further investigation in the light of the relation between a word's lexeme and its part of speech as proposed here and in the above study.
8 To illustrate this is the following example combining "conversion" and "word formation" provided by a colleague (private communication): "she's been employment-equitying her way up the system for years, and it's about time somebody called her on it."
9 See for example, Curme, 534–8; Christophersen and Sandved, 115–17; Schibsbye, 123–8.
10 Poutsma 1926, 192; cf. also Zandvoort, 265–77.
11 The traditional expression "part of speech" is adopted here because it is closer to the ordinary speaker's experience: words are parts of the speech, the sentence, being constructed.

12 "To signify conjointly; to mean or signify when combined with something," *OED*.
13 My translation.
14 As already mentioned, it would be more precise to say that "vocables" are universal since some languages do not include a grammatical import in their minimum sayable units. This distinction need not be introduced here, however, since we are concerned with English.
15 See my *Language in the Mind* for an introduction to the theory of the word this leads to.
16 Farrell (128) makes a similar claim concerning the lexeme, but his view of the part of speech is quite different from that proposed here: "words such as *bag* and *kiss* are not inherently associated with the syntactic categories 'noun' or 'verb'. Rather, they are associated with meanings that can manifest as either of these categories, by virtue of being compatible with different contextually imposed profiling scenarios." That is, the part of speech is not a morphological system, an integral part of the word's meaning, but a syntactic category imposed on the addressee by the syntactic context. Adopting the addressee's point of view implies an understanding of what constitutes a word very different from that proposed here.
17 Discussion of the example later brought out that it might also be interpreted as a different activity associated with the metal object, one arising after the winning performance, i.e. receiving the medal during the awards ceremony.
18 See my *Lessons on the English Verb* for the detail of how a lexeme is formed by the different subsystems of the verb.
19 Guillaume (1992, 47) even speaks of "words being processes, processes creating linguistic results." He sees them as momentary results that are immediately integrated into the sentence being constructed. The idea is developed in my 2002b article.
20 Cited by Mark Abley in *the* (Montreal) *Gazette*, 30 August 2008.
21 Cited in Fine and Josephson, 13.

CHAPTER SIX

1 To be noted here is the difference between this notion of lexemes in tongue as viewing ideas monitoring the speaker's extra-linguistic experience, and Geeraerts' notion of words focusing on a portion of their extension during speech: "words are searchlights that highlight, upon each application, a particular subfield of their domain of application" (260).

What Geeraerts is referring to is discussed in my 2009 study in terms of extension and extensity.

2 It is interesting to see that psychological analyses of sensory processing have led to similar conclusions. Ramachandran and Blakeslee, for example, speak of "a dynamic interplay between sensory signals and high-level stored information about visual images from the past" (112), and later specify that this is "high-level semantic knowledge" (275). Cf. also Arguin et al.

3 Guillaume attempted to compare language types on this basis in what he called *La théorie des aires glossogéniques du langage:* literally, the theory of glossogenetic areas of language. The bare outlines of this theory are found in the lessons of his later years (cf. Guillaume 2013). The only applications of the theory available in English are Lowe's comparison of word-making in Eskimo and English (1985, "Introduction") and his 1996 article on the word in Eskimo.

4 For various texts where Guillaume comments on different aspects of the complex relation between thought and language, see the volume translated into English (1984, 135–65).

5 As in a binary system such as number in the substantive, where -*s* signifies one position in the system, -ø the other.

6 The allusion here is to case in the substantive, which has no visible sign within the word (except for some personal pronouns). The "synaptic" case in tongue is not actualized by either of its possibilities, support or import function, until the word takes its place in the sentence, and so can be signified by its position there. For more detail, see the discussion in my 2009 study, 53–67, 358–67.

7 An observation I owe to Claude Guimier (private communication).

8 Interjections such as *Wow!* do not appear to have a formal significate, and so establish no syntactic relations with other words.

CHAPTER SEVEN

1 For a more detailed discussion of Ruhl's approach see Cruse 1992.
2 All references in this chapter are to Ruhl 1989, except where indicated.
3 *Webster's Third New International Dictionary.*
4 My translation.

CHAPTER EIGHT

1 "Many" here is surprising since it implies that a grammatical element, either morpheme or word, could consist of a phonetic manifestation without meaning.

2 James Michener, PBS, 13 August 1979. References are given only for examples that are in any way exceptional from the point of view of the rules given in grammars.
3 *Esquire Magazine*, May 1983, 138.
4 *Concise Oxford Dictionary* 1976, 1027.
5 *Esquire Magazine*, February 1981, 28.
6 Cf. my 2007 study on the verb.
7 See my 2007 study on the verb, 93–4.
8 Cf. Tobin, 64, where *see* is considered to be "marked for result" as compared to *look*, "unmarked for process / result." Although Tobin's study does not deal with the polysemy of *see* as such, it does bring out how the process / result relationship can be observed in the usage of different pairs of verbs.
9 See chapter 14 for a discussion of metaphor.

CHAPTER NINE

1 See Hirtle and Bégin 1990 and 1991 for more detail and references.
2 See my 2007 study on the verb for this analysis of the progressive form.
3 Cited in Osselton (454), who remarks that the example "was readily interpreted by all correspondents as meaning 'was experiencing at that moment,' that is, in his helpless state on the operating table." He further observes that the simple form *knew* "would have simply implied that the man had learnt the meaning of loneliness at some earlier unspecified stage in his life."
4 Bennett, 566.
5 Adamczewski, 483.
6 An example cited in Visser 1976 – *But they are not worrying him, because he is knowing that if ever he is appealing to Mayor Paget in person, all is well.* – is, according to Osselton (1980, 454) "quite baffling in its oddity" for native speakers. This is hardly surprising since the author puts this and other such misuses into the mouth of a character to indicate that he is a non–native speaker. The fact that competent observers rejected this example shows that introspective observation of meaning can provide a valid basis for data.
7 See Hirtle and Bégin 1990 for details and references.
8 See Visser 1973 and Osselton (53) for sources of these examples.
9 The only example found so far where the noun phrase subject does not imply a duration is the following cited in Visser 1973: *All these months we have been studying this rock ... To-day ... for the first time we are entirely certain. This stone is being an altar of your Druid peoples.* Like another example from Visser discussed in a previous note, this strikes one as a misuse, intended by the author to characterize a non–native speaker of English.

CHAPTER TEN

1 Langacker (2002, 83) also considers that "the auxiliary verbs *be, have,* and *do* designate highly schematic processes, i.e. they have little content beyond that which characterizes verbs as a class," though his view of their meaning (135–6) differs from that proposed here.
2 See chapter 12 for a discussion of the relation between comprehension and extension.
3 The adjoining of *so* or *not* is often a useful means of distinguishing between the two uses.
4 See my study of the verb (2007, 277–90) for a more detailed discussion.

CHAPTER ELEVEN

1 As already pointed out, the potential meaning may vary for speakers over a certain length of time, as they come to understand more about some object of their experience (as in scientific studies) or even learn more about how a word can be used.
2 This may turn out to be the sort of thing suggested by Lehrer (1): "If polysemy can be generated or predicted according to very general principles, then it is not necessary to state multiple meanings for each word, since secondary meanings for large classes of words could be predicted by general rules."
3 See Tobin 1993 for many useful comments on the lexical distinctions between verbs.

CHAPTER TWELVE

1 This is not to say that synonyms, such as two ways of naming some new device or procedure, may not persist in a speaker's usage for some time, but it seems that in the long run either they become differentiated, or one of them drops from usage.
2 See the discussion in Aitchison, 79–82.
3 *Maud* naming different persons might be considered the same word by those who adopt the addressee's point of view and consider the sign as the unifying component of a word, as seen above.
4 The case of trade names such as *Guinness* will not be discussed here, nor will proper names such as *New Zealand, The Hebrides,* and the like, since our aim is merely to see the difference, if any, between the lexical import of common and proper substantives. See Quirk et al. (288) for the distinction between proper substantives and names.

CHAPTER THIRTEEN

1 New terms such as these have the advantage of calling to mind the operativity involved in producing a word, the need to actualize or generate each of its main components.
2 Kipling, 110.
3 This in spite of the contrast between physical and mental entities in our experience: if I share a pie with someone, I no longer have all of it; if I share an idea with someone, we both have the whole of it.

CHAPTER FOURTEEN

1 Ortega y Gasset, 39.
2 See the discussion in Glucksberg, 8.
3 There are of course examples such as *the foot of the mountain* where some may understand 'foot' in a metaphorical sense, others not. This appears to reflect a difference in the potential meaning of particular speakers, the latter having generalized the lexeme to include what was once a metaphorical sense.
4 Cf. Clark (300) for whom expressions with "shifting senses" are "*contextual expressions*": "Their senses depend entirely on the time, place, and circumstances in which they are uttered." This includes "novel metaphors" (328n1).
5 My wife finally pointed it out to me.
6 This view is quite different from the "conceptual metaphor" approach based on recognition but has much in common with Glucksberg's "property attribution model," which considers that the noun phrase predicate in *Our marriage is a roller-coaster ride* "functions as an attributive category in that it provides properties that could be attributed to the topic" (cf. Glucksberg, 98).
7 Recanati (77) expresses a somewhat similar idea concerning the "sense extension" of metaphor: "those dimensions of meaning which stand in conflict to the specifications of the target are filtered out." This manner of depicting how a word's "meaning is adjusted" in context by the listener does not imply the speaker's actualization process to be proposed here.

CHAPTER FIFTEEN

1 A suggestion made by Bruno Courbon (private communication).
2 It has yet to be determined if uses like *poor little thing* to designate a human involve metaphor or depict the same impression as *it* in somewhat similar uses (cf. my 2009 study, 335–6).

3 Paradis has seen a parallel opposition in adjectives, but since it applies only to "gradable" adjectives it is not an option open to all adjectives and so does not appear to be something built into forming the lexeme, as in the case of substantives.
4 Nor as a metaphor, the way the parallel expression *big is important* has been characterized (cf. Pinker, 241).

CHAPTER SIXTEEN

1 Guimier (47–67) distinguishes between predicative and non-predicative adverbs, a discussion we cannot enter into here.
2 See my 2007b study for an outline.

CONCLUSION

1 A study calling for a discussion of the role of determiners, particularly the articles.
2 Guillaume often reflected on the notion of support, finally identifying it with the grammatical category of person – "cardinal person" as he called it (1999, 128). No attempt has been made here to bring in these reflections, since this would call for a study extending well beyond the question of the lexeme to include pronouns as well.

References

Adamczewski, H. 1978. *Be + ING dans la grammaire de l'anglais contemporain.* Lille, France: Université de Lille III.

Aitchison, Jean. 1987. *Words in the Mind: An Introduction to the Mental Lexicon.* Oxford, UK: Basil Blackwell.

Allan, Keith. 1980. "Nouns and Countability." *Language* 56 (3): 541–67.

Allwood, Jens. 2003. "Meaning Potentials and Context: Some Consequences for the Analysis of Variation in Meaning." In Cuyckens et al., *Cognitive Approaches,* 29–65.

Arguin, Martin, Daniel Bub, and Gregory Dudek. 1996. "Shape Integration for Visual Object Recognition and Its Implication in Category-Specific Visual Agnosia." *Visual Cognition* 3 (3): 221–75.

Artigas, Mariano. 2001. *The Mind of the Universe: Understanding Science and Religion.* Philadelphia, PA & London: Templeton Foundation Press.

Bartlett, John. 1980. *Familiar Quotations.* 15th ed. Boston: Little, Brown.

Bauer, Laurie, and Salvador Valera, eds. 2005. *Approaches to Conversion / Zero-Derivation.* New York: Waxmann Münster.

Bennett, A. 1930. *Imperial Palace.* London: Cassell.

Berlands-Delepine, S. 1974. *La grammaire anglaise de l'étudiant.* Paris: Éditions Ophrys.

Bloomfield, L. 1933. *Language.* New York: Holt, Rinehart and Winston.

Bolinger, Dwight. 1963. "The Uniqueness of the Word." *Lingua* 12: 113–36.

– 1977. *Meaning and Form.* London and New York: Longman.

Bolinger, Dwight, and Donald A. Sears. 1981. *Aspects of Language.* 3rd ed. New York: Harcourt Brace Jovanovich.

Bontekoe, R. 1986. "The Function of Metaphor." *Information Communication* 6: 52–73.

Buyssens, E. 1968. *Les deux aspectifs de la conjugaison anglaise au XXe siècle.* Bruxelles: Presses Universitaires de Bruxelles.

Christophersen, P. 1939. *The Articles: A Study of their Theory and Use in English.* Copenhagen: Munksgaard.

Christophersen, P., and A.O. Sandved. 1969. *An Advanced English Grammar.* London: Macmillan.

Clark, H.H. 1983. "Making Sense of Nonce Sense." In *The Process of Language Understanding*, edited by G.B. Flores d'Arcais and R.J. Jarvella. Chichester, UK: John Riley & Sons: 297–331.

Comrie, B. 1976. *Aspect: An Introduction to the Study of Verbal Aspect and Related Problems.* Cambridge, UK: Cambridge University Press.

Croft, William, and D. Alan Cruse. 2004. *Cognitive Linguistics.* Cambridge, UK: Cambridge University Press.

Cruse, D.A. 1986. *Lexical Semantics.* Cambridge, UK: Cambridge University Press.

– 1992. "Monosemy vs. Polysemy." *Linguistics* 30: 577–99.

– 2000. "Aspects of the Micro-structure of Word Meanings." In Ravin and Leacock, *Polysemy*, 30–51.

Crystal, David. 2008. *'Think on My Words': Shakespearian Vocabulary.* Cambridge, UK: Cambridge University Press.

Cuyckens, H., R. Dirven, and J.R. Taylor, eds. *Cognitive Approaches to Lexical Semantics.* Berlin: Mouton de Gruyter.

Curme, George O. 1931. *Syntax.* Boston: Heath.

– 1935. *Parts of Speech and Accidence.* Boston: Heath.

Dalrymple, Theodore. 2006. "The Gift of Language: No, Dr. Pinker, It's Not Just from Nature." *City Journal*, Autumn.

Damasio, Antonio. 2010. *Self Comes to Mind: Constructing the Conscious Brain.* New York: Pantheon Books.

Davis, Joel. 1993. *Mother Tongue: How Humans Create Language.* New York: Carol Publishing Group.

Dawson, Christopher. 2008. *The Formation of Christendom.* San Francisco: Ignatius Press.

Dillon, George L. 1977. *Introduction to Contemporary Linguistic Semantics.* Englewood Cliffs, NJ: Prentice-Hall Inc.

Dilworth, Ira. 1951. "Foreword." In *Klee Wyck*, Emily Carr, v–xvi. Toronto: Clark Irwin.

Duffley, Patrick J. 1992. *The English Infinitive.* London and New York: Longman.

Einstein, Albert. 1981. *Ideas and Opinions.* New York: Dell.

Eliot, T.S. 1963. *Collected Poems 1909–1962.* London: Faber and Faber.

Evans, Vyvyan. 2009. *How Words Mean: Lexical Concepts, Cognitive Models and Meaning Construction*. Oxford, UK: Oxford University Press.

Farrell, Patrick. 2001. "Functional Shift as Category Underspecification." *English Language and Linguistics* 5 (1): 109–30.

Fine, Edith H., and Judith P. Josephson. 2004. *Nitty-Gritty Grammar: A Not-So-Serious Guide to Clear Communication*. New York: Scholastic Inc.

Frisson, Steven. 2009. "Semantic Underspecification in Language Processing." *Language and Linguistics Compass* 3 (1): 111–27.

Frye, Northrop. 1971. "Ethical Criticism: A Theory of Symbols." In *Critical Theory Since Plato*, edited by Hazaro Adams, 1117–47. New York: Harcourt.

Fowler, W.S. 1962. *The Development of Scientific Method*. London: Pergamon Press.

Gardiner, A. 1960. *The Theory of Speech and Language*. 2nd ed. Oxford, UK: Clarendon Press.

Geeraerts, Dirk. 1993. "Vagueness's Puzzles, Polysemy's Vagaries." *Cognitive Linguistics* 4 (3): 223–72.

Gethin, Amorey. 1999. *Language and Thought: A Rational Enquiry into Their Nature and Relationship*. Exeter, UK: Intellect.

Gilson, E. 1969. *Linguistique et philosophie*. Paris: Vrin.

Glucksberg, Sam. 2001. *Understanding Figurative Language*. Oxford, UK: Oxford University Press.

Goddard, Cliff. 1998. *Semantic Analysis: A Practical Introduction*. Oxford, UK: Oxford University Press.

Guillaume, Gustave. 1919/1975. *Le problème de l'article et sa solution dans la langue française*. Paris: Nizet; Québec: Presses de l'Université Laval.

– 1984. *Foundations of a Science of Language*. Amsterdam and Philadelphia, PA: John Benjamins.

– 1987. *Leçons de linguistique de Gustave Guillaume 1947–1948, Série C, Grammaire particulière du français et grammaire générale (III)*. Québec: Presses de l'Université Laval; Lille, France: Presses universitaires de Lille.

– 1990. *Leçons de linguistique de Gustave Guillaume 1943–1944, Série A, Esquisse d'une grammaire descriptive de la langue française (II)*. Québec: Presses de l'Université Laval; Lille, France: Presses universitaires de Lille.

– 1992. *Leçons de linguistique de Gustave Guillaume 1938–1939*. Québec: Presses de l'Université Laval; Lille, France: Presses universitaires de Lille.

– 1998. Leçons de linguistique de Gustave Guillaume 1951–1952, Psychosystématique du langage: Principes, méthodes et applications (IV). Québec: Presses de l'Université Laval; Paris: Klincksieck.

– 1999. *Leçons de linguistique de Gustave Guillaume 1942–1943, Série B, Esquisse d'une grammaire descriptive de la langue française (I)*. Québec: Presses de l'Université Laval; Paris: Klincksieck.

- 2005. *Leçons de linguistique de Gustave Guillaume 1941–1942, Série B, Théorie du mot et typologie linguistique: limitation et construction du mot à travers les langues.* Québec: Presses de l'Université Laval.
- 2013. *Leçons de linguistique de Gustave Guillaume 1957–1958.* Québec: Presses de l'Université Laval.

Guimier, Claude. 1988. *Syntaxe de l'adverbe anglais.* Lille, France: Presses universitaires de Lille.

Györi, Gàbor. 2000. "Semantic Change as Linguistic Interpretation of the World." In *Evidence for Linguistic Relativity,* edited by S. Niemeier and R. Dirven, 71–89. Amsterdam: John Benjamins.

Hatcher, A.G. 1951. "The Use of the Progressive Form in English." *Language* 27: 254–80.

Hawkes, T. 1972. *Metaphor.* London: Methuen.

Hirtle, W.H. 1982. *Number and Inner Space.* Québec: Presses de l'Université Laval.
- 1992. "La métaphore: une idée regardante?" In *ALFA* vol. 5, 137–50.
- 1995a. "The Simple Form Again: Analysis of Direction-Giving and Related Uses." *Journal of Pragmatics* 24: 265–81.
- 1995b. "Meaning, Data, and Testing Hypotheses." In *Meaning as Explanation: Advances in Linguistic Sign Theory,* edited by Ellen Contini-Morava and Barbara Sussman Goldberg, 153–68. Berlin and New York: Mouton de Gruyter.
- 2002. "*Do* – One Sign, One Meaning?" In Reid et al., *Signal, Meaning and Message,* 157–70.
- 2002b. "Les mots étant des procès." In *Actes du IXe Colloque international de l'Association Internationale de Psychomécanique du Langage,* edited by Ronald Lowe, 48–59. Québec: Presses de l'Université Laval.
- 2007. *Lessons on the English Verb: No Expression without Representation.* Montreal & Kingston: McGill-Queen's University Press.
- 2007b. *Language in the Mind: An Introduction to Guillaume's Theory.* Montreal & Kingston: McGill-Queen's University Press.
- 2009. *Lessons on the Noun Phrase in English: From Representation to Reference.* Montreal & Kingston: McGill-Queen's University Press.
- 2009b. "Wording or How *Access* 'Got Verbed.'" In *LACUS Forum XXXV,* 45–56. http://www.lacus.org/volumes/index.php?volume=35.

Hirtle, W.H., and Claude Bégin. 1990. "*To Be* in the Progressive: A New Use." *Canadian Journal of Linguistics* 35: 1–11.

Hirtle, W.H., and Claude Bégin. 1991. "Can the Progressive Express a State?" *Langues et linguistique* 17: 99–137.

Hirtle, W.H., and V.N. Curat. 1986. "The Simple and the Progressive: 'Future' Use." In *Transactions of the Philological Society 1986*, 42–83. Oxford, UK: Basil Blackwell.
Huddleston, Rodney, and Geoffrey K. Pullum. 2002. *The Cambridge Grammar of the English Language*. Cambridge, UK: University Press.
Humboldt, Wilhelm von. 1988. *On Language: The Diversity of Human Language-Structure and Its Influence on the Mental Development of Mankind*. Translated by Peter Heath. Cambridge, UK: Cambridge University Press.
Jackendoff, Ray. 1983. *Semantics and Cognition*. Cambridge, MA & London: The MIT Press.
Jacob, François. 1981. *Le jeu des possibles; essai sur la diversité du vivant*. Paris: Fayard.
James, William. 1890/1983. *The Principles of Psychology*. Cambridge, MA: Harvard University Press.
Jespersen, O. 1924/1975. *The Philosophy of Grammar*. London: Allen and Unwin.
– 1954. *A Modern English Grammar*. London: Allen and Unwin.
Kipling, Rudyard. 1899. *Stalky and Co*. New York: Doubleday and McClure.
Koerner, E.F.K. 1978. *Toward a Historiography of Linguistics: Selected Essays*. Amsterdam: John Benjamins.
Konrad, Hedwig. 1958. *Étude sur la métaphore*. 2nd ed. Paris: Vrin.
Kosslyn, Stephen M., and Olivier Koenig. 1992. *Wet Mind: The New Cognitive Neuroscience*. New York: The Free Press and Macmillan.
Langacker, Ronald W. 1987. *Foundations of Cognitive Grammar*, vol. I. Stanford, CA: Stanford University Press.
– 1991. *Foundations of Cognitive Grammar*, vol. II. Stanford, CA: Stanford University Press.
– 1991/2002. *Concept, Image, and Symbol. The Cognitive Basis of Grammar*. Berlin: Mouton de Gruyter.
Le Guern, Michel. 2003. *Les deux logiques du langage*. Paris: Honoré Champion.
Lehrer, Adrienne. 1989. *Polysemy, Conventionality, and the Structure of the Lexicon*. Duisburg, Germany: L.A.U.D. Series A, 240.
Lowe, Ronald. 1985. *Siglit Inuvialuit Uqausiita Ilisarviksait. Basic Siglit Inuvialuit Eskimo Grammar*. Inuvik, NWT: Committee for Original Peoples Entitlement.
– 1996. "The Internal Syntax of the Eskimo Word." In Tollis, *Psychomechanics*, 74–99.
Lucy, John A., and Suzanne Gaskins. 2003. "Interaction of Language Type and Referent Type in the Development of Nonverbal Classification

Preferences." In *Language in Mind: Advances in the Study of Language and Thought*, edited by D. Gentner and S. Goldin-Meadow, 465–92. Cambridge, MA: The MIT Press.

Lyons, John. 1968. *Introduction to Theoretical Linguistics*. Cambridge, UK: Cambridge University Press.

McGirr, Robert. 1984. *Verbs that Tend to Avoid the Progressive: The Verbs of Perception*. Unpublished MA thesis. Québec: Université Laval.

Michael, Ian. 1970. *English Grammatical Categories and the Tradition to 1800*. Cambridge, UK: Cambridge University Press.

Miller, G.A. 1991. *The Science of Words*. New York: Scientific American Library.

Mittins, W.H. 1962. *A Grammar of Modern English*. London: Methuen.

Mounin, Georges. 2004. *Dictionnaire de la linguistique*, 4th edition. Paris: Presses Universitaires de France.

Nerlich, Brigitte. 1992. *Semantic Theories in Europe 1830–1930: From Etymology to Contextuality*. Amsterdam and Philadelphia, PA: John Benjamins.

Nerlich, Brigitte, Zazie Todd, Vimala Herman, and David D. Clarke, eds. 2003. *Polysemy: Flexible Patterns of Meaning in Mind and Language*. Berlin and New York: Mouton de Gruyter.

O'Grady, William. "The Emergentist Program." http://www.ling.hawaii.edu/faculty/ogrady/Emergentist_program.pdf. Accessed 1 March 2013.

Ortega y Gasset, José. 1986. "First Installment on the Dehumanization of Art." In *Contemporary Literary Criticism*, edited by Robert Con Davis, 33–43. White Plains, NY: Longman.

Ortony, Andrew, ed. 1979. *Metaphor and Thought*. Cambridge, UK: Cambridge University Press.

Orwell, George. 1984. *Nineteen Eighty-Four*. London: Penguin Books.

Osselton, N.E. 1979/1980. "Points of Modern English Syntax." *English Studies* 60 and 61: 49–53, 450–5.

Palmer, F.R. 1981. *Semantics*. 2nd ed. Cambridge, UK: Cambridge University Press.

Paradis, C. 2001. "Adjectives and Boundedness." *Cognitive Linguistics* 12: 47–65.

Pinker, Steven. 2007. *The Stuff of Thought*. New York: Viking.

Polanyi, Michael. 1969. *Knowing and Being*. Chicago, IL: The University of Chicago Press.

Poutsma, H. 1921. *The Character of the English Verb and the Expanded Form*. Groningen, Netherlands: Noordhoff.

– 1926. *A Grammar of Late Modern English: Part II The Parts of Speech: Section II The Verb and its Particles*. Groningen, Netherlands: Noordhoff.
Quirk, R., S. Greenbaum, G. Leech, and J. Svartvik. 1985. *A Comprehensive Grammar of the English Language*. London: Longman.
Ramachandran, V.S., and Sandra Blakeslee. 1998. *Phantoms in the Brain*. New York: William Morrow.
Ravin, Yael, and Claudia Leacock. 2002. *Polysemy: Theoretical and Computational Approaches*. Oxford, UK: Oxford University Press.
Recanati, François. 2004. *Literal Meaning*. Cambridge, UK: University Press.
Reid, T.B.W. 1956. "Linguistics, Structuralism and Philology." In *Archivum Linguisticum* VIII, 28–37.
Reid, Wallis. 1991. *Verb and Noun Number in English: A Functional Explanation*. London: Longman.
Reid, Wallis, Ricardo Otheguy, and Nancy Stern, eds. 2002. *Signal, Meaning and Message: Perspectives on Sign-Based Linguistics*. Amsterdam and Philadelphia, PA: John Benjamins.
Richards, I.A. 1936/1965. *The Philosophy of Rhetoric*. New York: Oxford University Press.
Ricoeur, Paul. 1975. *La métaphore vive*. Paris: Éditions du Seuil.
Ruhl, Charles. 1989. *On Monosemy: A Study in Linguistic Semantics*. Albany: State University of New York Press.
– 2002. "Data, Comprehensiveness, Monosemy." In Reid et al., *Signal, Meaning and Message*, 171–89.
Sacks, Sheldon, ed. 1979. *On Metaphor*. Chicago, IL: University of Chicago Press.
Saeed, John I. 2009. *Semantics*. 3rd ed. Oxford, UK: Wiley-Blackwell.
Sapir, Edward. 1921. *Language: An Introduction to the Study of Speech*. New York: Harcourt, Brace and World.
Saussure, Ferdinand. 1916/1955. *Cours de linguistique générale*. Paris: Payot.
Schaff, A. 1962. *Introduction to Semantics*. Warsaw: Pergamon Press.
Scheffer, J. 1975. *The Progressive in English*. Amsterdam: North-Holland.
Schibsbye, Knud. 1970. *A Modern English Grammar*. London: Oxford University Press.
Searle, J.R. 1983. *Intentionality: An Essay in the Philosophy of Mind*. Cambridge, UK: Cambridge University Press.
– 1984. *Minds, Brains and Science*. Cambridge, MA: Harvard University Press.
Shea, William R., and Mariano Artigas. 2003. *Galileo in Rome: The Rise and Fall of a Troublesome Genius*. New York: Oxford University Press.

Slobin, Dan I. 1996. "From 'Thought and Language' to 'Thinking For Speaking,'" In *Rethinking Linguistic Relativity*, edited by J.J. Gumperz and S.C. Levinson, 70–96. Cambridge, UK: Cambridge University Press.

Spencer, Andrew. 1991. *Morphological Theory: An Introduction to Word Structure in Generative Grammar.* Oxford, UK: Basil Blackwell.

Stern, Gustaf. 1931. *Meaning and Change of Meaning: with Special Reference to the English Language.* Reprint edition. Bloomington, IN and London: Indiana University Press.

Sweet, Henry. 1898/1958. *A New English Grammar Logical and Historical II.* Oxford, UK: Clarendon Press.

Sykes, Brian. 2002. *The Seven Daughters of Eve.* New York and London: W.W. Norton.

Taylor, John R. 1989. *Linguistic Categorization. Prototypes in Linguistic Theory.* Oxford, UK: Clarendon Press.

– 1992. *How Many Meanings Does A Word Have?* (Series A, General & Theoretical Papers, No. 322.) Duisburg, Germany: L.A.U.D.

– 2002. *Cognitive Grammar.* Oxford, UK: University Press.

Tennyson, Alfred. 1913. *Poems of Tennyson.* London: Oxford University Press.

Tobin, Y. 1993. *Aspect in the English Verb: Process and Result in Language.* London and New York: Longman.

Tollis, Francis, ed. 1996. *The Psychomechanics of Language and Guillaumism, LynX* 5. Valencia, Spain: Departament de Teoria des Llenguages.

Tuggy, D. 2003. "The Nawatl Verb *Kīsa*: A Case Study in Polysemy." In Cuyckens et al., *Cognitive Approaches*, 323–61.

Turvey, M.T., and M.A. Moreno. 2006. "Physical Metaphors for the Mental Lexicon." *The Mental Lexicon* 1 (1): 7–33.

Tyler, Andrea, and Vyvyan Evans. 2003. *The Semantics of English Prepositions: Spatial Scenes, Embodied Meaning and Cognition.* Cambridge, UK: Cambridge University Press.

Ullmann, Stephen. 1957. *The Principles of Semantics.* Oxford, UK: Basil Blackwell.

Valin, Roch. 1981. *Perspectives psychomécaniques sur la syntaxe.* Québec: Presses de l'Université Laval.

– 1996. "The Comparative Method in Historical Linguistics and in the Psychomechanics of Language." In Tollis, *Psychomechanics*, 37–45.

Vendler, Zeno. 1977. "Wordless Thoughts." In *Language and Thought. Anthropological Issues*, edited by William C. McCormack and Stephen A. Wurm, 29–44. The Hague and Paris: Mouton.

Victorri, Bernard, and Catherine Fuchs. 1996. *La polysémie: construction dynamique du sens.* Paris: Hermes.

Visser, F. Th. 1969. *An Historical Syntax of the English Language, Part III, First Half*. Leiden, Netherlands: Brill.
– 1973. *An Historical Syntax of the English Language. Part III, Second Half*. Leiden, Netherlands: Brill.
Vygotsky, L.S. 1962. *Thought and Language*. Cambridge, MA: MIT Press.
Waldron, T.P. 1985. *Principles of Language and Mind*. London & Boston: Routledge and Kegan Paul.
Webster's Third New International Dictionary of the English Language. 1969. Springfield, MA: Merriam.
Whorf, B.L. 1964. *Language, Thought, and Reality: Selected Writings of Benjamin Lee Whorf*. Edited by J.B. Carroll. Cambridge, MA: The MIT Press.
Wierzbicka, Anna. 1988. *The Semantics of Grammar*. Amsterdam and Philadelphia, PA: John Benjamins.
Zandvoort, R.W. 1957. *A Handbook of English Grammar*. London: Longman Green.

Index

act of language, 23, 161, 223–4
actual meaning. *See* potential and actual meaning
adjective, 210–13
adverb, 215–18
Aitchison, Jean, 57, 162

Bauer, Laurie, and Salvador Valera, 63–4
Beardsley, 184
Bloomfield, L., 34–5
Bolinger, Dwight, 35, 38; and Donald A. Sears, 47
Bontekoe, R., 186

Carr, Emily, 15
characterizing traits, 50, 160, 162–5, 171, 192–5, 199–207, 216
Christophersen, P., 173, 177
Clark, H.H., 239n4
comprehension or intension, 49, 160. *See also* characterizing traits
Condillac, Étienne Bonnot, 12
conversion, 60–5, 71–2
Croft, William, and D. Alan Cruse, 47–8, 58, 92
Cruse, D. Alan, 57–8, 111

Davis, Joel, 59
Delacroix, 23
denotatum, 161. *See also* referent
designatum, 161. *See also* referent
discourse: constructing sentences, 31. *See also* tongue
Dillon, George L., 47
Diver, William, 33, 35

Eliot, T.S., 15
Einstein, Albert, 14
Evans, Vyvyan, 49
expressive effect, 50–2
extension, 49, 160. *See also* range of representation

Farrell, Patrick, 235n16
formal significate, 53. *See also* lexeme: and part of speech
Frisson, Steven, 48
Frost, Robert, 16
Frye, Northrop, 15–16

Gardiner, A., 26–7, 45
Geeraerts, Dirk, 47, 92, 235n1
Gethin, Amorey, 16, 77
Gilson, E., 18, 20

Guillaume, Gustave, 28–30, 75–6, 85, 210, 226, 236n3–4
Györi, Gàbor, 78

Hegel, Georg Wilhelm Friedrich, 12
homonym, 48–9, 81, 169
Huddleston, Rodney, and Geoffrey K. Pullum, 61, 63, 65, 173, 175, 177
Humboldt, Wilhelm von, 25, 214
hyponym/hyperonym, 164–8, 171, 191–4

ideogenesis. *See* lexeme: actualizing; representing role. *See also* word
incidence, 187, 207, 216–18
intended message, 44. *See also* message

James, William, 43–4
Jespersen, O., 168–9, 172, 174, 195

Konrad, Hedwig, 193–4.

Langacker, Ronald W., 35, 48, 55, 89, 174, 233n6, 238n1
language: as interface, 17–23, 77; classifying experience, 18–20
lexeme: actualizing, 180–2, 199–201, 204–7, 212–13; and part of speech, 53–5, 173–6, 214–15, 218–19; potential meaning, 47–9, 52, 80–3, 100, 159; representing role, 78–80, 201–2; viewing role, 76–8, 201–2
lexical and grammatical meaning. *See* lexeme and part of speech
lexicon, 57–9, 65, 71

linguistic determinism/relativity, 28, 78–9
Lucy, John A., and Suzanne Gaskins, 77, 78
Lyons, John, 34, 160, 183

Mandelstam, Osip, 17
mass vs. count. *See* substantive: bounded vs. unbounded
material significate, 53. *See also* lexeme
meaning: *See* characterizing traits; expressive effect; lexeme; lexical and grammatical meaning; observing meaning; polysemy; potential and actual meaning
message: intended, 44–6, 146, 161; final, 45–6. *See also* lexeme; referent; viewing ideas
metaphor, 183–95, 204–7
Michael, Ian, 66
Miller, G.A., 35
Mittins, W.H., 51
morphogenesis, 85. *See also* words
Murry, J.M., 184

Nerlich, Brigitte, 25, 28; et al., 49
notional chronology, 151–2
noun, 212

observing meaning: 93–109, 112–27, 128–37, 139–45; in context, 50–2; difficulties in, 37–40, 54–5; scientific impossibility of, 34–5; providing scientific data, 36–7; and situation, 45–6; within the word, 52–4, 85
O'Grady, William, 58
Ortony, Andrew, 187

Orwell, George, 13

Palmer, F.R., 168
part of speech, 63, 66–9
polysemy, 89–92, 125–7, 137–8, 141–4, 212–13, 223–6; related senses, 147–56, 204–10. *See also* verb; substantive
potential and actual meaning, 47–52, 146–7, 180–1
psychogenesis, 172, 179

Quirk, R., et al., 61, 62–3, 140–1, 172, 177

Ramachandran, V.S., and Sandra Blakeslee, 236n2
range of representation, 49, 160–3, 185–6, 204–7
reference, 44. *See also* referent
referent, 45–6, 73, 146, 161
Recanati, François, 239n7
Reid, T.B.W., 34, 35
Reid, W., 174
Reisig, Christian Karl, 25
Richards, I.A., 19–20
Ruhl, Charles, 91–2, 109–10, 146–7, 177
Russell, Bertrand, 12

Saeed, John I., 44, 59, 231n13
Sapir, Edward, 26, 35
Saussure, Ferdinand, 66
Searle, J.R., 45, 89
semiogenesis, 172
Shakespeare, William, 17–18
Shea, William R., and Mariano Artigas, 7
Shelley, Percy Bysshe, 17

Slobin, Dan I., 78
speaker-centered approach, 4–5, 49, 91, 116
Stern, Gustaf, 27, 34
Sweet, Henry, 176
substantive: 207–10, 215–6; bounded vs. unbounded, 172–82; common vs. proper, 159–71, 199–200, 203–4
support, 187; spatial, 207–12, 215–18

Tennyson, Alfred, 16
thought: languaged, 12–4, 23, 25, 45–6; pre-language, 14–17, 23, 25, 45
Taylor, John R., 46, 48, 77, 184
tongue: constructing words, 31, 159; a mental construct, 55; a viewing universe, 76, 79. *See also* discourse; word
Tuggy, D., 92, 233n2
Turvey, M.T., and M.A. Moreno, 58
Tyler, Andrea, and Vyvyan Evans, 57, 59

Ullmann, Stephen, 27

Vendler, Zeno, 14
verb, 215–16; auxiliary vs. full, 153; notional chronology, 151–2; stative vs. developmental, 153–5, 181
Victorri, Bernard, and Catherine Fuchs, 110
viewing ideas, 76–8, 82–3, 163, 188–90, 202
Vygotsky, L.S., 17, 22, 23

Waldron, T.P., 13, 22, 23
Whitney, 25
Whorf, B.L., 26, 76–7, 78
Wierzbicka, Anna, 67, 234n2
word: constructing while speaking, 30–2, 67–72, 84–5; ideogenesis and morphogenesis, 84–5, 142, 159, 218–19; makeup, 66–9; a universal, 29. *See also* lexeme and part of speech; observing meaning